Conversations with Caryl Phillips

Literary Conversations Series
Peggy Whitman Prenshaw
General Editor

Conversations with Caryl Phillips

Edited by
Renée T. Schatteman

University Press of Mississippi
Jackson

www.upress.state.ms.us

The University Press of Mississippi is a member of the Association of American University Presses.

Copyright © 2009 by University Press of Mississippi
All rights reserved
Manufactured in the United States of America

First printing 2009
∞
Library of Congress Cataloging-in-Publication Data

Phillips, Caryl.
      Conversations with Caryl Phillips / edited by Renée T. Schatteman.
            p.   cm. — (Literary conversations series)
      Includes index.
      ISBN 978-1-60473-209-2 (alk. paper) — ISBN 978-1-60473-210-8 (pbk. : alk. paper)
1. Phillips, Caryl—Interviews. 2. Authors, West Indian—20th century—Interviews.
I. Schatteman, Renée. II. Title.
      PR9275.S263P47275 2009
      823′.914—dc22

                                                                                    2008044535

British Library Cataloging-in-Publication Data available

Books by Caryl Phillips

Strange Fruit. Ambergate: Amber Lane Press, 1981.

Where There Is Darkness. Ambergate: Amber Lane Press, 1982.

The Shelter. Oxford: Amber Lane Press, 1984.

The Wasted Years. London: Methuen, 1985.

The Final Passage. London: Faber and Faber, 1985; New York: Penguin, 1985.

A State of Independence. London: Faber and Faber, 1986; Straus and Giroux, 1986.

Playing Away. London: Faber and Faber, 1987.

The European Tribe. London: Faber and Faber, 1987; London: Picador, 1992, with a new
    foreword by the author.

Higher Ground. London: Viking, 1989; Penguin, 1990.

Cambridge. London: Bloomsbury, 1991; Alfred A. Knopf, 1992.

Crossing the River. London: Bloomsbury, 1993; Alfred A. Knopf, 1994.

Extravagant Strangers: A Literature of Belonging, ed. London: Faber and Faber, 1997.

The Nature of Blood. London: Faber and Faber, 1997; New York: Alfred A. Knopf, 1997.

The Right Set, ed. London: Faber and Faber, 1999.

The Atlantic Sound, London: Faber and Faber, 2000.

A New World Order: Selected Essays. London: Secker & Warburg, 2001.

A Distant Shore. London: Secker & Warburg, 2003; New York: Alfred A. Knopf, 2003.

Dancing in the Dark. London: Secker & Warburg, 2005; New York: Alfred A. Knopf, 2005.

Foreigners: Three English Lives. London: Secker & Warburg, 2007; New York, Alfred A.
    Knopf, 2007.

Contents

Introduction

The *New York Times* describes Caryl Phillips as one of the great literary giants of our time,[1] an appraisal supported by the sheer number of novels, collections of essays, plays, screenplays, travel books, anthologies, and radio and television dramas and documentaries he has produced in his twenty-nine years as a writer and by the broad scope of his focus on issues concerning belonging, identity, and homelessness as they are manifested in multiple points of the African diaspora. Born in St. Kitts in the West Indies, raised in Leeds, England, and currently residing in New York City, Phillips's own history makes him uniquely positioned to address these concerns. Having personally experienced the "unbelonging" that was imposed upon Caribbean immigrants in his early years and having devoted his later years to the exploration of dislocation, Phillips uses his fiction and his nonfiction to imagine the lives of people least represented in history even though they are often the ones most adversely affected by historical circumstances. His resulting works, in particular the nine novels and three works of nonfiction he has written to date, have firmly established Phillips as one of the most important and talented writers of the late twentieth and early twenty-first centuries.

Since 1987, Caryl Phillips has given some fifty interviews that have appeared in a wide range of scholarly journals, newspapers, magazines, online sites, and—increasingly—the popular media. He is an ideal interviewee: articulate, collegial, sincere, charming, and witty. A social being who appreciates the camaraderie of others, Phillips has an easy informality about him that causes many of his interviews to resemble a good conversation between friends at a pub, and, in fact, a number of the shorter interviews were conducted in such a venue. At the same time, Phillips is always completely serious about his writing, answering each question he is asked with a precision and intelligence that speak to his deep knowledge about and commitment to his subject matter. Recently, Phillips suggested that his willingness to give interviews comes in part from his appreciation of the clarifications about the purpose and direction of his writing that tend to emerge from a conversation that asks challenging questions. He explains, "[an interview] gives you an opportunity to really think about [a] subject, about an author, about a particular book, about yourself, about your own development—questions that I never ask myself when I'm sitting at my desk" (Schatteman 2006). The resulting interviews, and profiles that are based on information gleaned through interviews, can be viewed as Phillips's thinking aloud and can be used as important supplements to his writing, for they contain his insights into the factors that have motivated his career and inspired particular texts as well as his perceptions about the aesthetic and thematic concerns that make up his writing. As such, the interviews open up new interpretive spaces in understanding the many writings that constitute Phillips's oeuvre while providing illuminating connections between Caryl Phillips, the writer, and Caryl Phillips, the man.

Phillips's willingness to speak so freely about his work may seem out of character for an author who, by his own admission, remains largely inconspicuous in his writing. As he comments to Louise Yelin when asked about where he positions himself in his novels, "*I'm* not present. The characters are totally in the fore, I'm invisible . . . I hide behind the characters and let them have the issues." Phillips has offered multiple reasons for ceding center stage to his characters and refraining from authorial commentary: to avoid polemic, to seek out understanding rather than judgment, to provide room for his readers to dwell in the gray areas, and to let his characters have a voice since they are so frequently excluded from other, more official narratives. This tendency to stand in the wings is in keeping with certain elements of Phillips's public persona, for while he is strikingly open about this intellectual life, he carefully guards his personal life and avoids anything that smacks of celebrity. As he tells Charles Wilkin, "People are always interested in the lives of artists, painters, musicians, writers, poets; they want to know the man or woman behind the work. I'm quite reluctant to let things drift in that direction."

When considering an entire body of interviews from more than twenty years, one might expect that the shifts over time would prove the most interesting, but that is not the case with Phillips's interviews. What is most striking is the consistency of his reflections and the particular points that are repeated in many interviews, albeit in a variety of forms. This consistency is most obvious in his recollections of his personal history. Phillips holds no cloak of privacy over his past as he does his present; instead, he is particularly forthcoming, especially about those touchstone moments that were critical to his identity formation. His recollections, which work their way into nearly all of his interviews to some degree, are focused around three specific times in his life: his early years as a black youth growing up in a white working class neighborhood in Leeds, his college years at Oxford and the supplemental learning he did in response to Oxford's deficits, and his return to the Caribbean in his twenties, especially his first trip there since his original departure at only three months of age. The fact that memories from his past have had such resonance in Phillips's work gives credence to Stephen Clingman's point about the notable degree "to which the personal, the biographical, and [the] writing are interlinked" in Phillips's work.

Phillips has never softened the recounting of his childhood. As he tells Maya Jaggi, "Objectively, my childhood was massively dysfunctional and traumatic. I have no happy memories of it. But I never felt deprived; I played with the cards I was dealt." The causes of his trauma were multiple. Being from the only black family in a white community, Phillips recounts the verbal and physical abuse of being chased down the street by other boys, the emotional turmoil of being best friends with someone one day and ignored the next—an event he says that "was often tinged with racial overtones" (Schatteman 2001)—, and the discomfort of being torn between a British and West Indian culture. Phillips also faced challenges in his home setting that added to the precariousness he felt as the child of immigrants in the outside world. He felt confusion about his Caribbean heritage because his parents, who were of the pioneer generation, were anxious to root themselves in England and consequently didn't talk about life back home. This was particularly difficult, Phillips tells Pico Iyer, because Leeds was "a very rooted part of England, very working class, extended family. . . . Everybody is going to see their mam, their gran, or their aunt . . . I had my mother, and my father, and my brothers, and that's it. So, the primary displacement I felt was growing up in such a tight community without a sense of extended family." Home was made even more elusive for Phillips when his parents divorced and afterwards when his mother struggled with serious illness. For a period of time, he and his brothers had to be fostered out, or, as he expresses it, "cargoed around between white families in the north of England" (Jaggi), and later he lived with his father from the ages of fourteen to eighteen, due also to his mother's continued health problems.

Phillips's childhood was also one in which gender and class figured prominently. Growing up working class in England shaped his identity as much as did his race, and living primarily in a female-ruled household made him especially sensitive to the struggles of female characters. Various interviewers have commented on Phillips's ability to successfully capture female voices, and he himself admits to being drawn to women's viewpoints because they are often more honest, impassioned, and complex than men's and because gender issues are so inextricably linked to issues of race and class. Describing his childhood as a time of profound silence about his identity, Phillips suggests that this deprivation led him to use his writing to give voiceless people a chance to tell their own stories and consequently write themselves into history. Additionally, he often makes note of the importance of his learning about anti-Semitism and the Holocaust when a teenager because he could finally relate the hardships of his own life to a people's story, even if it was not his own people or his own story. His first short story, in fact, was about a Dutch Jewish boy and was written in 1973 after watching a TV documentary about the German occupation of the Netherlands.

Phillips's early years are so critical to his writing because it is during this period that he gained the experiential knowledge of themes that would later infuse his fiction. The other touchstone moments from his past reflect periods when he began to understand the causes of the crucible he had had to endure. During his college years, he began to demythologize the concept of class when he learned that students who came from supposedly better stock were no more intelligent or sophisticated than he. He also experienced racism anew, even though he was one of the more outgoing and socially active students on campus, but now he could contextualize the racial slurs against him in relation to the race riots that were taking place in Notting Hill in 1976. He also gained a heightened identification with blackness when he visited the United States during the summer before his last year at college and learned of the African American literary tradition. In the story that he refers to as "the old Laguna Beach story" (Iyer) because of how often it has been cited, he purchased a copy of Richard Wright's *Native Son* while visiting California and began reading it one morning. He finished the novel as the sun was setting in the ocean, and he rose out of his chair with the firm intention of becoming a writer himself. The importance of his identification with African American identity issues in the absence of a well-articulated black British identity cannot be overestimated. When he returned from his trip, he intended to do thesis work on African American literature, "as a not too subtle way of trying to synthesize Laguna Beach with Oxford" (Schatteman 2001), but he discovered that the university library did not have any of the resources needed even though American fiction was supposedly an available option. His frustration at this under-representation of minority voices would give Phillips the determination to make sure that his own books would one day be found in the Bodleian stacks.

Phillips started writing plays after college, but it was his trip to St. Kitts in 1980 that gave him distance from England and attachment to his place of origin, both elements he needed to begin to write fiction that could contain his own story. As he tells Maya Jaggi, "The trip liberated me. It kicked my brain out of a British perspective. I realized that narrative didn't begin in Leeds or Brixton." Phillips returned repeatedly to the Caribbean and even established a third household there for a period of time. This setting would serve to launch his career as a novelist as his first two novels, *The Final Passage* and *A State of Independence,* are set at least in part in the West Indies and present narratives about the first Caribbean immigrants to England, the Windrush Generation, and their relationship with their homes and families back on the islands.

Phillips's interviews also include considerable attention of his aesthetic choices, particularly in discussions about his use of characterization and form, both elements that are unique enough in his work to warrant investigation. As early as 1991, only six years after the publication of his first novel, Phillips identified form as the most important aspect of a writer's work. He says to Graham Swift, "It seems to me that the real test of a writer's ability is the degree to which the writer applies himself to the conundrum of form, to the task of imposing a form upon these undisciplined stories." What distinguishes Phillips's form in the majority of his works is, of course, his fragmented style and the resulting leaps he makes across his various narratives. It is often assumed that he did not begin splicing together stories from different times and spaces until the 1989 publication of *Higher Ground,* his third novel, but Phillips clarifies, in his interview with Carol Margaret Davison, that it was in the 1983 play entitled *The Shelter* that he actually began "exploring this way of writing and connecting across centuries." Phillips speaks eloquently about the logic and relevance of this form which he invented for himself, as he had no models to work from, and which he has used to varying degrees in all of his fiction with perhaps the exception of *A State of Independence.* In the Pico Iyer interview, he states, "I keep trying to write a book with a beginning, a middle, and an end, and then failing spectacularly. Something happens during the process where the linear structure seems to break down. It's almost like I've crafted this wonderful ceramic fruit bowl, and I'm two pages from the end of the book just doing the final glazing, and I deliberately drop it, and it shatters, and I have to start again." He fragments his narratives so dramatically, he explains to many interviewers, because his characters' lives have been so deeply disrupted by forces of history, forces such as slavery and migration. "It hasn't seemed right to write a novel about people whose lives are fractured and ruptured," he notes, "without trying to reflect some of that fracture and rupture in the narrative" (Schatteman 2001).

Phillips is equally emphatic and reflective in his interviews about his characterization, which is not surprising given that he began his literary career directing and then writing plays. As with his drama, Phillips's fiction writing starts with character, and he speaks often of how he views his characters as real individuals, people he must wait upon who continually surprise him despite his efforts to determine their actions. What has drawn readers' attention and interviewers' questions about Phillips's characterization is his tendency to depict individuals who are highly ambiguous and deeply flawed in at least one regard—Emily Cartwright from *Cambridge,* the African translator from *Higher Ground,* Bert Williams in *Dancing in the Dark,* and the father that sells his own children in *Crossing the River* being obvious examples—at the same time that he depicts individuals who are mere victims of the historical and cultural forces beyond their control—such as Eva from *The Nature of Blood,* Solomon from *A Distant Shore,* and Irene and even Rudi from *Higher Ground.* Phillips has argued that characterization automatically introduces ambivalence into fiction because characters resist the easy reduction of history and contemporary events to sloganeering; he capitalizes on the potential for ambiguity by often including individuals whose views he doesn't share so that he can, as he tells Jenny Sharpe, "transgress such artificial boundaries as good and evil, black and white—I mean black and white in the broader sense—right and wrong in fiction." To bring out these voices, Phillips draws upon what he describes as "confessional materials," or first-person accounts, which he fictionalizes in a way that explores the "self-serving nature behind the narratives" (Sharpe). Despite his characters' shortcomings, though, Phillips is unwavering in his refusal to judge them. "Part of the magic of writing," he stresses to Graham Swift, "is that you cannot be too judgmental about a character. You have to find some kind of trust, some form of engagement. You attempt to breathe life into these people and if you're lucky they breathe life into you."

The interviews also cover common ground in their discussions of the interrelated themes that are so pervasive in Phillips's work: those of displacement, home/homelessness, race and identity, Eurocentrism, victimization and complicity. Whether he is depicting slavery, migration, the Holocaust, or genocide; whether his narratives are set in England, the Caribbean, the United States, or Africa; whether he is writing about the contemporary moment or centuries ago, Phillips is always seeking out the stories of people who have been displaced and are not allowed to enjoy the basic human rights of security or visibility within the context of their particular place in history. Keenly aware that the powerful desire to be rooted carries with it the violent potential for exclusion, Phillips has adopted a pluralist notion of home for himself and advocates for a more fluid sense of human identity in his writing. His engagement with the world, as evi-

denced for example in the major reading tours he has given in twenty-one different countries in the past twenty years, suggests that Phillips has moved beyond
the need for affiliation as it is configured in conventional terms. In so doing, he
has joined the ranks of other transnational writers who write across borders and
who identify with a sense of belonging that emerges from the movement between
spaces rather than from an attachment to a specific locale. He names as his colleagues those writers who cannot be easily identified within one particular national tradition like J. M. Coetzee, Salman Rushdie, Michael Ondaatje, Pico Iyer,
Edwidge Danticat, Jhumpa Lahiri, and Rohinton Mistry. It is also significant that
Phillips repeatedly identifies James Baldwin as the person who asserted a great influence on his early writing since Baldwin, whose interest lay in matters involving
race consciousness, also declared a transatlantic identity for himself.

One final thread that runs through his interviews has to do with Phillips's
insistence on remaining true to his artistic convictions even in the face of criticism from various directions. A telling anecdote he recounts to Stephen Clingman involves an African American woman who was extremely angry at him
for including the white woman Joyce as one of the children claimed by the African father in *Crossing the River*. Phillips refuses to invest in notions of racial
solidarity and many of his works—particularly *Cambridge* and *The Nature of
Blood*—demonstrate his interest in examining the way that history has affected
white people as well as black. Other unpopular views that Phillips has willingly
voiced throughout his career include an unflattering representation of Caribbean
men in *The Final Passage,* the suggestion of a corrupt government in St. Kitts in
A State of Independence, the accusation of European barbarianism in *The European Tribe,* the indictment of Africans in the slave trade in *Higher Ground,* the
critique of the African Americans' idealization of Africa in *The Atlantic Sound,*
and the acknowledgment of a vexed relationship between African Americans and
Caribbean immigrants in *Dancing in the Dark.* J. M. Coetzee has commented that
Phillips's fiction has a single aim—"remembering what the West would like to
forget"[2]; clearly, Phillips's recollecting proves challenging for many different audiences, given the complicated dynamics of race, class, and power in the diaspora
as a whole.

Phillips's interviews also reflect shifts in his perspective that occur naturally over time as he moves from England to other locations, as he advances
from one academic position to another, as he develops a stronger sense of himself as a writer, and as he gains a fuller sense of the relationship and the inter-
relationship between his fiction and his nonfiction. But, as argued earlier, it is

the consistencies of Phillips's reflections over the past two decades that are more prominent, and they indicate that he likely had a general vision of his purposes from early on. When asked in a recent interview if he intended his texts to build on one another, he answered: "I'm increasingly aware of the territory that I'm trying to cross and recross. In that sense, inevitably the texts do speak to each other. Or maybe I should put it this way: they will eventually all speak to each other. But right now it's pretty much a matter of just staying on the scent of whatever it is that is pulling me forward" (Schatteman 2006). The driving forces behind Phillips's writing seem to be his commitment to the reworking of history to reveal new layers of analysis about the past and his ethic of empathy and hope for those who have been overtaken by historical injustices. In a number of interviews, Phillips is asked whether he sees himself as an optimist or a pessimist. While his answers vary, he more frequently suggests that some degree of hope does emerge from a heightened understanding of the causes of suffering, even if that understanding cannot yet offer immediate or practical remedies. As Jenny Sharpe notes, "[Phillips] is skeptical of facile solutions to the deep and pervasive problems left by history, but he holds out on the possibility that, even beset by tragedy, one can and should meet these challenges open-eyed and with courage." Phillips's works ultimately affirm those things that people cling to as they struggle to survive— love, faith, family—, as they call for the need of alternative social systems that do not impose unnecessary suffering on the marginalized. His is a moral imperative based in understanding and analysis which implicitly calls for reform, even if the means of transformation are never outlined in the texts themselves.

Phillips's overall uniqueness as a writer is affirmed by the way that he represents himself and his literary purposes in his many interviews. He is always challenging borders, whether in terms of racial divisions, distinctions of genre, or geographical identities. He resists being labeled by embracing many labels at once, seen, for example, in the way he allows himself to be identified as a black British writer, a Caribbean writer, or a postcolonial writer without feeling the need to rank his affiliations in a particular hierarchical order. He epitomizes a cosmopolitanism that is based on a sense of homelessness that has over time transformed into an affiliation with multiple homes at once. The resulting complexity of Phillips's writing and life has clearly made a significant impression on his readers, for he has received significant critical attention for his overarching project throughout his career. He has been given honorary degrees from Amherst College (1995), Leeds Metropolitan University (1997), University of York (2003), Leeds University (2003), and Yale University (2006); he has received numerous literary fellowships, including the Guggenheim Foundation Fellowship in 1992; his novel *Crossing the River* was shortlisted for the Booker Prize in 1993; his fiction has been translated into eleven different languages; he has been honored at an international conference entitled "Caryl Phillips: Twenty-five Years of Writing" which was held at the University of Liège, Belgium, in 2006; and he has been the recipient of many prestigious prizes, ranging from the Malcolm X Prize for Literature which he received in 1987 to the PEN/Beyond Margins Award which he was awarded in 2006.

The seventeen interviews and two profiles based on interviews that have been selected for this collection are generally longer and include more sustained discussions of particular texts than those not included. They are deliberately unedited with only silent proofing so as to be of maximum value to readers and scholars. They are presented in full, with the exceptions of the Michael Kransy and John McLeod interviews, which included questions from an audience in their original form. The interviews are arranged chronologically in the order that they took place, and the location of each interview is indicated to illustrate Phillips's spatial movements over time. There is a degree of repetition in the interviews, as is to be expected in a collection such as this, but this proves valuable in highlighting the sustained intensity of Phillips's vision and in underscoring how his ideas about writing and about displacement, race, and belonging have expanded over time as he has moved outward from his starting place as a writer in England. The interviews not selected here offer additional information on Phillips's biography, and a number of them include his reflections on his early work as a playwright.

A project of this scope involves many people. My gratitude goes to Seetha Srinivasan, director of the University Press of Mississippi, for seeing the significance of Phillips's oeuvre and the need for this collection; to Walter Biggins, editor, for fielding my many questions about the exact details of the publication; to Michele Yulo, my steadfast graduate assistant, for her enthusiastic dedication to the work of obtaining permissions and transcribing interviews; to Bénédicte Ledent, author of the first monograph on Phillips, for creating and maintaining an online bibliography of Phillips's writing since 2000, and to Maya Wainhaus, Phillips's assistant, for her help in tracking down sources. But my primary thanks go to Caryl Phillips himself for offering the kindness, patience, and collaborative spirit that have been critical in seeing this project through to its completion, for being so generous to scholars who realize the seriousness of his work, and for understanding the importance of giving his readers the opportunity to listen in on the meaningful conversations he has engaged in over the course of his career.

RS

Notes

1. George Garrett, "Separate Prisons," *New York Times Book Review,* February 16, 1992: 25.
2. "What We Would Like to Forget," *New York Review of Books* Volume 44, Number 17, November 6, 1997: 41.

Chronology

1958   Caryl Phillips is born on March 13 in St. Kitts, West Indies, to Malcolm and Lilian, above a rum shop owned by mother's family. At twelve weeks, he is taken by parents to England, where they relocate to a white, working-class neighborhood in Leeds.

1969   Passes eleven-plus exam and attends Leeds Central High School.

1976–79   Wins a place at the Queen's College, Oxford University, where he studies English language and literature and directs plays.

1978   Travels across the United States during the summer of his second year of college and is introduced to the African American literary tradition.

1979–80   Spends a year in Edinburgh after graduating from Oxford, writing plays and scripts.

1980   First play, *Strange Fruit,* is produced at the Crucible Theatre in Sheffield. Returns to St. Kitts for the first time since infancy.

1980–82   Is named Arts Council of Great Britain Writer-in-Residence at the Factory Arts Centre in West London.

1982   *Where There Is Darkness* is produced at Hammersmith Lyric Theatre, London.

1983   *The Shelter* is produced at Hammersmith Lyric Theatre, London. Visits St. Kitts again to witness the independence of the country and to produce a documentary for the BBC.

1984   Radio play *The Wasted Years* is awarded the BBC Giles Cooper Award. Tours Europe for nine months to gather material that would later appear in *The European Tribe.*

1985   First novel, *The Final Passage,* is published by Faber and Faber. Receives the Malcolm X Prize for Literature for *The Final Passage.*

1986   *A State of Independence* is published by Faber and Faber. Writes the screenplay for *Playing Away,* which premieres at the London International Film Festival.

1987   *The European Tribe,* his travelogue and first work of nonfiction, is

published by Faber and Faber. Awarded Martin Luther King Memorial
Prize for *The European Tribe*. Becomes writer-in-residence at the University of Mysore, India.

1988–89   Lives in St. Kitts.

1989   *Higher Ground* is published by Viking Press. Becomes writer-in-
residence at the University of Stockholm, Sweden.

1990   Visiting writer at Amherst College in Amherst, Massachusetts.

1991   *Cambridge* is published by Bloomsbury Press.

1992   Becomes writer-in-residence and co-director of Creative Writing
Center at Amherst College. *(London) Sunday Times* names him Young
Writer of the Year for *Cambridge*, and he is awarded a Guggenheim
Fellowship.

1993   *Crossing the River* is published by Bloomsbury and shortlisted for the
Booker Prize. Granta lists him as Best of Young British Novelists of
1993.

1994   Is awarded the James Tait Black Memorial Prize for *Crossing the River*
and wins the Lannan Literary Award for Fiction. Becomes professor of
English at Amherst College.

1996   Adapts and co-produces *The Final Passage* as a two-part television
series.

1997   *The Nature of Blood* is published by Faber and Faber. Edits *Extravagant Strangers: A Literature of Belonging*, an anthology of short pieces
by British writers not born in Britain, which is published by Faber
and Faber. Travels from the Caribbean to England on a transatlantic
freighter to relive his parents' experience of migration and to gather
material that would later appear in *The Atlantic Sound*.

1998   Becomes professor of English and Henry R. Luce Professor of Migration and Social Order at Barnard College, Columbia University, New
York, as well as series editor of Faber Caribbean Series.

1999   Edits *The Right Set*, a tennis anthology published by Faber and Faber,
and is named the University of the West Indies Humanities Scholar of
the Year.

2000   *The Atlantic Sound*, his second book of nonfiction, is published by
Faber and Faber. Elected fellow of the Royal Society of Literature and
is named Director of Initiatives in the Humanities at Barnard College,
Columbia University.

2001   *A New World Order: Selected Essays* is published by Secker and Warburg. Writes screenplay for V. S. Naipaul's 1957 novel *The Mystic Masseur,* which is made into a Merchant Ivory film.

2002   Becomes fellow at the Centre for Scholars and Writers, New York Public Library.

2003   *A Distant Shore* is published by Secker and Warburg.

2004   Wins the Commonwealth Writers Prize for *A Distant Shore* and the Caribbean American Heritage Award for Outstanding Contribution to Literature.

2005   *Dancing in the Dark* is published by Secker and Warburg. Becomes professor of English at Yale University.

2006   Receives the PEN/Beyond Margins Award for *Dancing in the Dark.* Elected honorary fellow of the Queen's College, Oxford University.

2007   *Foreigners* is published by Secker and Warburg.

Conversations with Caryl Phillips

Interview by Kay Saunders

Kay Saunders/1986

From *Kunapipi* 9.1 (1987), 44–52. Reprinted by permission of Kay Saunders and *Kunapipi*. Interview conducted in London, on June 5, 1986.

KS: In both your novels, *The Final Passage* (London: Faber and Faber, 1985) and *A State of Independence* (London: Faber and Faber, 1986) you explore the notion of colonialism in its destructive role in the Caribbean. Did you write each novel separately or did you envisage them as a cycle?

CP: They were conceived of separately because *The Final Passage* was a first novel, right? The main problem was just to write a novel. I didn't have any Trollope-like idea of constructing a nine-novel sequence . . . I finished that novel and I didn't have any other novel in mind or any idea of what more I might do, About six months after having finished *The Final Passage,* I thought of an idea for another novel. As it happens, they were both linked by the notion of colonialism, simply because I don't think it is really possible to address the Caribbean in any literary way without touching upon colonialism. Colonialism sustained Caribbean history for 250 to 300 years.

KS: The changing of masters from Britain to the United States is depicted very clearly in *A State of Independence.*

CP: Well, that is something I witnessed in 1983 when St. Kitts [and Nevis] became independent. I was there doing a programme for the BBC and I remember standing there when the British flag came down the pole, I was five yards away when the new flag of the nation went up. I just kept thinking to myself: "This is nonsense because already the place is completely infused with an American colonialism; not just because you can pay for stuff with U.S. dollars, but the TV, the music, the food, the cars, etc." It didn't strike me that there was going to be any intervening period where an indigenous Caribbean cultural form of expression could flourish. Britain has had no interest in the Caribbean since 1834 when it was no longer possible to exploit free labour and the bottom fell out of the sugar market, and more recently since she joined the EEC. It is inevitable that a country the size of St. Kitts and Nevis is going to be dependent upon colonial masters of

3

some sort, even if one calls them "special relationships." You cannot be independent if you're a country of 35,000 people . . . And given the geographic proximity to America, the outcome was obvious. It was sad—but inevitable.

KS: Your novels are very historically authentic. Did you engage upon research or have you imaginatively reconstructed either parts of your own life and observations or that of your parents?

CP: First, *A State of Independence* is based on absolute historical veracity to the point of being dodgy in terms of my relationship with the government of the country I come from [*St. Kitts*]. I was there. I saw it. I witnessed the event. It did rain at precisely the moment when the flag was hoisted. Everything is almost authentic and the minister is based upon a real person. If I hadn't been there, I would have had to do some research. *The Final Passage* is historically rooted in the late 1950s. It came from talking to not just my parents but others as well. I did actually dig up a few old things from papers in the fifties and sixties on the Caribbean and here in London; so it wasn't a research job in the sense of having an idea, then moulding the characters to make a novel. I had the characters and the people and the land and the story and I just wanted to pin it down a bit in history. There are facts which are important facts. Sometimes we forget the numbers and the hardships, the pressures that caused those people to migrate.

KS: In Beverley Bryan's *The Heart of the Race* [*Black Women's Lives in Britain,* Virago Press, 1985] the people interviewed in London talk about very similar experiences that you do in *The Final Passage;* even though, of course, it becomes far more optimistic because black women are now able to mobilise themselves into a political force in a way that they could not do in the 1950s.

CP: Well, yes. I think the role of black women in Britain is very different from that in the Caribbean. You'd have to ask a woman, I suppose, for an insider's view of this. But from my own perspective, it seems to me that there are curious kinds of contradictions in the Caribbean. Women seem to have much more of a responsible role in the family—perhaps because men are far more irresponsible. Women have a far more central role in the bringing up of children and being responsible for the running of the place on a day-to-day basis, But their actual access to power—political power, social power—is as limited as it was in prewar Britain. Their role in the larger Caribbean society seems to be pretty . . .

KS: Minimal?

CP: Yes, minimal. They don't have any access to real power, to making structures in those societies. Yet, paradoxically, they seem to be more dominant figures in the day-to-day business of organising on a family level. In England, more recently, black women have been able to express themselves more in terms of being able to grasp the reins of their own destiny, and shape their lives the way they want them to be, irrespective of what men want—black or white. But I still can't understand why it is that they occupy such a dominant role in the Caribbean society on the one hand, but seem to be excluded, on the other hand, from things that, being in London, I'd take for granted, like women in Parliament, in top positions in colleges and hospitals, lawyers. There are very few in the Caribbean. When a lot of black women in this country go back, they find it very, very difficult to come to terms with life there. They've grown to accept one form of being treated and relating to men in this country. Then in the Caribbean, irrespective of their educational attainment, they're just treated like shit basically by a very male, macho society.

KS: Well, I thought when I was in the Caribbean that it was very much the operation of a nineteenth-century concept of "separate spheres" where, as you say, women are very dominant in the family and it seemed that men reneged on their familial responsibilities.
CP: Totally.

KS: Yes, and left women to run the family often with a huge number of children—and in great financial difficulties.
CP: That's what I meant when I said the responsibility which women seem to have in the Caribbean might not be what they want, but rather it is a by-product of the irresponsibility of some of the men. I suspect that the notion of women's traditional role is not because they have been given responsibility because men think they are so trustworthy, but because there is a long tradition of wilful or unwilful neglect or absence on the part of men. They had to perform migratory labour. But there is also wilful irresponsibility.

KS: It emerged also out of the experience of slavery when family life was unstable.
CP: You know that's a familiar argument, but I really don't buy it. That was 150 years ago. It is a convenient cop-out for a lot of blokes, "Well, we've not actually owned our children."

KS: And why should we start now?
CP: Yes. It's very convenient. It's nice for them. It is rooted in some pseudo-historical jargon to appear respectable.

KS: The campaign that the government in Jamaica is now having to promote contraception is falling on very deaf ears with Jamaican men.

CP: Yes, I know. But that would happen anywhere. The received wisdom is: "Contraception is a women's problem and responsibility." Blokes there think contraception is not on, full stop ... "It's not natural." Eric Williams once said about the Caribbean that it was a twentieth-century people trapped in a nineteenth-century economy. Well, I often find that sometimes they are twentieth-century people trapped in nineteenth-century ideas.

KS: That's why I said "separate spheres" operates very strongly there. This applies to a theme which you can see in Walker's *The Color Purple*. And, in some ways, you suggest in *The Final Passage* that perhaps women's happiness may lie in women-centred relationships rather than them worrying about all the hassles connected with negotiating life with men. Although you don't have a sexual relationship between Leila and Millie.

CP: No. But the only happy relationship Leila ever had was with her friend, Millie. I don't think that I would be able to take it as far as Alice Walker in *The Color Purple*. She's quite explicit because she does suggest that there's a lot more satisfaction and stability in that relationship with women (between Shug and Celie); I'm not really qualified to talk about the relationship between those two women in terms of either a sexual relationship or an on-going physical relationship of any kind. But I would suggest that for this particular woman, Leila, the man she married, Michael, has all those things we've just been talking about—an irresponsibility born of ... an aimlessness of the life which has been bestowed on him by colonialism. What I was trying to say by using his buddy Bradeth in a kind of mirror is that you don't have to be like that. One feels sorry for Michael because he's riding around the island on his motorcycle aimlessly.

KS: He's trapped like in Joan Didion's *Play It As It Lays*.

CP: Yes, he can't get out. But Michael's friend Bradeth is there to show it up. We meet the two of them sitting outside of a bar pissed. We think "A right pair of rogues." But a third of the way through the novel one of them grows up. Bradeth decides—yes, he has got this woman pregnant; yes, he is going to marry her; yes, he will change his life to accommodate his circumstances. He actually ends up physically threatening Michael and says, "You've got to grow up too." So, I mean, what I was trying to suggest is, that Leila's problem is not so much with men but with that particular man.

KS: You have a similar scenario in *A State of Independence* when you're dealing with gender relations between Bertram Francis and his girlfriend, Patsy Archibald, and it is unclear in this novel as to whether the child she bears is Francis's.

CP: Well, it's more than hinted at. The kid is hers really. And it is his as well. He is very vague. In *A State of Independence* the relationship between the men and the women is very problematical. At the time Bertram left, Patsy was much more grown up than he was. He had to go away in order to grow up and face his responsibilities. She realises very early on, something which is implicit in the title: there is no such thing as a "state of independence," either for the country or for them as individuals. Before his departure for England, Patsy says, "Well, what about me?" He says, "I've got to do this on my own," despite the fact that he obviously loves her and cares for her. When we see him on his return, and he sits with her, it becomes apparent that she was the one who survived. She was the stronger of the pair.

KS: She's a wonderful character, particularly in the way that she tries to explain to him in very emotional terms what life is like there. He has to find out after many, many hard knocks, though to what degree he ever understands, is problematical. He understands it in the wider political context, but whether he understands it as a person, I don't know.

CP: Well, again you've touched upon something vital which runs through both novels; because I do believe that, to a certain extent, there is a greater maturity amongst Caribbean women than amongst the men. And that maturity is born of responsibility and understanding that there is no such thing as independence— that you are interdependent upon each other as families, as lovers, as friends and that you can't just shirk that responsibility. Women, especially when they are involved in motherhood, know intuitively what it means to be independent and what it means not to be independent; what it means to rely upon somebody; what it means not to rely upon somebody. And that is, if you like, a microcosm of the Caribbean. The whole notion of being independent in the Caribbean is what screwed it up for many, many years. Particularly, in recent Caribbean history, the notion that a land of 100,000 people can state: "We are a country with our own flag, our own national anthem, our own way of doing things, and sod the islanders ten miles across the water that we see every day." Given that 99 percent of the leaders in the Caribbean have been men, that attitude is mirrored in the attitudes of a lot of men towards the family.

KS: As if they are just autonomous individuals.
CP: That's neither true for the islands nor for the individuals.

KS: Women are not usually in a position to renege on their responsibilities.
CP: Exactly, especially to children who are a metaphor for the next generation.

That's why I call the kid in *A State of Independence* "Livingstone." It does suggest that there is a new beginning; whether that beginning is going to be correct or whether the island is going through another kind of awful exploitative rebirth is anybody's guess. But . . . the clue is the name, "Livingstone." I really don't think they are going anywhere.

KS: You have Livingstone working as a gardener in a big American hotel. So his fate is set.

CP: It's like a new colonial product really.

KS: In the novels of V. S. Naipaul, the family is totally enveloping. You can see the different aspects if you consider whether you're talking about a negro family or an Indian family. Trinidadian history is in itself a very different experience from other parts of the Caribbean.

CP: The first time I ever went to Trinidad, I was shocked to discover how many Indians were there. Roughly 50 percent Indians, 50 percent black. I'd always found a certain difficulty with Naipaul's work because in it I'd never been able to recognise the Caribbean in which I lived. They are specifically Trinidadian Indians, emerging out of a different cultural tradition. The Indian family in Britain tends to be more of a stable structure. It feeds off itself and tends to be more self-reliant. In V. S. Naipaul's work I've never really recognised the splintered, messed-up, crazy relationships between men and women, women and children, men and children and grandparents which I'd always recognised as being specifically West Indian. V. S. Naipaul doesn't feel any sense of belonging anywhere; but I do feel a sense of belonging there. It's a responsibility for me to address myself to the questions that are for me more urgent. I cannot feel detached about the Caribbean, V S. Naipaul is laconic about the whole thing. He's a fine writer. There's no reason why he shouldn't be detached. He grew up there, he was schooled there, I wasn't. Maybe I'm trying to discover what he's trying to forget. The Caribbean has a funny tradition of writers who either seek to discover it or to escape from it. Most of its major writers in the past have left, trading nomadic lives like Claude McKay or have settled in America or Europe. It provokes a very odd attitude in writers towards how to address it.

It's very hard because I wasn't brought up in the Caribbean, so I'm still discovering things about it I made an effort to discover, perhaps more than most of my generation, because I've been fortunate enough to go back there sometimes and do things. I've made it my business to find out about the Caribbean. What you have is somebody who left there very early and feels attached to the place; it's an emotional attachment but it's more than that because it is a territory of the world that cries out to be written about and debated about. I think its position, sitting there between Latin America and that great brooding land of the brave above, its geographical proximity to both makes it fascinating. Its influences, European, American, African, South American, Indian, have produced such an explosive society, not just politically but culturally as well. But it's really tricky because I don't think there's anybody of my generation in Britain who has trodden that path—the reverse path of having been brought up here—and is now actually engaged actively in the Caribbean. Most people criticise me quite a lot for not writing more about Britain. They say, "Shit, the riots, how come you're not writing about Britain?" I do write about Britain, in other things I do for radio and television or whatever. I suppose, however, that my main concern is the Caribbean. Because of the volatile nature of the relationship between black people here and British society, everybody is telling me I should be writing about Britain. But I'm not really feeling engaged with that. This creates more of a desire to find out more about the Caribbean. Then in the West Indies they're always saying I'm putting down West Indian guys. Well, I don't think that's too difficult to do.

KS: What do they want? Travel brochures?

CP: Well, I think they'd like to see, to use a well-worn expression, the West Indian male highlighted in a more sympathetic light. It comes back to the notion of responsibility and inter-dependence which is what is desperately needed in the Caribbean. This generation's political leaders in the Caribbean today are like the first or second generation leaders they had in Africa. Basically, collaborators to some extent with the colonial masters. They're getting what they can out of it. They want to have what the people who ruled before them had and they want it *now*.

KS: Those leaders are compradors. My own observations of the Caribbean were, even at the most personal level, that West Indian men tended to be predatory. You could translate this metaphor into a wider sense as well.

CP: There's an underdeveloped sense of history in the Caribbean. In *A State of Independence* I said: "We're too small to have a past." Patsy says, "We're too small an island"—that attitude of living for today and tomorrow. It's not good enough to conceive of history in terms of "Slavery and here we are now—Toyota." There's a whole bigger sense of development which is ignored and is tied up with the sense of being predatory—of stalking and being on the look-out for the easy opportunity.

I'd like to think, in conclusion, that I was a Lamming who could cling on to the Caribbean. He's not super-popular in Barbados but he's a survivor. He says, "Screw it. This is where I'm from and I'll stay here." It's a difficult place to keep your head above the water if you're in any way critical, and make critical observations. People there just hate self-criticism. The critical tradition just hasn't developed. And because it's such a macho society, any condemnation of behaviour of the West Indian male is taken personally. I don't know how it will be resolved . . . Writers are notoriously scaly and headstrong, liable just to say anything . . . The general tone of the society is that you lose friends by simply being critical.

Caryl Phillips Interviewed by Graham Swift

Graham Swift/1991

From *Kunapipi* 13.3 (1991), 96–103. Reprinted by permission of Graham Swift and *Kunapipi*. Adapted from a public interview conducted at the Institute of Contemporary Arts, London, in March 1991.

I first met Caryl, or Caz as I've come to know him, a few years ago at a literary jamboree in Toronto. I think we fulfilled all our official duties, but we spent a lot of time in a place in downtown Toronto called the Bamboo Club—one of those places which has acquired since a sort of metaphysical status, because whenever Caz and I have met again in some far-flung corner of the globe, it seems our first instinct has been to find out where the "Bamboo Club" is. Caz, I confess, is a little bit better at finding it than I am.

Caz was born in 1958 in St. Kitts, one of the Leeward Islands in the Caribbean. He came to England when still a babe in arms and was brought up and educated here. In more recent years, he has travelled extensively and has made his temporary home in many parts of the world, including his native St. Kitts. In keeping with his nomadic inclination, it could be said that one of the main themes of his work is that of the journey or, put rather differently, of human displacement and dislocation in a variety of forms. The journey behind his first novel, *The Final Passage* (1985), was the one Caz himself took part in, albeit unwittingly—the emigration of the post-war years from the Caribbean to this country. The journey that lies behind both Caz's last novel, *Higher Ground* (1989), and his new novel, *Cambridge*, is a more historic, more primal and more terrible journey, the journey of the slave trade westwards from Africa.

Caz has maintained, however, a keen interest in Europe or, to be more precise, in Europe's pretensions and delusions about the place of European civilization in the world. His book of essays, *The European Tribe* (1987), was devoted to the subject. In *Higher Ground*, a novel in three parts, we travel from Africa in the slave trade days to North America at the time of the Black Power movement, only to end up in a Europe still nursing its wounds from the last war. In *Cambridge*, Caz has reversed the direction of this journey to bring a European consciousness face to face with Europe's global perpetrations. He does this through the person of Emily, a woman of the early nineteenth century who escapes an arranged marriage by travelling to her father's estate in the West Indies (her father being an absentee landlord), where she is exposed to and, indeed, exposed by the effects of slavery and colonialisation.

Like its predecessor, *Cambridge* is a novel in three distinct parts, the first and longest of which is Emily's own account of her journey and her observations when she arrives. From what seems at first to be an inquisitive, self-consoling travelogue there emerges a drama revolving around a handful of characters: Emily herself; Brown, an Englishman whom we understand has somehow ousted the previous manager of the estate; the Cambridge of the title, a negro slave who has suffered the singular and equivocal fate of having lived in England and having been converted to Christianity; and another slave, Christiania, who, despite her name, indulges in decidedly un-Christian rites and appears to be on the verge of madness.

The second part of the book is Cambridge's own account of how he came to be Anglicized and Christianized. The third, written in the form of a report (which we guess to be far from reliable), describes how Cambridge comes to be executed for the murder of Brown. And the brief epilogue of the novel tells us the effect of all this on Emily. These last few pages are particularly astonishing. Coming at the end of a novel of enormous accumulative power, they pack a tremendous punch and, written in a prose of tense intimacy, they show how facile it is to assess either Caz's work as a whole, or his heroine, by any crude cultural or racial analysis. Caz is interested in human beings. Emily's plight at the end of the novel plainly has its cultural and racial dimension, but it's essentially one of personal trauma—psychological, sexual, moral, and (a word Caz will no doubt love) existential.

GS: How did *Cambridge* arise? What was the germ, the idea behind it?
CP: You know that period when you've finished a book and you don't know what to do? We generally have lunch during these periods in that place around the corner from the British Library, as one of us is pretending to be "working" in there. Well true to form, I was doing little more than scrambling around in the British Library, having just finished *Higher Ground,* and having a month and a half on my hands before I was due to go down to St. Kitts. It was during this period that I happened upon some journals in the North Library. One in particular caught my eye. It was entitled *Journal of a Lady of Quality,* and written by a Scotswoman, named Janet Schaw, who at the beginning of the nineteenth century travelled from Edinburgh to the Caribbean. What attracted me to this story was the fact

that she visited St. Kitts. Right beside what was once my brother's place, up in the mountains in St. Kitts, is a broken-down Great House. Janet Schaw described going to a dinner there when it was the centrepiece of one of the grandest plantations in the Eastern Caribbean. I began to realize then that there was a whole literature of personal narratives written primarily by women who had travelled to the Caribbean in that weird phase of English history between the abolition of slavery in 1807 and the emancipation of the slaves in 1834. Individuals who inherited these Caribbean estates from their families were curious to find out what this property was, what it would entail to maintain it, whether they would get any money. The subject matter began to speak, but that's never enough, for there's another and formidable hurdle to leap; that of encouraging a character to speak to you. At the back of '88 when we used to meet, I was concerned with the subject matter and the research, but as yet no character had begun to speak.

GS: And how did the character of *Cambridge* evolve?

CP: Actually, he came second. Emily, the woman's voice, came first, partly because for the last ten years I'd been looking for a way of writing the story of a Yorkshire woman. I'd grown up in Yorkshire and I had also read and reread *Wuthering Heights,* so I'd this name in my head, Emily. Emily, who wasn't anybody at the moment.

GS: The novel's called *Cambridge,* but Emily certainly has more prominence in terms of pages. I wondered whether you'd ever thought of Cambridge as the main character, or indeed if you'd still think of him as the main character?

CP: No. Emily was always going to be the main character, but Cambridge was conceived of as a character who would be ever-present. He doesn't appear often in her narrative, in terms of time, but he's always in the background of what she's doing, and what she's saying, and what she's thinking. And then, of course, in the second section of the novel, he has his own narrative.

GS: There's a lovely irony to *Cambridge*'s narrative. We've had many pages of Emily and then we get Cambridge's account: Emily figures in Cambridge's mind merely as that Englishwoman on the periphery—scarcely at all, in fact.

CP: There is a corrective in having Cambridge's perspective. Cambridge's voice is politically very important because it is only through painful application that he has acquired the skills of literacy. There are so few African accounts of what it was like to go through slavery, because African people were generally denied access to the skills of reading and writing. Reading and writing equals power. Once you have a language, you are dangerous. Cambridge actually makes the effort to acquire a language. He makes the effort to acquire the skills of literacy and uses them to sit in judgement on himself and the societies he passes through.

GS: Did your feelings about *Cambridge* change as you wrote the novel? He is a very ambiguous character.

CP: You know you cannot be too judgmental about your characters. Novels are an incredibly democratic medium. Everyone has a right to be understood. I have a lot of problems swallowing most of what Emily says and feels. Similarly, I have difficulties with many of Cambridge's ideas and opinions, because in modem parlance he would be regarded as an Uncle Tom. But I don't feel I have the right to judge them.

GS: Emily seems to be a mixture of tentative liberal instincts and blind prejudice. And it could be easy for us, with our twentieth-century complacent hindsight, to judge her quite harshly, but you are very sympathetic—and we can't do anything but sympathize with her, pity her. I wonder if your feelings about her changed as you wrote her long narrative?

CP: (pause) Maybe.

GS: Did you have the end even as you wrote the narrative?

CP: No. No. I think she grows. She has to make a journey which begins from the periphery of English society. I could not have told this story from the point of view of a man. She was regarded, as most women of that time were regarded, as a "child of lesser growth" when placed alongside her male contemporaries. She was on the margin of English society, and I suspect that one of the reasons I was able to key into her, and to listen to what she had to say, was the fact that, like her, I also grew up in England feeling very marginalized. She also made a journey to the Caribbean for the purpose of keeping body and soul together, which is a journey I made ten years ago. So in that sense, looking at it coldly now, through the prism of time, I can understand why I would have listened to somebody like her and why she would have entrusted me with her story. And through the process of writing . . . you are right, I did begin to feel a little warmer towards her. She rose up above her racist attitudes.

GS: She became alive in her own right.

CP: Because she was courageous. It may be a small and somewhat unpleasant thing in the context of 1991 to find a woman expressing some warmth and affection for her black maid, but in the early nineteenth century it was remarkable that a woman, and particularly this woman, was able to confess to such emotions. A nineteenth-century man couldn't have done this, for men have a larger capacity for bullshit and for self-deception, even when they are talking only to themselves. I am not sure that I would have trusted the narrative of a nineteenth-century man engaged in the slave trade. The only time I read men's narratives which seem to me to be lyrical is when the men, nineteenth century or otherwise, are in prison.

GS: Emily, in a way, is about to be sold into a kind of slavery—her arranged marriage—which gives her a perspective on what she sees. Is that how you saw it?
CP: Yes. I don't want to push it too hard, for the two things are obviously only analogous on a minor key. However, an arranged marriage to a widower who possessed three kids and a guaranteed income was a form of bondage. Emily finds the strength, the wit, and the way out of this. I admire her for this. What makes her grow are a series of events which are particularly painful and distressing for her. As I have already stated, part of the magic of writing is that you cannot be too judgmental about a character. You have to find some kind of trust, some form of engagement. You attempt to breathe life into these people and if you're lucky they breathe life into you. You love them with passion; then, at the end of two or three or four years, you abandon them and try and write another book.

GS: You said a moment ago that men could only become lyrical when they are in prison. The second part of *Higher Ground* actually consists of letters from prison in a very distinct male voice. In that novel generally, you seemed to depart from your previous work in using strong first person voices. In *Cambridge* again, there is an emphasis on first person narrative. Was that a conscious decision or did that just happen?
CP: It was conscious. There are any number of stories that you can tell. You are populated with the potential for telling stories from now until doomsday, for these things are circling around in your head. But it seems to me that the real test of a writer's ability is the degree to which that writer applies him or herself to the conundrum of form, to the task of imposing a form upon these undisciplined stories. I had written two novels in the form of the third person and somehow I couldn't address myself again to such a manner of telling a story. It was as though I had to find some way of expanding my repertoire. So the first part of *Higher Ground* is written in first person present tense, the second part as a series of letters and the third part is in the third person but with these rather strange flashbacks. Each segment of the novel demanded a different point of attack. It was a way of breaking out of what was becoming, to me, the straightjacket of the third person. We used to talk about this when you were writing *Out of This World*. I remember you saying that there was an intimacy about the first person which

you found attractive. Well, me too. And like you, I am interested in history, in memory, in time, and in the failure of these three things. It seems to me, at this stage anyhow, that the first person gives me an intimate flexibility which I can't find in the third person.

GS: Nine-tenths of *Cambridge* is written in a pastiche of nineteenth-century language. Certainly, the final few pages of it are your language, the language of the twentieth century. This sense of a language that can talk about certain things suddenly bursting through Emily's own language in which she can't, is very volcanic. It is a brilliant conclusion to a novel. I wonder if we could broaden things out and talk more generally about your writing. You say in *The European Tribe* that you wanted to be a writer while sitting by the Pacific in California with the waves lapping around your ankles . . .

CP: Alright, alright! The summer of my second year in college, I travelled around America on a bus until my money ran out in California. And I went into this bookshop and bought this book, *Native Son,* by Richard Wright. There weren't many black people writing in England. So it never occurred to me that writing as a profession was a possibility. But when I was in the States, I discovered such people as Jimmy Baldwin and Richard Wright and Toni Morrison.

GS: Do you think it was necessary to go to America to become a writer?
CP: I was slouching towards a writing career. Being in the States shifted me into high gear and out of the very slovenly third that I was stuck in.

GS: How old were you when you first went back to St. Kitts?
CP: Twenty-two. I had written a play, *Strange Fruit,* in 1980, which was done at the Crucible Theatre in Sheffield. And with the royalties from that, I went back to St. Kitts with my mother, who had left in 1958 when she was twenty. It was strange, because I had grown up without an overbearing sense of curiosity about the Caribbean. My mother hadn't been back either. She held it in her memory. But when we arrived in St. Kitts, many of the things that she remembered were no longer there: her school had burnt down, people that she knew had died, and someone she dearly wanted me to meet had long since emigrated to America. For her it was like discovering a ghost town. But for me, it fired my curiosity about myself, about England, about the Caribbean. Naturally, the "rediscovery" confused and confounded me, but that was no bad thing for, after all, writers are basically just people who are trying to organize their confusion.

GS: Your first two novels were very much about the Caribbean, coming from and going back to. How much was that actually paralleling your life and exorcising your own feelings about the Caribbean?

CP: My first novel, *The Final Passage,* was published in 1985. I had started it some five years earlier, on the inter-island ferry between St. Kitts and Nevis. I looked back at St. Kitts and began to write some sentences down. I wanted to try and tell the story of the journey from the Caribbean to England, which seemed to me to be, in terms of fiction in this country, an untold story. People had written novels and stories about this journey, but not people of my generation. The second novel, *A State of Independence* (1986), although not autobiographical, followed the emotional contours of my life, in that it dealt with the problems of returning to the Caribbean and thinking, they are not sure if I am one of them, and yet feeling that I am not sure if I am one of them either. However, I have certainly not exorcised my feelings about the Caribbean. I have no desire to do so. The reason I write about the Caribbean is that the Caribbean contains both Europe and Africa, as I do. The Caribbean belongs to both Europe and Africa. The Caribbean is an artificial society created by the massacre of its inhabitants, the Carib and Arawak Indians. It is where Africa met Europe on somebody else's soil. This history of the Caribbean is a bloody history. It is a history which is older than the history of the United States of America. Columbus didn't arrive in the United States. He arrived in the Caribbean. The Caribbean is Marquez' territory. He always describes himself as a Caribbean writer. It's Octavio Paz' territory. It's Fuentes' territory. The Caribbean for many French and Spanish-speaking writers has provided more than enough material for a whole career. For me, that juxtaposition of Africa and Europe in the Americas is very important.

GS: But now it's not just Europe, America has moved in. How do you feel about that? You are living in America now, teaching there.

CP: The reason I am living in America is because, like yourself, like many people, business occasionally takes me to the United States. When I'm not there all I have to do is turn on the TV, or open up the papers, and I am bombarded with images of America. In other words, over the years I have come to think of myself as somebody who knows America because I have some kind of a relationship with it. However, I'm not sure that anybody can seriously claim to "know" a country as large and as diverse as the United States. It seemed important, given the opportunity of spending a year or maybe two years in the United States, to make a concerted effort to get to know a part of the country more intimately. That's really why I'm living there. Furthermore, the Caribbean is now, to some extent, culturally an extension of the Florida Keys, and I really want to understand a bit more about American people rather than simply imagining them all to be characters out of *Dallas,* or a nation whose soul is reflected in the studio audience and guests of *The Oprah Winfrey Show.*

GS: I've one last question and it's quite a big one. We always have a lot of fun together, whenever we meet we have some laughs. Yet your work doesn't really glow with optimism. You are very hard on your characters; most of your central characters are lost people, they suffer. Pessimism seems to win through. Is that ultimately your view of the world?

CP: I am always surprised that people think I am a pessimist. *Cambridge* is to some extent optimistic. Emily grows. Okay, she suffers greatly, but she still grows. It's the price of the ticket, isn't it? The displacement ticket. Displacement engenders a great deal of suffering, a great deal of confusion, a great deal of soul-searching. It would be hard for me to write a comedy about displacement. But there is courage. Emily has a great amount of courage. As does Cambridge. And in *Higher Ground* there is faith. I don't necessarily mean faith with a religious gloss on it. I mean the ability to actually acknowledge the existence of something that you believe in, something that helps you to make sense of your life. You are right when you say that the characters are often lost, and that they suffer. But I would like to claim that the spirit and tenacity with which my characters fight to try and make a sense of their often helplessly fated lives is in itself optimistic. Nobody rolls over and dies. If they are to "go under," it is only after a struggle in which they have hopefully won our respect.

Crisscrossing the River: An Interview with Caryl Phillips

Carol Margaret Davison/1994

From *Ariel* 25.4 (1994), 91–99. Reprinted with the permission of the Board of Governors, University of Calgary, Calgary, Alberta. Interview conducted in Toronto.

Taken to England at the "portable" age of twelve weeks from St. Kitts, one of the Leeward Islands in the Caribbean, thirty-five-year-old Caryl Phillips grew up in Leeds, was educated at Oxford, and has spent his literary career probing the ramifications of displacement, a complex condition that he claims characterizes the twentieth century and "engenders a great deal of suffering, a great deal of confusion, a great deal of soul searching." Describing writers as "basically just people who are trying to organize their confusion," he has opted, it would seem, for the right calling. The rapidly growing list of honours for his prolific output certainly validates his choice. The author of five novels, Phillips was the recipient of the Malcolm X Award for his first novel, *The Final Passage* (1985), and the Martin Luther King Memorial Prize for his travel-commentary *The European Tribe* (1987). While *The Final Passage* and *A State of Independence* (1986) were "written out of a sense of great elation at having 're-discovered' the Caribbean," his third novel, *Higher Ground* (1989), encompasses everything from Africa in the days of slave trading to post–World War II Europe and the Black Power Movement. With the publication in 1991 of his fourth novel, *Cambridge,* which chronicles the story of Emily, a nineteenth-century woman who escapes an arranged marriage by travelling to her father's West Indian plantation where she is exposed to the effects of slavery and colonialism, Phillips garnered more serious attention in North America. Back "home" in England, he was subsequently named *(London) Sunday Times'* Young Writer of the Year in 1992 and listed among GRANTA's Best of Young British Novelists of 1993. He is also a well-established playwright and currently is Visiting Professor of English at Amherst College in Massachusetts, USA.

Phillips's fifth novel, *Crossing the River,* shortlisted for Britain's prestigious Booker Prize in 1993 and published in January 1994 by Knopf, Canada, is a sophisticated, sometimes-sorrowful meditation upon the painful dislocations, longings, and "weird" relationships borne of the aptly named "peculiar institution" of slavery. Three years in the making and spanning 250 years of the African diaspora, *Crossing the River* is a fragmented work plagued by questions of identity, paternalism, and spiritual growth. The novel is framed by an African father's melancholic reflections on his desperate act of selling his three children into slavery following his crop's failure and relates their life stories. In each instance, Phillips conjures up largely unchronicled moments in black history: Nash becomes a Christian missionary repatriated to the new land of Liberia in the 1830s; Martha, at the end of the nineteenth century, accompanies some black pioneers west in search of her beloved daughter; and Travis is stationed as an American GI in a small Yorkshire village during the Second World War.

This interview was conducted by telephone on 14 February 1994, when Phillips was engaged to read from *Crossing the River* at Harbourfront, in Toronto, Canada.

CMD: *Crossing the River* has been called your most ambitious work to date. Do you think that's an accurate description?

CP: Not really. I think they're all pretty ambitious. When you sit down with an idea—to turn it into a novel, it's always a big risk, it's always a danger. So there's an element of ambition always. In the formal sense, however, it probably is my most ambitious work. But it's not in the more specific way of looking at the desire to write a book and the ambition. They're all as hard as each other.

CMD: What was the seed of this book?

CP: Originally, I had lots of ideas in my mind, including doing a piece about something in the Second World War. That was the idea to start with and then it just got out of control.

CMD: The novel reminded me somewhat of your 1983 play *The Shelter*. You span a great deal of time there too, moving from Act One, set in the eighteenth century, to Act Two in the 1950s. You also deal there with interracial relationships.

CP: That's interesting. Most people haven't made any references to *The Shelter*, a play I wrote back in 1982–83, because they don't know of it. It's not as easily accessible as most of the novels, but if I were to look at one piece of work of mine which has the beginning of this structural paranoia and schizophrenia, that would be it. You could say that I've been writing or exploring the way of writing and connecting across centuries for ten years.

CMD: What was your principal aim in writing *Crossing the River*? What did you feel you wanted to do here that you hadn't done in your earlier work?

CP: Well, I wanted to make a connection between the African world which was left behind and the diasporan world which people had entered once they crossed the water. I wanted to make an affirmative connection, not a connection based upon exploitation or suffering or misery, but a connection based upon a kind of survival. This is an unusually optimistic book for me. I don't have a deliberately downbeat feel, but there's never been a redemptive spirit to the things that I've written. There's always been a sense that things have been rough and people have just about managed to limp by and survive, but I don't think there's any reason why one should be "positive." I have never really had a very optimistic view of things.

CMD: In some of your earlier interviews, however, you have expressed surprise about being pegged as a pessimist.

CP: I have been surprised because I've never really considered myself to be a pessimist, but I've never really given people any good reason to think otherwise.

CMD: As your wonderful portraits of the elderly Western pioneer, Martha, and the restrained British housewife, Joyce, attest in *Crossing the River,* you have a tremendous ability to do cross-gender writing. By that I am referring to the ability to enter the consciousness of a woman—and in the case of Joyce, here, and Emily in *Cambridge,* you have the added difficulty of traversing racial difference too. Do you have any thoughts about assuming a female voice? Do you think this involves a special ability at all?

CP: I don't feel it requires any particular strengths. The deal is really that we all play to our own strings, and you find out where you feel most comfortable. Women's position on the edge of society—both central in society, but also marginalized by men—seems to me, in some way, to mirror the rather tenuous and oscillating relationship that all sorts of people, in this case, specifically, black people, have in society, and maybe there is some kind of undercurrent of communicable empathy that's going on. Again, I don't want to make too much of anything because I don't really see it as that much of a mystery. It doesn't appear to be that way to me, and I don't want to find a logical reason in case the ability to do so somehow goes away. I do think that to write only from the point of view of a male is to exclude half of the world and I obviously want to include as many different points of view as I can, so I'm very pleased that I've never really felt a problem doing that.

CMD: There are certainly many different literary influences in *Crossing the River.* Several critics mention the echoes of Toni Morrison's *Beloved* in the Martha

Section. It also seems to me that the father figure here whose voice frames the four narrative segments encompasses the voices of the African diaspora just as Saleem Sinai encompasses the whole of India in Salman Rushdie's *Midnight's Children*. Could you speak a bit about the various literary influences at work here?

CP: I haven't sat down and thought too clearly about what books have perhaps influenced me in putting this novel together, but you have certainly named some authors who are big influences. *Beloved* has been particularly influential. It's always easier for an author to see these things in retrospect and, looking back, yes, I can see the influences of all of these people. It's a novel which is fragmentary in form and structure, polyphonic in its voices, which means that a lot of my reading and a lot of the people whose work I've enjoyed have made their way in. Obviously there's ample room for echoes of all sorts of people. It's great for me as a writer because it allows me to switch gear or switch direction, shift perspective, and at each new turn I'm able to employ something else which, obviously, I have learned by reading other people's work.

CMD: Another book that kept coming to mind while I was reading *Crossing the River* was Edward Brathwaite's jazzy Caribbean poem-trilogy, *The Arrivants*. I decided finally to pull it off the shelf and, lo and behold, I discovered that Chapter Five is entitled "Crossing the River."

CP: Is it? I know him. He's going to murder me. Is it really? I'm going to write that down. That's probably where I got the original title because I first thought of this title ten or eleven years ago.

CMD: There is a haunting, reiterated Biblical question throughout this novel, namely, "Father, why hast thou forsaken me?" Nash mentions this about his white "father" Edward; Martha seems to be addressing God when she repeats the same phrase in Section Two. In the larger picture, of course, they are addressing their flesh-and-blood father who has sold them to the slave traders. The connected issues of paternalism and responsibility are often meditated upon here. What exactly fascinates you about these subjects?

CP: It seems to me that the very nature of the relationship between the master and the slave, the colonizer and the colony, Britain and the Caribbean, is paternalistic. The whole question of relationships between black and white historically has tended to be paternalistic and perhaps enshrouded in some air of patronage at times, and so I've always been interested in those kinds of power relationships. It has such Biblical overtones as well because it is also a reference to religious themes. In the immigrant experience in Britain, the father was often pretty absent from the home. There are so many broken families in the black community in general, not just in the migrant community. There tends to be a preponderance of single mothers. I'm very interested in the whole question of how, on the personal level, that has emerged out of the larger development of slavery and all of those kinds of diasporan movements. There is a very commonly held theory that one of the reasons there is such a preponderance of single mothers is *because* of slavery, an institution which greatly disrupted the black family. There is an idea that if you take away a man's responsibility for his children, which is what happened in slavery when the man was replaced by the master as head of the family, it does something to the psyche of the man of African origin. It induces an irresponsibility. I don't know whether this is true or not. I'm not a sociologist or an anthropologist, but all of these issues make me interested in that whole power-father-paternalistic-patronage issue. They all seem to be pretty linked.

CMD: I want to ask you about your changing ideas about the writer's responsibilities. In the introduction to your play *The Shelter,* you speak of the various burdens on the writer; in particular, you state that you were then motivated by the luxury of inexperience and felt that your "only responsibility was to locate the truth in whatever piece I was working on, live with it, sleep with it, and be responsible to that truth, and that truth alone." In *The European Tribe* [1987], written a few years later, you seem to be more aware of the power the writer has along political lines. You state towards the end of that book: "I had learnt that in a situation in which history is distorted, the literature of a people often becomes its history, its writers the keepers of the past, present, and future. In this situation a writer can infuse a people with their own unique identity and spiritually kindle the fire of resistance." What do you feel today about your responsibility as a writer?

CP: I think that the second piece from *The European Tribe* is a development from what I thought earlier. It doesn't displace what I thought earlier, because I do think that that remains true—your first responsibility is to locate the truth and to deal with the truth, particularly as it relates specifically to the characters—but I think that by travelling and writing a bit more and becoming hopefully a bit more knowledgeable about writing and the world and about other writers' lives in other communities, I did realize—and I think that I already knew it, but I wasn't able to articulate it—that there is a particular responsibility in *certain* situations for the writer to take up. He doesn't have to become a politician, but the writer has to be aware of the writer's power, his capacity for good as well as his ability to duck larger social responsibility. I agree with the position I had in *The European Tribe,* but I would go further than that and say that it seems to me increasingly important since then that one, as a writer, does try to locate the truth in one's work. You do become aware of the possibility of being somebody who can identify a history and perhaps do something about redressing the imbalance of some of the ills and falsehoods that have been perpetrated by others about your own history. But beyond that, I think a writer really has a responsibility to at least acknowledge that he was produced by very specific social circumstances. We weren't, any of us—male, female, black, white, whatever—immaculate conceptions dropped out of nowhere without a history. One shouldn't feel a guilt for one's history and one shouldn't feel ashamed of one's history, one should just take responsibility for it.

CMD: Do you ever feel, though, that you have to compromise conveying your own personal "truths" because they clash with your responsibilities as a writer, or is it your primary responsibility to tell the truth, the whole truth, and nothing but the truth, so help you God?

CP: The latter. I don't think I could actually write properly if I felt that in any way, even in any small way, that I was somehow in my life as well as in my writing, not tackling issues of injustice and speaking up when they appear. I just don't think I could do it, because I think that eventually those kinds of lies and that kind of self-deception do seep into your work. It has honestly never occurred to me to pull a punch a little bit or change gears. I don't think you can do that. I mean I just don't see how you can. You just have to continually risk coming up against irate people.

CMD: As you are certainly aware, today is not only Valentine's Day. Today marks the fifth anniversary of the *fatwa* declared against Salman Rushdie. Do you have any comments about Rushdie's situation and the issue of censorship and writing in general?

CP: I just got of the phone with him. He and I speak a lot. To tell you the truth, I don't think that I have got anything to say that hasn't already been said and maybe said better by others, but I was talking to somebody earlier today about his situation. It seems to me clearly that one of the most unfortunate things in the *fatwa* is the way a lot of people in the West have taken it as a convenient excuse to hammer Islam, and it's not Islam that needs to be hammered. It's a particular extreme branch of Islam. It really is like judging the whole of Christianity on the actions of the Spanish Inquisition. It doesn't really make any sense. That has nothing to do with Salman personally. That is just my own discomfort at watching writers and other people, including a lot of people who should know better, who claim to be defending Salman Rushdie making incredibly sweeping and stupid comments about Islam, but not taking into consideration that this isn't Islam. There are many Muslims all over the world who think this is an outrage.

CMD: What were your feelings about being nominated for the Booker Prize? Were you surprised?
CP: That's a good question. Was I surprised? Well, I suppose I was a little bit. To tell you the truth, I was more surprised that *Cambridge* wasn't nominated because everyone kept telling me it would be. So by the time this came around, I was pleased but I just didn't care because I realized how much of a lottery it was. I wondered about it in the days leading up to it when it was *Cambridge*. This time I didn't even know that it was the day of the announcements or anything. I came into my office and there was a message from Salman on the machine. I was pleased because of the sales.

CMD: What were your feelings when Roddy Doyle received it?
CP: Oh, that was fine. I know Roddy. I was sitting right at the next table. I didn't mind you see because it wasn't really about winning it. I was just pleased to be on the shortlist. After a while, you need to get sales because the more sales you get, the more money you get. The more money you get, the more time you have, and that's the deal. I'm not sure that I would want to be like Miss World for a year, which is what you would be if you won. I was pleased that Roddy won because he is a nice guy. At the Booker Prize dinner everybody talked to everybody. The person that I knew the best was David Malouf and, in some ways, I would have liked David Malouf to have won simply because he's twenty-five years older than Roddy and I who are both thirty-five. I'll get another chance as will Roddy, even though he doesn't really need another chance, but I would have liked David Malouf, whose work I really admire, to have won it and gained this recognition at this stage of his career. As Kazuo Ishiguro, who called me up the morning of it, said: "Just remember, it's an exercise in public humiliation."

CMD: Speaking of influences, taking into consideration both their life and their work, who stands out as the most important single literary influence on you?
CP: I would probably have to say, if it's a combination of their life and their work, James Baldwin. I hesitated because there's no other person who I've ever met who is a writer who has been as important to me. I think that this is partly because at the time when I met him I was a sort of "wanna-be" writer. To meet a real and a great writer, I was incredibly lucky. He was also incredibly generous with his time.

CMD: The novel seems to have a firm hold on you. Would you ever consider writing another play?

CP: Oh yes, I'm probably going to write another play next year or later this year. I prefer the theatre to film. There are just too many people involved in television and film. I have worked in both mediums, and I don't particularly enjoy them that much.

CMD: Have you ever been approached by anyone about adapting one of your novels for the screen?

CP: I have often been approached by people who have wanted to do that. I'm afraid that I'm not usually very good at replying. I get my agent to speak to them, but it's not a world that I feel particularly comfortable in anymore. A number of my friends have had bad experiences having their novels adapted or even adapting them themselves. I'll tell you the truth. I look upon adaptations of my work for the screen as something that I would like to be involved in and I would like to see happen at a time when I don't feel quite so fertile about producing original work. There may be a time down the line, whether it's in five or twenty-five years' time, when I just feel I don't have anything else to say, or I dry up, then it would be fun to go back and look at some of the early work and try to find new ways of saying that stuff and working on the screen. But right now, I'm too keen and eager and hungry to write prose, so I don't want to waste time on screen work.

Of This Time, of That Place:
A Conversation with Caryl Phillips
Jenny Sharpe/1995

From *Transition* 68 (1995), 154–61. Reprinted with the permission of *Transition*. Interview conducted in Los Angeles.

Caryl Phillips, novelist, essayist, and playwright, was born in St. Kitts in 1958 and taken to England by his parents while still an infant. He was raised in white working-class areas of Leeds and attended Oxford University. As an adult, Phillips has traveled widely and lived in the Caribbean and the United States, as well as in England. In his first two novels, aspects of Phillips's own history—his life as a West Indian in Britain and his attempted return to the Caribbean—serve as points of departure. His first novel, *The Final Passage* (1985), tells the story of a West Indian woman who moves her family to England where she faces bigotry and poverty. In *A State of Independence* (1986), a West Indian man returns to the Caribbean after two decades in Britain. Feeling himself more educated and sophisticated for his time in England, he finds that his former countrymen give little thought to the Commonwealth and are instead under the cultural and economic shadow of the United States.

Phillips's concern with the West Indian experience is immediate. There are moving depictions of the squalor in which West Indians live in Britain and of the social ills such as alcoholism and unemployment that beset former colonies in the Caribbean. However, his project is not that of a chronicler of one culture. His third novel, *Higher Ground* (1989), is a tripartite novel whose third story, "Higher Ground," recounts the experiences of a young Jewish woman who leaves her native Poland for England; there she finds safety from the Nazis, but also alienation and loneliness. *Higher Ground*'s middle section is a collection of letters written by a black man unjustly imprisoned, whose time in prison is a moving and admirable journey of reflection. The first story, "Heartland," is concerned with the effects of the African slave trade; Phillips's most recent novels, *Cambridge* (1991) and *Crossing the River* (1993) share similar subjects. *The European Tribe* (1987), a collection of travel writings, explores Europe's deep-seated xenophobia and the hostility faced by such groups as West Indians in Britain, Algerians in France, and Turks in Germany.

Though the scope is broadened, Phillips's works still have a common element: peoples who have been displaced and who lack a comforting or stabilizing history or tradition. Yet, although all his works can arouse outrage at the injustices of war, slavery, racism, or imperialism, they are not sweeping calls to social action. In part, this kind of polemicism is precluded by his formal explorations. Large portions of Phillips's novels are narrated from the consciousness of individuals with reprehensible views, and the reader rarely has access to an omniscient perspective that allows categorical statements to be made. Instead, the stage is the thoughts and actions of individuals; characters come to grief in Phillips's work through not understanding the larger events of history that are responsible for how they come to be where they are and for the problems they face. This formal focus on the individual is a reflection of Phillips's more general attitude toward the problems faced by displaced peoples: he is skeptical of facile solutions to the deep and pervasive problems left by history, but he holds out the possibility that, even beset by tragedy, one can and should meet these challenges open-eyed and with courage. Though his characters often fail in this regard or meet with misfortune despite their best efforts, there is still for the reader an exhortation to self-knowledge, and the faith that one can, however fleetingly, find some tranquillity.

Jenny Sharpe: In *The European Tribe,* you describe your sense of exile from British culture. You say that reading Ralph Ellison's *Invisible Man* and Richard Wright's *Native Son* during a visit to Los Angeles made you decide to become a writer. How do you see your relationship to, on the one hand, black American culture and, on the other, black Britain?

Caryl Phillips: My relationship to black American literature—or, more importantly, black American society—was very important to me when I was a college student, because I didn't have any coherent sense of a black British tradition. We didn't have any role models. When I first came to America in 1978, I was amazed that there was such a thing as a black middle class, that there were these self-confident people who thought of themselves as part of, as responding to, a tradition. And black literature was an incredibly important part of it. When you're an aspiring writer, there are always people you want to be like, books you wish you had written. For me, growing up, there were plenty of books I wished I had written, but none of them had been written by people who looked like me.

The longer I stay here in the States, the more I realize how underdeveloped the black British sense of identity is. And rather than making me feel that I want to sit down and write a novel in the black American tradition, it makes me bullishly determined to do something about overturning the insular view the British have of themselves as a nation. It's not a new thing, of course, for a writer to look back at the country they've left and realize that their engagement with that country is actually a lot stronger than they realized.

JS: You also mention in *The European Tribe* about having a need to visit the Caribbean after traveling through Europe, and you say that your Caribbean journey heightened your awareness of Europe. Did you return to your birthplace in St. Kitts?

CP: Yes. I was there on and off for about three years—I still have a place there. For much of the late eighties and early nineties I was dividing myself between St. Kitts and England. As soon as I started to teach at Amherst College in 1990, I found myself doing a sort of triangular thing, which is both prohibitively expensive and incredibly exhausting. So I had to make a decision as to which one of the three places would fall out of the equation, and it turned out to be St. Kitts. I do go there every year, but only for a month or two.

JS: The triangular relationship you describe is very common among Caribbean writers. Is that something that is inevitable given both the geography and the history of the Caribbean region?

CP: I think that it's inevitable that people from the Caribbean should think of themselves in relation to both Europe and North America. We are now, more than ever, at a point in history in which the Caribbean is undergoing a struggle—to orient itself away from Europe, after two or three hundred years of a fractured and difficult relationship, and towards a new and equally difficult relationship with North America. Most people, like my own family, have brothers and sisters or aunts and uncles who live in Miami and Manchester. Most families are split up that way. A person from the Caribbean just naturally thinks in terms of that triangle. And this is true for writers, as well: for every George Lamming who went to England, you have a Claude MacKay who came to the States. Then there are people like Sam Selvon, who went to England and then came to Canada. I think the cross-Atlantic pattern is part of the twentieth-century Caribbean experience.

JS: Your most recent novel, *Crossing the River,* locates the beginnings of the African diaspora in the Atlantic slave trade. I was wondering if you could talk a little bit about the relationship between history and cultural identities. In particular, I would like to hear your response to Stuart Hall's position on this issue: "Far from being grounded in a mere recovery of the past which is waiting to be found and which when found will secure our sense of selves into eternity, identities are the names we give to the different ways we are positioned by and position ourselves within the narratives of the past."

CP: It's certainly true that identities change—my own identity changes all the time. I'm not a William Faulkner, a proud chronicler of a little patch of earth in Mississippi. I am the product of a diaspora. The way I look at my past is changing all the time—it's being reclaimed by so many different writers.

Alex Haley wrote *Roots* when I was eighteen years old. Though it may be of dubious literary merit, the book had a huge impact psychologically—it allowed a lot of us, writers or not, to begin to reclaim Africa with a certain degree of confidence. Suddenly our past was different. One moment we came from a past which was shrouded in mystery, lost to us; we couldn't quite see it clearly. The next minute it's on TV, getting the highest ratings of any TV show in history. Our past was different after that moment; our past had grown.

It was like that, too, when I came to the Caribbean for the first time as an adult. I saw cousins and aunts and uncles I'd never seen before, but who looked like me, like members of my family. And when I'm in the United States, when I'm among African Americans, I'm constantly reclaiming that part of my past. They're both linked. The only difference was that, two centuries ago, one boat docked in Barbados, while another boat docked in Charleston.

JS: This is one aspect of the notion of diaspora that you work with, but there's another that addresses the impossibility of a simple return or recovery of the past.

CP: I agree with Stuart Hall. There isn't a sense in which one can identify a past, pull it on like it's a nice new overcoat, and then stride purposefully to the future. The past is complicated; it requires further exploration. When I was little, growing up in England—this was true for all of us black British children—there was nothing in the textbooks, nothing in the geography around me which actually acknowledged that I had a past. The past is never going to fit comfortably, no matter how much more of it is excavated, despite the best efforts of our writers and historians and academics. It's always going to be something for further exploration.

One can never go back. The old Garveyite dream of returning to Africa makes no sense. A lot of the people are saying that in England now. Older folk, pensioners, have begun to understand that there is no return to Trinidad or Barbados.

JS: In *Crossing the River*, the African father who sold his children into slavery listens for "the many-tongued chorus of the common memory." You suggest, through the historical expansiveness of your narrative and the African father's recognition of the impossibility of his children's return, that memory does not involve recovering the past, but reworking it.

CP: The larger historical question regarding memory has to do with our own collective memory of history as a community, as a society. So my way of subverting received history is to use historical documents, use first-person voices, digest what they're saying, and somehow rework them. It's a reworking that can get us to understand, for instance, the rather troubled relationship between captured slaves on the west coast of Africa and those who stayed behind. That's what I want to do.

JS: The first section of *Crossing the River* shows the disappointment of Nash, an ex-slave, upon his arrival in Liberia, which he believed to be the one true home for his race. He not only feels estranged from the West Africans who treat him like a white man but discovers that the slave trade is still thriving along the coast. The section "Heartland," which appears in your third novel, *Higher Ground,* also addresses the African participation in the Atlantic slave trade. Is this complicity something that remains unspeakable?

CP: There's enough spoken about it now, though it remains something of a taboo. I felt that very strongly when I was in West Africa.

JS: Where in West Africa?

CP: I was in Ghana for a while. It was a very strange moment. I was doing a talk at Cape Coast University, and there was a big slave fort there, and there was an even bigger one, Elmina Castle, further down the coast. And after I did my talk, these lecturers took me to the place, and I remember two things struck me very forcefully. One, I didn't feel as much of an emotional charge as I thought I would, and I think that's directly related to the fact that I'd written "Heartland." I had already written out the emotional complexity of being a black person in a slave fort on the west coast of Africa. I'd imagined it. And I had, in a way, already dealt with it. So then, actually standing there, in that fort, I looked around and thought to myself: I sort of understand this. They showed me where the slaves were kept, the rings on the wall for the chains, and I looked. But it worried me slightly that I was feeling quite so logical about this.

And then I began to feel really uncomfortable, and I realized that it was because something about my relationship to these lecturers had suddenly changed. Hitherto, we'd had a really cool time—going out for beers and talking—but suddenly everything went quiet. It took me a few days to figure out what had happened, which was that guilt had intervened into our relationship. A huge, unspoken question came between us—how come they remained behind, and I was one of the people who left. And finally, during that meeting, somebody, one of them, turned to me and said, "Sorry." I didn't understand why he was sorry, but it just added to the discomfort. It was out of the sense of guilt and discomfort I felt on that day that I began to write *Crossing the River*.

JS: Your use of historical documents addresses the memory of slavery that also haunts the West. The section "Crossing the River" places the reader inside the mind of an English slave trader through his ship log, which you base on an actual eighteenth-century document, John Newton's *Journal of a Slave Trader*.
CP: I especially enjoy reading first-person historical material because it gives the most interesting window on the past. But I'm also interested in subverting, if you like, the form, because all too often there's a self-serving nature behind these narratives—that interests me too.

JS: You undermine the available historical record, Newton's journal, by interspersing the ship log of your fictional captain with the highly sentimental letters he writes home to his wife.
CP: Yes. I look at John Newton's *Journal of a Slave Trader* and I think, This is an interesting document, let me write my own version of it. But let me also add something which shows us the huge paradox of this guy's mind, some insight into the mind of a slave trader. As he's wreaking havoc on other people's families, he's dreaming of beginning a family of his own. He can't see that, can't recognize his own contradictions, but hopefully we can. That's the larger point I wanted to make. As black people's lives were being subjected to all these forces—the dispersal, the brutality, the historical hurt—white people were still dreaming of having families, of bringing up their kids, and of what schools they were going to send them to. They couldn't actually see the people before them as human beings, as fathers, brothers, mothers, daughters, sons.

JS: Yet, your novel does not condemn the English slave trader or the African father who sells his three children into slavery because of a crop failure.
CP: One of the things I try to avoid in my fiction is judging my characters.

JS: This is what I find so effective in your writing. Rather than being positioned behind the characters to judge them, your authorial voice disappears into the characters and becomes them. Let me give you an example of what I mean. When I taught *Cambridge* to undergraduates, the opening narration by Emily

Cartwright led many students to believe that Caryl Phillips, the author, was an Englishwoman like her.

CP: Good!

JS: The first-person narratives of the white women that you give are particularly powerful. Is that deliberate?

CP: Oh, I don't know. Linking questions of class and gender with the whole question of race has always been important to me. The defining characteristic of my childhood was the shifting emphasis of my identity: being working-class black some days, black working class others. Those sorts of questions and connections are much clearer in Britain, I suspect.

Gender has always interested me, too—probably because I was brought up by my mother. In the case of Emily, I was interested in exploring the parallel situations that a woman might find herself in and that black people were definitely in in Britain at the turn of the nineteenth century. The power structure operated in a different way, but the power source was the same. At the time I was writing that book, actually, I was thinking about the Brontë sisters. And wondering, What did the Brontës know about slavery? It turns out they knew a lot, they knew a hell of a lot. I was very, very interested in a working-class woman's relationship to slavery.

JS: One of the things that interests me about Emily's narrative is that she has very clear ideas about what is wrong with slavery. Yet, she can only see slaves through a racially inscribed lens. I have colleagues who don't like *Cambridge,* and I think the reason they don't like it is because Emily's narrative is so seductive for the reader. As a woman who is obliged to marry a widower many years her senior, she is a somewhat sympathetic character. But at the same time, her racist attitude makes the reader feel very uncomfortable. The seductiveness of the ethnographic voice lures us into seeing slave society through her racist eyes. It's enormously complicated, because her narrative expresses the racism of the antislavery position. In much of your fiction you get at those contradictions rather than oppose the evil defenders of slavery to the enlightened liberators of slaves.

CP: I think that one should be seduced into seeing the problematic nature of the antislavery position. One should also be seduced into seeing the problematic nature of the pro-slavery position. One should be able to transgress such artificial boundaries as good and evil, black and white—I mean black and white in a broader sense—right and wrong, in fiction. That's what fiction is supposed to do. It challenges our own feelings and our own assumptions, and the best way of doing that is through an engagement with a character whose views you don't share. And that engagement gives us an insight into their mind.

I just read a terrific book by William Trevor, an Irish writer, called *Felicia's Journey,* in which one of the central characters is a guy who is big, overweight, a kind of Rush Limbaugh type who specializes in seducing homeless girls, sexually molesting them, and killing them. I felt bloody uncomfortable reading this book, because I felt empathy with this total bastard. But that's what fiction should do for us. It should expand our minds. And I'm sure there are a lot of people who feel uncomfortable with a lot of what I do. Good.

JS: I find the black woman characters in *Cambridge* and *Crossing the River* the most difficult to understand. In *Cambridge,* you are careful to show that what the reader knows about Stella and Christiana is highly circumscribed by the first-person narratives in which they appear. For example, you show Emily interpreting Stella in a particular way and Stella's response escaping her. But at the same time, these black women characters—including Martha—remain somewhat enigmatic. We're not satisfied at the end of your novels, because we don't have their stories.

CP: We don't have their stories. You do have Martha's story, and I think Martha's at least as well rounded as anybody else. There's a difficulty with her in the sense that we move from the first person to the third person, third to first, which makes you shift perspective from intimate to distant and back again. But you don't get Stella's story, any more than you get Isabella's, because she's not a main character. Thinking back to *Crossing the River* and Martha, I tell you it would have been so much easier to have written about a black guy—a cowboy—which is what I wanted to do originally. But it struck me that there wasn't really any first-person documentary material I could draw on for a black woman in the nineteenth century. There was plenty of stuff for black guys. But it just struck me that I'd never seen a film in which there was a black person on one of those wagons heading west, let alone a black woman. A lot of the photographs of frontier towns contain women who were obviously doing the cooking and the cleaning and the laundry and what have you in the forts and towns all across the West. So that's why I wanted to write about the American frontier from the perspective of a black woman.

JS: What direction do you see your writing heading?

CP: I wish I knew. I can tell you the next book I write is not going to be about slavery, though that doesn't mean it's exhausted as a topic, for me or for anybody else. I'm still quite interested in those people who came over to England in the fifties and sixties from the Caribbean and are trying to get back to the Caribbean to die. There's a sort of endgame that's being played out. There is a whole generation who never thought they'd die in England and who are now having to face the fact that they're never going to get back.

JS: Aren't many black British of Caribbean origin returning to the Caribbean because of the intensified racism they are encountering in Britain?

CP: The older ones want to go, but they don't have the money. The younger ones can at least look forward to getting a job and taking their degree, if they have one, back there. I sympathize with that position. Obviously, though, in my position, as a writer and a scholar in constant circulation between three "homes," I have the luxury of being able to turn my back on Britain. As the years tick by, I feel the necessity to engage with Britain, rather than disengage, because I see that not everybody is going to be able to get up and leave, and what we are gong to find is a whole generation who are going to have to digest the historical nonsense which I had to digest. This is why we have to say, Stop! And get it all down, make a record of all this. I don't just mean writers. We must all say, Stop!

Caryl Phillips: Lannan Literary Videos
Pico Iyer/1995

From Lannan Foundation Literary Videos, March 7, 1995. Reading from *Crossing the River* and interview directed by Dan Griggs. Reprinted with the permission of the Lannan Foundation. Interview conducted in Los Angeles.

Iyer: Well, I have a sense that what you'd really like to talk about are the competing merits of the British and German soccer teams, but we will sidle into that in a different way. Let's talk about passion. Actually, when we were just talking backstage, you were saying very powerfully to me that it is difficult for you to read some of these passages [from *Crossing the River*] because you get so immersed in the characters. So, it sounds to me as if fiction is really a way for you to try to understand people utterly different from yourself.

Phillips: I think that's a pretty fair summary. It's a strange process. I think every writer has a different relationship to character. I get quite involved with my characters because I feel they are entrusting a story to me, and I have to be quite patient, or try to cultivate a certain degree of patience during the process of writing, and just listen. Rather than crazily searching for them I try to be patient and tease out a voice. And then, I do have a sense, without being too new-age about this, that they are entrusting me with something. In the case of this particular novel there are a number of central characters. Normally, one would write a novel with maybe one, two, or three central characters; there are quite a few in this one.

Iyer: But any love affair has to work in both directions. The trust has to be on your part too. You have to trust them to tell you interesting things, and you have to do the hard work to draw them out in some way.

Phillips: Yes. I think Toni Morrison said that very correctly—everything she said is correct as far as I'm concerned. She did say that once you have the first line, you have the novel. And I think that there is some truth in that. Once there is a certain tone, it's like a tuning fork you can hear. You hear the right note. It can take a long time until that note is sounded, but I think once it happens, you are up and running.

Iyer: But it must be quite a jolt when you move very abruptly as you do in this book, from a nineteenth-century black woman to an eighteenth-century white slave trader. You abandon her in midstream, as it were, and open yourself up to him. Do you feel a betrayal in that kind of process?

Phillips: I feel like a kind of hit and run lover. You're here and then you're gone, and then you're there, and then you're gone. There is a sense of guilt. In the first novel I wrote I didn't feel like that because that was the first set of characters I had ever communed with. And then I wrote another novel and I suddenly realized, oh my God, I have forgotten about that first set of people. I had these images of them wandering around in black saying, "Bastard, you've forgotten us." So, in each successive novel, it's like mud dried on your boots. You can't kick it off; the guilt is accumulating.

Iyer: So it would be very difficult for you to write about these characters unsympathetically or to inhabit some of these skins without falling in love with them?

Phillips: I don't think it's a matter of falling in love. It's certainly feeling a deep desire to understand them, a deep desire to get to know them. They're not always characters you'd like either. And certainly not always characters with whom I would want to have a drink, but certainly people I do want to understand.

Iyer: It seems that fiction would be the opposite of polemic for you. It's a way of cutting through polemic and coming to understand any position.

Phillips: I think fiction has to be the opposite. Polemic is easy in a sense. One can make a very important, very powerful, and very correct point polemically, but what is missing is the craft. And I think eventually every writer, no matter how many characters are zipping about in them, no matter how many stories they feel compelled to tell, they come up against the same problem time after time after time which is, "how do I tell the story?" This means they have a problem which is known as form. That is what seems to me to separate the passion that becomes polemic from the passion that becomes fiction.

Iyer: And how in a very practical sense do you address that problem and solve it?

Phillips: Slowly. I don't know. I think each book is different. They have these handbooks that are knocking around the place: "How to write a novel" or "You too can be a writer." The funny thing is that none of the people who write these handbooks have written any books. If one could go into a store and buy one of these books that could tell us how to solve the problem of form, then it could save all of us, yourself included, a lot of time. But it doesn't really seem to work like that, and also one learns something from the last novel about the necessity of being patient, the necessity to listen, to trust, to be determined when it's time to be determined, to give up research when the time has come to put research to one side. Some of these things are applicable to the next book, but it seems that the next book always presents problems which require you to find new methods which will get you through. So I don't really know. Each new book presents a whole new set of problems for me.

Iyer: It's interesting what you've been saying now and also in the last section you've read where you're speaking for the voices of Sao Paulo and Dominica, all of the world really, is about acceptance and about trying to internalize every aspect of the world. Yet, one striking thing about your life, I know, is that you teach at Amherst, you have a house in Saint Kitts, and you have a flat in London. To some extent you must feel a foreigner wherever you are. I sometimes sense that when you are in England, you are aware of your African heritage, and when you're in Africa, you're aware that you grew up in England. Is it a sense that you are forever displaced?

Phillips: Actually, increasingly I don't really feel the trauma of displacement nearly as much as I used to. I don't think I've ever felt it as strongly as trauma—that's something of an exaggeration—but certainly the discomfort of displacement. I used to think that one had to have a home. You know I grew up in Yorkshire which is a very kind of rooted part of England, very working class, extended family. A place where everybody is going to see their mam, their gran, or their aunt. And I grew up at school where people would say, "I went so and so this week, and I saw my cousin." I didn't have any grandparents, aunts, uncles, or cousins because they were all in the Caribbean. We were first generation migrants. I had my mother, and my father, and my brothers, and that's it. So, the primary displacement I felt was growing up in such a tight community without a sense of extended family. I think that engendered in me a very deep desire to have all those things such as family, and a sense of place, and a sense of home. When I began to write, one of the authors I admired the most was Faulkner. I used to think lucky sod; he's got his little square of Mississippi that is forever home. He has his maps and things. And I thought, God, wouldn't it be great to also have a sort of literary home as well. But I don't really feel that so much anymore maybe because of the amount of traveling I do and maybe because I suspect my literary influences and people I consider to be my peers have changed, and a lot of those people don't have a sense of home. So I've begun to think maybe its okay not to have a sense of home.

Iyer: Where is your sense of literary affinities? Are they for example with the displaced people in England like Ishiguro and Rushdie, or are they with the black Americans like Richard Wright or Toni Morrison, or are they with the West Indians like Derek Walcott, and Naipaul? All of them? None of them?

Phillips: Well, the first and the third. I think the second one is a bit more problematic for me because African American literature has a very strong and powerful tradition of its own, and I don't really think they need me as a sort of exotic adjunct to it. They seem to be doing perfectly well without me. In a Caribbean tradition, I do feel some kind of affinity to the place I was born in. I left there when I was very young, but I am a dual citizen. I'm a citizen of Saint Kitts and a citizen of Britain as well. The Caribbean is where my cousins, aunts, and uncles are. I do feel some affinity to the place and also some sort of literary solidarity, albeit as a foot soldier to Derek Walcott's field marshal. I do feel a relationship with him in that sense, and with other Caribbean authors, but I think my primary literary relationship, or sense of community, is with the people you mentioned who are not only my peers but in many cases my friends—our friends I mean. You know how important that is. These people who do have more than one cultural background to draw upon and who are based in Britain do form a group of British writers who are quite strongly identifiable.

Iyer: Indeed, and I think in Rushdie's last book, he writes very poignantly that home like hell is other people. The strongest sense of home he has ever had is in the friends he makes wherever he goes. At the same time, as you were suggesting, the striking thing about your books is that nearly all the characters are at sea literally and metaphorically. They are always in motion, they are always in passage between different worlds, and they don't really belong to either one. Lots of them are intermediaries; slaves who translate for white men who won't be accepted by the native community as well by the white community. You must feel a strong connection with that, a sense of being caught in between every world.

Phillips: Yes. For a long time I used to think that was the deal—that I was caught between something. When I was a student, you may know this because as you mentioned in the introduction we were students at the same time, I remember walking down the streets in Oxford and coming across a book in a bookstore called *Between Two Cultures: A Study of Immigrants in Britain,* with a chapter on Cypriots, a chapter on West Indians, a chapter on Pakistanis, et cetera, et cetera. I thought, hell, that's it, isn't it? I'm between two cultures. But I realized that I wasn't between two cultures at all. I mean this wasn't an instant discovery on the streets of Oxford. I took it away and panicked for a few years but eventually I came to understand that the very title of the book is deeply disturbing because I don't believe people are between two cultures. I think people inhabit two cultures or more.

Iyer: And then become communities of one person in some sense, isn't it?
Phillips: Yes. I think the synthesis of one country with another, of one culture with another is actually an incredibly positive and powerful synthesis. But you know Britain is a country likes to project herself as this homogenous, exclusive society. You know over two hundred years ago Defoe pointed out that Britain is actually a mongrel nation and it has been forever thus. This notion that Britain still likes to put out to the world that somehow "we know what a British man is. He is in a pin-striped suit, and he's like John Major." This is the image that Britain exports of what is British, except, of course, you will notice, when it's time for the Olympics.

Iyer: But you and I are typical Englishmen now, in part because we're living a long way from England. I think the most vogue English phrase about all those things you've been talking about is the empire is back. Everyone has noticed how the most prominent novelists in England like yourself, Ishiguro, Okri, Rushdie— all people from the ex-colonies—have actually come and claimed the center of English literature, very self-consciously. For example, in your book *Cambridge* when somebody picks it from a bookshelf, they expect to read some bucolic comedy about a sylvan, ivory tower city in England, and they're reading *Cambridge* is the name of a very poorly treated black slave. That seems to be an almost conscious wish to take the very terms of English, and the traditions of English literature, and turn it on its head. To see Jane Austen from the perspective of Saint Kitts as well. Is it something you're conscious about doing?
Phillips: I am, increasingly, because I think I feel quite passionate about the desire to remake Britain as a country. After all, it's the country which I grew up in. I'm in a very peculiar position, as you are, as a writer. We have a luxury, we have a choice, we don't have to live there, we can move around. But I'm increasingly aware of the fact that there is a generation, not only my generation, but another generation behind, who are growing up in Britain, who are facing a lot of the same problems, a lot of the same discrimination, a lot of the same ignorance that I had to face growing up. And that's why I think as each year passes, it seems to be increasingly important in whatever small way or small manner that I have at my disposal, that I do something about yoking that country's head around and making it look in the mirror and see people like you and me or perhaps more importantly people who are unemployed, people who have been discriminated against

in the work place because of what they look like, because they don't look like John Major.

Iyer: And also in terms of history forcing us to see the eighteenth and nineteenth centuries from a radically different perspective, as in the passages you were reading, to take the very texture of English literature and put it in the voice of a black person.

Phillips: Again, most British people don't know their own history because most of it didn't take place in Britain. It took place on somebody else's soil. So I think it's very important to make the connection between the British notion of, "We had the Industrial Revolution, we are the first industrialized nation in the world." You could ask, "Yes, but where did the money come from?" People say, "Isn't Bristol a terrific city? Look at the architecture, look at the wonderful crescents in Bath," but I wonder where do they think the money came from to build this stuff? I mean the evidence of the greatest rogues' gallery in the world is the bowels of the British museum where there is pillaged art from every conceivable place you can think of. I don't want people to feel guilty about that; I just want them to actually come clean.

Iyer: And as a connoisseur of displacement and as a great champion of the possibilities of cultures fusing, that's probably part of what brought you to America and why you are enthusiastic about that.

Phillips: I enjoy teaching, but one of the things about teaching in Britain is you don't get any money. What has been done to the British educational system is a disaster. I know because my mother was a teacher at secondary and tertiary levels. That's one aspect of it. It's not facetious, but I would be dishonest if I didn't say that. The other aspect is that one of the things about teaching in a country which is not your own country is that it's a terrific way to learn about that country because you're continually engaging with young people who are going to go out in the future and shape the country. The academic world is an ivory tower, but it is a good vantage point for me to learn about the United States.

Iyer: And America has liberated you personally because I think you said you first realized you could be a writer in Laguna Beach in California when you were a student and you picked up a copy of Richard Wright and suddenly it opened horizons to you.

Phillips: Oh, the old Laguna Beach story!

Iyer: But it's true?
Phillips: It's true.

Iyer: When we were studying at Oxford there was no black writing. There was nothing written by anyone who didn't look like John Major or Jane Austin.
Phillips: No, there wasn't.

Iyer: You had to come here to find it.
Phillips: I did, and thank God. I'll tell you a story, and this is absolutely true. After I came back from the U.S in 1978, I had one more year to go at university. I had by that time made my somewhat embarrassing belated acquaintance with Richard Wright and James Baldwin, and Ralph Ellison, and Zora Neale Hurston and all the people who are writers and who look a bit like me. So I was going back to Oxford and I had one more year to do this English degree and I thought, well, let me do some sort of special paper on American literature. I thought it was a not too subtle way of trying to synthesize Laguna Beach with Oxford. So, I went into the library at the University English faculty library, and I looked up Baldwin and came across one book. It was *Critical Essays on James Baldwin,* and no novels whatsoever, no copy of Wright's *Native Son.* This was a disgrace, so in a sense I say thank God for Laguna Beach because I certainly wasn't going to find those books even in the University library where they purported to offer American fiction as an option.

Iyer: And now the hope is that ten years from now somebody studying English literature at Oxford will be reading you, Ishiguro, and Rushdie and will be able to make connections with his own circumstances.
Phillips: Yes, hopefully. That's one of the reasons why, as I was saying, I do feel it's important to continue to wrestle with Britain. I don't see Britain in that perhaps parochial way that a couple of generations of writers that came before me did, those who viewed themselves as little Englanders. I don't think many people in my generation, in our generation, see it in that parochial way anymore. I think of many writers in Britain, people like Ian McEwan, Julian Barnes, Michelle Roberts, who are beginning to write novels which deal with Europe, deal with Germany, deal with France. After all, Britain is only just coming to terms with the fact that she is a part of Europe. It's only just dawned on Britain that she's actually in Europe. I also think that there are another group of novelists who are making connections to Hong Kong, to the Caribbean, to India, and to Africa. So, in a sense, I think it's a generational thing. It's not just, the much used phrase, the "empire is writing back" group. I think Britain has a whole generation of authors now who are wrestling with the problem of what it means to be British.

Iyer: To be a suburb of America in some ways too.
Phillips: Yes, I think that if you read Martin Amis's *Money* or Will Boyd's *Stars*

and Bars, you will understand that the relationship that Britain has with America is also something that these authors have begun to take up and deal with quite vigorously.

Iyer: One of the striking things, to go back to your reading, about your writing is that you write about slavery often without writing about race because you think all of us are slaves to some extent. Slaves to conventions, slaves to expectations, women in particular have always been in bondage in a variety of kinds. And an unusual thing about your writing is that the women often seem much more sympathetic than the men. It seems like you trust women in your life and your art more than you do men. Is that the case? Is that a rhetorical question?

Phillips: One of the interesting things that I found looking at historical documents for research—not just for *Crossing the River,* but for the novel before, *Cambridge*—is that the voices of women when they are writing diaries, journals, and nonfictional accounts of journeys to former colonies and so on, their voices always seem to be much more honest and direct in tone. In the voices of men there is always an agenda, which is obviously part and parcel of the economic and political purpose behind that journey. The women's voices seem to me to be clearer, more impassioned, more complex. And that's why I think I often appropriate a woman's voice because it offers me much more room as a fiction writer to move around and I suppose to gain some form of sympathy.

Iyer: And voices of understanding more than some form of assertion or argument.

Phillips: I'm not saying that the women can't be strident and polemical in their journals or their discourse. They certainly can, but the few times that I have used a woman's voice, it's been precisely because of the lack of drum-bashing on the part of whomsoever the character is who has presented herself.

Iyer: All three of the last novels have really involved a whole set of documents, three or four voices just placed side by side, and then it's up to the reader to join them up or try to balance them in his imagination. Do you anticipate writing a book in which you weave them all into a whole?

Phillips: I wish. I mean I've tried. I keep trying to write a book with a beginning, a middle, and an end, and then failing spectacularly. Something happens during the process where the linear structure seems to break down. It's almost like I've crafted this wonderful ceramic fruit bowl, and I'm two pages from the end of the book just doing the final glazing, and I deliberately drop it, and it shatters, and then I have to start again. In some way, it's like I don't trust the linearity of time. I don't trust it. I think a lot of people in the world don't trust it anymore. So a beginning, a middle, and an end in that order, with one set of characters, is an old nineteenth-century form. I don't mean old in any pejorative sense, but the old nineteenth-century realistic novel does not seem applicable to the subject matter that I'm addressing. I think that's why I drop the bowl every time.

Iyer: Yes, and also because it sounds like you see the world as a collection of fragments of diasporic souls with pieces of this over here and that over there and the most we can do is just get an overview of as many pieces as we can. I feel we can go on talking like that without even getting to English and German soccer stars. So, I'd better ask my final question which is that all your books clearly involve a huge amount of research and reading. It's interesting that in *Higher Ground,* the prisoner who is educating himself advises his sister to do it by reading and reading and reading. I'm just interested in, as somebody who travels a lot like myself, how do you get your writing done? Because you're constantly in motion. You were in Australia yesterday, you're going to England next week, and then you're going to the Caribbean. You taught in India; you taught in Sweden. When do you have the time, and how do you make the time just to sit down and collect your thoughts?

Phillips: Oh, I have to block off periods of the year to be quite honest, two or three week periods where I just decide that I'm going away somewhere to hide and work. I'm not one of those writers who write every day; in fact, I've not written a word of prose for two and half years now. It doesn't worry me. I'm lying; it worries me a little bit. But you have to block off periods of the year when you can get some work done. I've always worked in some sort of burst and even when I did have a bit more time that's how I work best. On the idea of crafting, the idea of how you approach it, every writer will give you a different answer, but for me I find it hard to write when I'm on the move. I find it pleasurable to read; in fact, it's what keeps me sane, I suspect with you too. Being able to travel around with an ever weightier bag with more and more books. Then I get to a place where I think, hell, should I mail this load back? Eventually you justify this ridiculous expense and mail them back. Then your bag is lighter again. Then you start to accumulate. So I read a lot when I'm traveling, but I don't really have the time to write.

Iyer: Do you have a sense where you're going, where the next book will take you?
Phillips: Yes, vaguely. I do feel only now that I'm beginning to understand something about the process, to be honest. I'm only now beginning to understand something about my own process and that's what I'm trying to deal with at the moment.

Iyer: Each time you will be able to take more and more of the world, is it the hope?

Phillips: I don't know. I think each time you must attempt to be more and more courageous and increasingly insightful. Whether or not you succeed other people are very good at telling you, and they will tell you in one way or another. But the desire is there to become increasingly successful at sharpening the blade of narrative and thereafter to become increasingly thrustful, and more and more insistent. I don't feel that I've realized even the beginning of what I imagine I have to say.

Iyer: That seems to be an eloquent and inspiring way to close. Thank you very much.

Phillips: Thank you, Pico.

An Interview with Caryl Phillips

Louise Yelin/1998

From *Culturefront* 7.2 (Summer 1998), 52, 53, and 80. Reprinted with permission of Louise Yelin and the New York Council for the Humanities, publisher of *Culturefront* (150 Broadway Suite 1700, New York, New York, 10038). Interview conducted in New York City.

Caryl Phillips was born in St. Kitts in 1958. When he was a few months old, his parents emigrated to England, where he grew up. He now divides his time between New York, London, and the Caribbean. He is the author of six novels, several screenplays and television scripts, and a collection of essays about Europe. His most recent novels reimagine the history of the modern west. *Cambridge* (1991) describes the system of plantation slavery in the British West Indies from the perspective of Emily, a British woman who travels to a plantation owned by her father, and Cambridge, a slave on the plantation who kills a brutal overseer. *Crossing the River* (1993) brings the African diaspora to life through the voices of multiple characters in different times and places, all set adrift in a history that begins with the transatlantic slave trade. *The Nature of Blood* (1997) meditates on racism by juxtaposing the stories of European Jews in fifteenth-century Venice and during the Holocaust; Othello, portrayed as a military hero isolated in a cultural milieu which treats him as an outsider; and Ethiopian Jewish refugees who suffer discrimination in contemporary Israel. Phillips is also the editor of a Caribbean literature series for Faber and Faber.

LY: Why did your parents leave St. Kitts for England?
CP: Mainly because of economic reasons. There was also, I suspect, an idea of going to where their friends and family were. They were quite adventurous, foolhardy, or courageous.

LY: Were they a source of encouragement for you?
CP: Yes. My parents were always very clear about education; they kept telling me that I was going to go to university. Given what England was like in the sixties and seventies when I was growing up, I don't think there was any other way that a young black person could have achieved or dared to aspire to excellence. If

you weren't encouraged in the home, you weren't going to do it, because society is prone to regard the Other as predestined to be permanently marginal.

LY: What was it like growing up in a northern, industrial city like Leeds in the sixties and seventies?
CP: In Leeds, you were marginalized because you were a Northerner, a regional hick. Britain is divided along a geographical fault line. The North is less sophisticated than the South and the butt of southern humor. It's a world of flattened vowels. When you're growing up, you think that's normal. It's only as you hit adolescence and listen to Southern-based radio and television coming from London that you become aware of it. I read the literature of Northern working-class writers—David Storey, John Braine, Stan Barstow, the plays of Trevor Griffiths, *Billy Liar, Room at the Top*—all of which end with some guy on a station platform getting a train south. I realized that I fitted into a long tradition of people who wanted to get out of there. It was okay growing up in Leeds until I began to realize that there's another world where you could find a more sophisticated life.

LY: In *The European Tribe* [a 1987 book of travel pieces that, taken together, make up an ethnography of European culture] you say that, when you were at Oxford, someone wrote "Nigger Go Home" next to your name on a list. Was this typical of your experience at Oxford in the seventies?
CP: That particular incident reminded me of the precariousness of being black in British society: I'm at Oxford in this college where I play soccer, rugby, cricket, track and field. I'm also in charge of the drama society. I have a socially central role, and I'm probably the best-known undergraduate in a college of 250 people. Whenever they need something, they come to me. That incident was a betrayal.

Now I see the ease with which one can move from the center to the margin, with nobody questioning it or publicly protesting. At the time, I wasn't able to articulate this; the initial feeling was hurt and anger and not really knowing whom to talk to. But I was aware emotionally of the precariousness of being visibly the Other, that it didn't really matter how much they needed you, you would become a crumpled tissue whenever it suited them.

LY: Is this the source of your portrayal of Othello in *The Nature of Blood* and as a "black European success" in *The European Tribe*?
CP: Yes. But more than that, *The Nature of Blood* also comes from my own sense of the Holocaust. When I think of Germany, I still find it incredible that, in an age of Einstein and Freud, nobody actually said, "Are you people kidding? What do you mean inferior? What are you talking about?" I find it incredible that

people could move from the center of society to *that*—or that Marc Chagall has to look for a way out of Europe because he's two steps away from being killed. So that incident at Oxford fed my own sense of precariousness in European culture, in which people define themselves by defining who they're not.

LY: How did you decide to become a writer?

CP: The things that I wanted to read didn't exist. I wanted to read stuff that included me, that was about the condition of people like myself. In college, I was directing plays—Pinter, Shakespeare, Tennessee Williams, Ibsen. I loved all this, but one day I was in the drama section of the local bookstore and I thought, What about something about me, about black kids growing up in England? There were a few plays by black British people, and a very good Shelagh Delaney play called *A Taste of Honey* which has a black character in it. I read it and watched the film and thought maybe I'd do a production of it. Then it became clear to me that I had something to say. That was at the end of my second year. Before my final and third year I came to America, where I finally began to read books by black people and realized, Yeah, why didn't I think about writing?

LY: What about George Lamming [a writer who was born in Barbados and emigrated to England in the 1950s]?

CP: Lamming's nonfiction about Britain was about exile from the Caribbean, but it wasn't available in Britain until the seventies, and it was about my parents' generation. Lamming's fiction, like V. S. Naipaul's, tended to be rooted in an exotic geography I didn't recognize. Black Americans wrote about an urban experience I understood, and they were angry. Angela Davis, Jimmy Baldwin: they were more in tune with what I was going through. The situation in England bespoke an urgency that the literature wasn't mirroring.

LY: Your first two novels are transatlantic. In *The Final Passage* (1985), a family is leaving the Caribbean; in *A State of Independence* (1986), a man is leaving England and returning to the Caribbean.

CP: They're not autobiographical in terms of facts and details, but they are emotionally. The journey out to England is the story of my parents' generation. The central character in *A State of Independence* spends half a life in England and goes back to the Caribbean. He's ostensibly home, but he's confused; it begs the question "What is home?" That's what I was feeling when I was writing that book.

LY: In *The European Tribe,* you say that you had to go to the Caribbean to go to Europe. How does the conflict between home and exile link that book and the two novels you were writing at virtually the same time?

CP: Once *The Final Passage* had been accepted and delivered to Faber, in early 1984, I decided to do a nonfiction book involving travel around Europe. The big questions that got me on the road were: Is Britain my home? Is Europe my home? Is this where I want to be? I kept encountering people to whom the question of home was crucial and problematic. By the time I got back to England at the end of 1984, this question had found a fictional form in *A State of Independence*. But I wasn't yet ready to tackle the multifaceted questions of home in essay form. So, when *The Final Passage* was published, I put *The European Tribe* on hold, and early in 1985 I went back to the Caribbean and finished *A State of Independence*. There is a common resonance among the three books; they're about journeys to places where you hope you might belong. In *all* of them, someone who has journeyed is asking, do I *belong*, do I feel I belong in this place, do I feel comfortable?

LY: Where do you feel your home Is now?

CP: I don't worry too much about the question of home. I feel comfortable in St. Kitts. My professional life is in New York and London. I feel equally comfortable in New York—not America, but New York—and London—but not Britain.

LY: You've written about England; you've written about the Caribbean; do you see yourself writing about New York?

CP: I'm writing about America now. I've written a long piece for the *New Yorker* about the death of Marvin Gaye. It's about the relation between African-American fathers and sons and the legacy of slavery, the historical pressures that drive a wedge between them. It deals with black American males' sense of themselves as providers for the family and with their sexual stuff, and with how they fail miserably in both departments. I'm thinking of Baldwin's relationship with his father, of Richard Wright's awful relationship with his father, and, obviously, of Marvin Gaye, whose father shot him.

I'm writing a nonfiction book now, about Charleston, South Carolina, Liverpool, England, and Elmina on the west coast of Africa: three points in the triangle of the slave trade; three cities with warped senses of their own history, with a deep historical sense of communal amnesia. Take Charleston. About thirty-two percent of African Americans passed through Charleston. But there's no monument, plaque, or statue to slavery there. It's as if they don't want to acknowledge that the region was built upon the slave trade. Liverpool interests me for similar reasons. It was the biggest slave port in Europe; it has a history of huge antipathy towards black people. Heathcliff in *Wuthering Heights* disappears, and he comes back *loaded*. He went to Liverpool! The only way he could make money like that was in the slave trade.

LY: Another reading of the novel is that he was a black child who was dumped on the streets. . . .

CP: The Brontës knew all about slavery; as did Jane Austen. The Brontës were right there; they weren't in favor of slavery, but they knew what the deal was. Anybody in the nineteenth century who was writing or making any reference to Liverpool was making a thinly veiled reference to the slave trade. When I was in school, *nobody* talked about the economic roots of slavery or the way in which the industrial revolution in Britain, and therefore in Europe, and therefore in the world, was founded on this institution. When I started to write, I began to read a lot and communicate with historians. But when I was studying literature, nobody would have dreamed of pointing out the reference to Antigua in Jane Austen.

Even now, in Hugh Thomas's big tome that came out last year [*The Slave Trade*], he tries to dismiss the economic argument about the abolition of the slave trade and downplays the role of black people in stirring the moral imagination of England. But there were all these black guys like Olaudah Equiano [an ex-slave and author of *The Interesting Narrative of the Life of Olaudah Equiano, Or, Gustavus Vassa, The African* (1792)] running up and down the country ruining their health giving hundreds of speeches a year. Equiano's narrative went into six or seven editions, he was quoted in the House of Lords whenever they were debating abolition, but this bastard only mentions Equiano (or any of the huge numbers of black people who were active on their own behalf) in passing, in the context of abolition.

LY: Your piece on James Baldwin in *The European Tribe* suggests that he influenced you. Which other writers influenced you? And which writers do you like reading now?

CP: Faulkner, Shaw, Tennessee Williams—a reasonably wide range. I don't like writers who keep their emotions in check. The writer I admire the most is a Japanese writer, Shusaku Endo. He tackled serious subjects but goes close to the heart. I always learn something from reading him; he's got a strong sense of characterization. I listen to a lot of music and watch a reasonable number of films because I'm always looking at form. Right now, because I'm working on nonfiction, I'm reading a lot of nonfictional writing about race. I tend to read where I'm going.

LY: You said that the impetus for your early novels was your desire to read about experiences that resonated with your own. Where do you get your ideas for your novels now?

CP: What matters is the idea that won't go away, the obsession. Usually it's a character or a voice. I have to have something I can work with, and it usually comes in human shape. I'm interested in Lewis and Clark; they had this black guy with them, York. I've always been interested in York. What was he doing with Lewis and Clark? But if I don't hear York's voice, or if there's not an incident in which York is a character, then he remains just an idea. Now, some novelists squeeze the voice out of the character. I'm more passive than that, I want the person to entrust me with their story, tiptoe towards me. So I spend a lot of time waiting, just to see what will happen.

LY: How did you get Eva [a young Jewish woman who survives the death camps but kills herself soon after the war] to talk to you, in *The Nature of Blood*? What made you hear her voice so clearly?
CP: Through the research effort, I was in Italy, and I was reading all this Holocaust material. It was driving me bloody mad, just painful, painful, painful stuff. It came to me stronger than anything else, and I knew she was dead. Initially I was going to do the novel from the point of view of an old woman who survived. But in Italy, it became clear to me that this old woman was dead, and that she died in England.

In *Crossing the River*, there's a section set in England during the Second World War, and its from the point of view of Joyce [a young British woman who falls in love with a black American G.I.]. Originally, it was to be from the point of view of the American soldier, who doesn't have a single word in the final version. At first I highjacked the wrong person to tell the story. You never know how structurally, formally, in terms of character, an idea is going to be transformed. One reason I write in other forms—film, theater, nonfiction—is that I have an idea and I know it's not a novel.

LY: What makes a novel, for you?
CP: *I'm* not present, the characters are totally in the fore, I'm invisible, I'm able to submit to the drive of the characters in the fictional world. At the same time the themes and ideas that it's tackling are absolutely essential to my own growth, intellectually and emotionally. I hide behind the characters and let them have the issues.

LY: In your novels, places are vividly imagined, but completely unspecified: in *Crossing the River*, "somewhere in England"; in *The Nature of Blood*, "somewhere in Europe."
CP: I don't like to get too specific; it might just flatten the energy. I want conflict, character, psychology. When people talk to me about the sections I set in Venice in *The Nature of Blood*, they talk to me about the evocation of Venice. Nobody

ever says *anything* about Othello. So maybe I don't bother too much with place, because I want the character in the forefront. I have a lot of unfinished business with Othello.

LY: Othello is clearly a leitmotif in your work. He reminds me of Cambridge, a black man with a certain power yet isolated in a white world.

CP: Well, Othello is so deeply rooted in the canon, while *Cambridge* was an imaginative act. But the same question is behind both those characters, the question which plagued me for the three years I was at Oxford, the fear of being in this atmosphere which did not celebrate, recognize, even acknowledge any worth in your culture. People could deal with me because I was there, 1 could drink more beer than them, and I was better at football, but they didn't know anything about my world, my values, my family. I was always aware that people were talking to me as though I was an exception. *They* may not have thought of this, but I knew it was just beneath the surface. I had to hold onto who I was in this place and who I was *out* of this place. I had to build the bridge.

My thing about Cambridge and Othello—particularly Othello—is that they had the whole burden of having to live in two worlds. There was no one who would help them, who could say, I understand the negotiation you have to do, and this is how to do it, because I've done it. It's okay; it can be done. But don't get tired too soon. Don't opt for the route of least resistance and put your burden down. Don't run scampering back to where you've left. And don't think that you have to kick away the ladder that you just climbed up, because you might need it again, not only to climb back down but also help others up there too. So don't kick it away and leave yourself up there at the top alone.

Disturbing the Master Narrative:
An Interview with Caryl Phillips
Renée Schatteman/1999

From *Commonwealth Essays and Studies* 23.2 (Spring 2001), 93–106. Reprinted with the permission of *Commonwealth Essays and Studies.* Interview conducted in Amherst, Massachusetts.

Caryl Phillips was born in the Caribbean and raised in England. His work deals with the African diaspora and related topics. Phillips has written a number of dramas and screenplays, but he is best known for his six novels: *The Final Passage* (1985), *A State of Independence* (1986), *Higher Ground* (1989), *Cambridge* (1991), *Crossing the River* (1993), and *The Nature of Blood* (1997). He has also published two collections of essays, *The European Tribe* in 1987 and *The Atlantic Sound* in 2000. This interview was conducted on April 29, 1999 at the University of Massachusetts as part of a research project on the writings of Caryl Phillips, Michael Ondaatje, and J. M. Coetzee. In this interview, Phillips praises Ondaatje and Coetzee, whom he admires for their resistance to easy categorization, and he speaks of his own need to upset narrative conventions in order to more accurately portray people whose lives have been disrupted by diasporic experiences. He also sheds new light on the stylistic and thematic choices he made in constructing *The Nature of Blood*, his most recent work of fiction.

—(Renée Schatteman [Georgia State University])

Renée Schatteman: There are numerous parallels between the "Heartland" section of *Higher Ground* and Coetzee's *Waiting for the Barbarians*. Both protagonists hesitate to act because they are secure in their positions. As a result, they both participate in oppressive structures they abhor, and in both cases their complicity gets expressed particularly in their sexual activities. Despite that fact that they both acknowledge the ambiguity of their relationship with the women, they also look to this bond as a means of redeeming themselves from their complicitous positions. Was the Coetzee text indeed an inspiration for this section?
Caryl Phillips: Definitely. I wrote that "Heartland" section just before I went to

West Africa for the first time. One of the reasons for writing it was the fact that I knew I was going to visit the slave forts and I wanted to experience it imaginatively before I experienced it physically. It was a way of imaginatively preparing myself. I'd been looking for a way, for a form to try to reflect the thorough isolation of somebody. I was reading Coetzee's work at the time because Rushdie and Graham Swift are both close friends of mine and they were both on the short list for the Booker Prize in 1983 when *Life and Times of Michael K* won. I knew *Waterland* and I knew *Shame* very well, and I wanted basically to see the book that had beaten them out. I read that and I thought it was really good, so I went back and started to read other Coetzee books. When, some time later, I was looking for a form which could express a heightened first-person narrative that could really express isolation, I remembered both *In the Heart of the Country* and *Waiting for the Barbarians* and I reread them. I think *Waiting for the Barbarians* was influential, more so than the other work, not so much thematically but just because it was set in a confined space and that's what I wanted to do with my narrative. So, yes, it definitely was an influence.

RS: Could you comment on your general impressions about Coetzee's writing?
CP: Well, to be honest, I'm pretty sure in my own mind that *Waiting for the Barbarians* is his best book to date. In some ways it is a masterpiece. It's a great, great piece of writing. My own impression of his work is that he has survived a political condition which has buried a lot of other writers, many of whom, I think, just rode a political wave. I always admired his oblique resistance to being categorized. It would have been all too easy to have become a Breyten Breytenbach or an André Brink or, to some extent, an Athol Fugard, writers who became identified with a sort of liberal white resistance to apartheid. It's not that I think these writers are bad, or that I think their politics are bad, but I've sort of quite admired Coetzee's stubborn resistance to being "identified." He even refused to turn up and get the Booker Prize in person, which is highly unusual. He's the only author I can think of who has not bothered to show up and I respect that. But I find his essays impossible. They betray his training as a mathematician and a computer scientist which is no bad thing but I find them very difficult to engage with. But I do think of all those writers who are his contemporaries, he has produced the most important work and the work that will endure.

RS: In *Higher Ground,* as in the other novels, you seem to be making a powerful accusation against slavery and racism while at the same time you express a compassionate acceptance of the fact that individuals are often deeply complicit in the forces that shape their lives. I'm thinking of your treatment of characters such as the African translator in *Higher Ground*, Cambridge in *Cambridge*, and the father who sells his children into slavery in *Crossing the River*. Is this an inherent tension in your writing between indictment of large-scale oppression on the one hand and acceptance of personal complicity on the other?

CP: Well, I think so. I've never really been able to accept the fact that one should regard slavery, or something like colonial incursion into Africa or the Caribbean, as being something to be just condemned in the way that a historian or a sociologist might condemn it. To me, individuals are ultimately much more complicated than historical forces or historical events. There is a tension because the individual is often mired in an ambiguous situation that historical narratives don't capture. As long as I'm writing about individuals whose lives are torn apart by events and circumstances that are out of their control, and who find themselves powerless to respond, there will inevitably be a tension. Those individuals who are washed ashore and find themselves marooned in a very strange place by history are often the people that interest me the most.

That word you use, "complicity," is very important too. I don't think Americans have this term, but in Britain they have this term which is usually applied to the BBC and the media which is "dumbing down" where everything is increasingly didactic and explicable. History is to be "dumbed down." You have this process occurring in this country too. For instance, CNN will have a debate about Kosovo; the idea is to achieve a "yes" or "no," it's either a good thing or a bad thing, and in twenty-five minutes they have reached a result. It's a bit more complicated than that. I think the type of fiction that I write, and the type of fiction that the two other people you are writing about write, is a fiction that resists the easy reduction of history and contemporary events to sloganeering. As long as you have characters in the centre of fiction, you have immediate ambiguity. If you are writing what is essentially a nineteenth-century novel of character (which both Coetzee and Michael do since they are both great believers in character-driven novels), even if the form is postmodern or post-post-modern or whatever, essentially at the heart of the novel is character. By placing character at the heart of these events, then you immediately have tension because characters resist the sloganeering. They just won't behave themselves. They do stuff that is at odds with what you might expect them to do.

RS: You've said often in your own writing process that you start with character and that you allow characters to live with you for a while.

CP: I have ideas, but the ideas don't mean anything until there is a character. I attempt to beat them onto the stage from the wings, and I encourage them to take centre stage and start to speak, but usually the most insistent ones are the ones that appear from the other side and just walk on and take over. So it's a matter of waiting for these people. I sometimes envy novelists like Rushdie who is able, it seems to me, with I wouldn't say effortless ease to sit down and knock off six hundred pages because his novels are novels of ideas. He doesn't have to wait for his characters in a sense because the characters are not the central component. He's like a puppet master organizing a few people around on stage but essentially the central character is him and his consciousness. The type of writer that likes to hide (i.e. me) and doesn't feel comfortable with juggling the ideas and balancing these historical things around and wants to wait for character often feels kind of helpless because you're just waiting and waiting and hoping that something, or even better, somebody comes along to move your idea.

RS: You mention the point about being a writer who prefers to hide. That raises another question. You seem to place a great value on the human heart and the concept of love in literature. In your book reviews of Naipaul's novels for example you complain that this element is missing in his work. Your own fiction certainly demonstrates deep compassion for people in the midst of struggle. But by using such a fragmented style to tell the stories of your characters' lives, is there not an element of self-consciousness or detachment on your part as a writer? How do you reconcile this investment in character and yet this distancing that comes from your narrative techniques?

CP: Well, I've always started out with the idea of writing a novel with a beginning, a middle, and an end, roughly in that order, with one set of characters, like a regular person might write a novel. But what has happened is not a lack of affection, or attachment, or investment in those characters or in their stories, but particularly in *Crossing the River* and perhaps even more so in *The Nature of Blood*, the idea of writing about people whose lives have been disrupted by what one might term diasporan concerns, by involuntary migration, by the wheel of history turning against them, the idea of not in a sense showing structurally or formally how this has affected them, hasn't seemed right to me. It hasn't seemed right to write a novel about people whose lives are fractured and ruptured without trying to reflect some of that fracture and rupture in the narrative. I would like to and I will write a novel, I'm sure, which is reasonably conventional in terms of remaining within the unities of time, but it just hasn't seemed possible in the last couple of books. The thematic concern of them just spun them in a different direction.

RS: You have spoken in other interviews about the importance of form and of finding a form that is appropriate to your subject matter. Did you have models or inspirations for choosing this kind of a fragmented structure?

CP: No, that's been one of the most difficult things of all, to tell you the truth. I think probably the nicest compliment anybody ever paid me was from Margaret Drabble, the English novelist. She said to me once, "The peculiar thing about reading your books is that you're training me how to read them." I don't have a model, somebody that I could sit down and say he or she is writing the type of novel that I would like to write. I feel it is risky because I write these books in isolation and then I hand them over, and I literally have no idea whether it will make any sense to the first person who reads them, who is usually my agent in London. I have no idea whether this hangs together, or whether this conceit is ridiculous on my part, because I'm not able to say there is a novel like this and it worked. So, no, there are no models for the overarching structure. But there are certain authors, and passages of their works I find influential. I have found that what they have done finds its way into my work.

RS: That's interesting because your fragmentary structure is the unique element of your work. But on the other hand there's a lot of intertextuality (influences of other writers) coming into the various sections of your novels. So there is an element of imitation at the same time that there is an element of uniqueness. On the issue of intertexuality, you use many first-person historical sources that you rework. In general, what attracts you to intertextual writing, and do you think your fragmented style makes it easier to be intertextual in your work?

CP: It must in some sense because otherwise you'd be doing a sort of pastiche of something. For instance, if I'd done *The Nature of Blood* as a Holocaust memoir (and there are literally hundreds of them out there), I would have felt why bother because there are so many other people who have written eloquently so why am I just mimicking that? So, as the novel became increasingly fragmented, it felt okay to have parts of it that were influenced by this book or by that text, some of which I do acknowledge and some of which I don't acknowledge.

I was talking to a French Caribbean writer yesterday, Maryse Condé, and she told me that she's teaching a course at Columbia next fall called "Cannibalism." Of course, my first question to her was "Are you crazy? You're going to get loads of students. Why do you want to teach a course with a name like that? Everyone will want to take it." But what she meant by "Cannibalism" is that she is teaching texts by Caribbean authors who have basically appropriated. She's done a book which is a take of *Wuthering Heights*. Then there's Walcott's *Omeros*, Jean Rhys's *Wide Sargassso Sea*, etc. Fancy name for the course, and she's going to get too many students, but it's about major intertextuality. I don't really have any interest in the larger scheme of doing that, such as taking *The Tempest* or taking *Othello* and writing a whole novel based on that. My idea of the novel is not pastiche, it's not Maryse's cannibalism, that's not what I would want to do.

RS: Well, you did do something interesting in *The Nature of Blood* in your treatment of *Othello*. Is your handling of the character meant to be a preface to the play that enables us to better understand his rage towards Desdemona, or are you offering an alternative perspective?

CP: Well, I think it's like a movie prequel. It's what happened before the play. I've been fascinated with the play for years since I was at school. When I was an undergraduate, we had to do two papers on Shakespeare. One was a general paper on Shakespeare and the other was a three-hour exam on one Shakespeare play. It changed every year, but as it just so happened it was *Othello* my year, which was a thirty to one shot. Actually, I did really badly on the paper. I thought I knew the play too well. I can't remember what I wrote but I think I was trying to be too clever and I didn't do very well. But, I've always been fascinated with it. I wrote about *Othello* in *The European Tribe* and I just felt I had unfinished business. What happened was that as soon as I started to write about Venice, I thought to myself well I have to go to Venice. Then I thought you don't need to go to Venice, you just want a holiday. I thought what I would do instead is sit down and watch Orson Wells's version of *Othello* again. The film got me thinking again about Othello and the whole relationship between Othello and Desdemona. I had already got in my mind, at that stage, the idea of what the end of the novel might be with the Ethiopian woman and Stephan Stern. So it began to present a nice mirror. I didn't want to go into the play itself because that would be too intertextual for me. I always figured that the "problem" with Othello was that he believed that marriage and love were somehow conduits into social acceptance, in the way in which a lot of Jewish people certainly believed the same thing in Germany between the wars. There was an element of self-delusion, deracination, of people not wanting to acknowledge that they were Jewish and marrying Gentiles, thinking it would keep them safe, and of course it doesn't because it goes back to your grandparents in terms of the Nuremberg laws etc. . . . . I was interested in the notion of "passing," if you like, and the social convention of marriage and I knew that Eva in the novel was going to regard marriage as a possible conduit to safety. When we're presented with Othello at the start of the play, he's already married in Act I, Scene 1. And I just thought let's just explore exactly the nervous condition, the psychological state that led him to think that it would be cool to get married, and let's just see how he did it. That's why I included all that about him wandering about at night and getting the boat out and marrying in secret. So it came out of all these concerns which had largely to do with my own notion of European safety, race, gender, and the convention of marriage.

RS: You said in an interview you gave before writing *The Nature of Blood* that your next book was not going to be about slavery. And while the text does move further afield from issues of the African diaspora than any of your earlier works, slavery still asserts its presence in the fact that Othello was enslaved at some point in his life before arriving in Venice as a mercenary general. What part does his previous enslavement play in your presentation of this character?
CP: I don't think it plays any real part to be honest. The kind of slavery that Othello talks about is pre-the Atlantic slave trade. So it's the type of slavery which could allow someone to still have a noble bearing. It's a pre-modern concept of the trans-Atlantic slavery. So, one could still have a certain nobility, and bearing, and individuality, one could keep one's name, and one could also be a slave and later be released. The Romans kept slaves who were essentially free. They weren't slaves in the way that we now think of slavery. *Othello* the play was written in 1600–1601 at a time when England was just starting the slave trade so it was Shakespeare's response to the beginning of the European slave trade and England's involvement. Shakespeare's Othello refers back to his nobility, and this slave history, right at the end before he commits suicide.

RS: That makes sense then because in your text when he arrives in Venice he still has his self-esteem fully intact.
CP: Yes, in his own country, he's enslaved and then freed and then he's a general. He arrives without that sense of stigma that slavery imposed on the people of Africa after about 1550. The English sailed about 1560, 1570, so after that most Africans' sense of themselves was tinged, tainted, tarnished with the idea of being looked upon in European eyes as perhaps inferior. One has to remember that until 1492 Spain was ruled by Africans. Until the Spanish kicked out the Africans, Spain was ruled and civilized by Africans. The whole of the irrigation system, the architecture of the southern half of Spain is all African, it's all Moorish. So there was no sense either in the Moor or in the European of African people as being ignorant because the evidence indicated the contrary. It was only once the slave trade started.

RS: What prompted you to become interested in the Jewish diaspora? Reinhard Sander, I believe, wrote that one of your grandfathers was Jewish. Did this contribute to your interest? And how did you come to this linkage between the Holocaust and slavery?

CP: The familial thing didn't contribute to my interest really. What triggered it off was that when I was about fourteen or fifteen, I watched a documentary about the Holocaust when living in England. I found it terrifying because for the first time I realized the precarious nature of identity in Britain. Curiously enough, these "problems" didn't necessarily have all that much to do with being black. I realized that in the middle of the twentieth century, in an era of Marx, Freud, Einstein, and so on, the German people had managed somehow to convince themselves that Jews were inferior right in the middle of a great flowering of Jewish intellectual vigour. To me, Jews were white people. I didn't know the difference between a Jew and a Christian. As far as I was concerned, the world was divided into white people and black people, and that was the Britain I was growing up in. Where I went to school, I was the only black kid and I knew there were some people called Catholics.

This program terrified me because I realized that even within the white community, there were vicious divisions around questions of identity, around questions of belonging. I realized that almost overnight one's identity, which had hitherto been accepted and perhaps cherished and valued, could be turned and used against you. I guess the obvious and rather theoretically simplistic point to make is that I thought if white people could do that to white people, what on earth are they going to do to me. Every kid, irrespective of background, has the experience of one day being at school talking to someone, and the next day, the person you thought was your best friend suddenly isn't your friend any more and is hanging out with a new group and you're suddenly the geek or the nerd. That happened to me, but it was often tinged with racial overtones, and so I realized that you could quickly be excluded. As a result, of course, I began to think about the Holocaust and that prompted me to think more about my own history and why was I growing up in Britain, why not where I was born in the Caribbean, and why had my parents come to Britain. Over the years, almost as a sort of parallel interest, every time I thought about my own history and about African people in the diaspora, I also thought about European history and particularly the Holocaust.

RS: You mentioned that there are a great number of Holocaust memoirs out there. I know that you traditionally do extensive research before you do your writing. Could you talk about sources for Eva's narrative other than Anne Frank's diary?

CP: For the first time I kept a list of books that I read. I don't know why I kept the list and I don't propose to do it again, but I did keep a list and there were way over two hundred books. And I made notes about what I thought of the books after I read them which ranged from "totally useless for my purposes" to "very moved." Anne Frank's narrative wasn't the most important narrative. The example of Anne Frank has obviously been important to "free me." There were any number of books that had a pretty profound effect on me, but there was no one story or one person about whom I thought let me try to recreate her voice. Eva's an amalgam of a number of voices, but then she's a voice and a person which had already been with me I feel for many, many years.

RS: Is she related to Irina in *Higher Ground*?

CP: No, but what's interesting is that two weeks ago I was in Germany and I read from *Higher Ground* at some conference. My publishers had told me that it had been ten years exactly to the day that that book was published, so 1 thought I haven't read from this book for many, many years now. So I opened it up and I chose to read something from Irina's section, and I was kind of surprised about the similarities. It did surprise me that she was clearly related in some way to the character that emerged in *The Nature of Blood*. I didn't think of her or read the novel again when writing *The Nature of Blood*, but she clearly is in some way related to Eva.

RS: One of the things that is fascinating about Eva is that through her memories we get so many scenes of the Holocaust, so it doesn't surprise me that you created her from many different stories. Her narrative does have such a breadth to it. Trying to imagine or envision the experience of the camp must have been a difficult writing experience to go through.

CP: Yes, much more difficult than anything I've written about on the slave trade. Much more problematic because I can understand slavery, the economics of it, the warped logic of those who would perpetrate it. At a very early stage of what became *The Nature of Blood*—I remember telling my agent this. We were having lunch, and I was saying this to him because he's Jewish. He and his father had just gone to Auschwitz. His father wanted to take him there. His father is a writer whom I know. I was asking him how it was for him, and I said during that conversation that one of the things I wanted to try and do was to give voice to the perpetrators, the Nazis, the camp commandant or something. Not for balance or fairness but just because I was curious about what on earth goes on in these people's minds. As a way to try and prepare my head for this, I read a book by Gitta Sereny called *Albert Speer*. She went to interview Speer in Spandau, at the prison he was kept in before he died, to try to understand him and understand what had made him do this. I got not very far into this book before just throwing it across the room because I was so disgusted at the self-justification. I was disgusted that this man had been given a platform to try to explain what I think was inexplicable and inexcusable, and it soon became clear to me that I didn't actually have the patience or the interest in trying to do what I think is an act of generosity. When you try to imagine yourself into somebody else's skin, it's an act of generosity to try to engage and listen, and I just thought I can't be bothered with these people. And it's how I felt when I watched *Schindler's List* with Ralph Finnes's character when Spielberg is trying to understand him when he's playing with the Jewish girl in his barracks. He obviously fancies her and he's trying to play with her, and Spielberg is trying to explore the warped sexuality. And I just thought, give me a break. I don't want to know. This guy is the same shit that we just saw standing on his balcony taking pot shots, and I just thought why am I supposed to be interested in what motivates this guy? Because there is nothing there that I feel compassion for. Now I can feel much more compassion for and interest in a slave ship captain because not only do I have the evidence that some slave ship captains deeply repented and in the end wrote narratives against the slave trade, I could also imagine the slave ship captain finding himself in this position through no fault of his own. I could also imagine that even somebody cruel could find themselves justifying what they were doing because of economic necessity or even economic greed. I can understand a variety of motives. But I just don't have the patience with your average Nazi. I just cannot be bothered.

RS: There are many camps featured in this novel. You form a link between Jews and blacks through the concept of ghettoization. Are we also meant to think of the way the term ghetto is used today, mainly to describe poor black communities in Europe and the U.S.?

CP: Yes, ghetto is an interesting word because it is a word in contemporary parlance which is almost universally associated with black people. But it's a word which emerged absolutely out of the Jewish experience. So today when you have a Jewish community and a black community in the States which for some bizarre, stupid reason are at loggerheads with each other, the use of the word "ghetto" is just one of the ways I try to show there is so much history which is very similar. Jewish people and black people are to some extent, I think, two great communities who exercise historical vigilance. They are always looking over their shoulder, always looking to the past, always hyperaware for obvious reasons of the fact that the present is conditioned by the past. In the Jewish tradition, you have so many books and so many narratives that are to do with roots and with the past, and with determining who is Jewish by looking to the past. And in the case of people in the African diaspora, having this very strange symbiotic relationship with Africa fosters an often mythical, romanticized notion of the past. So, I feel so many links, I also see lots of separation, but there are so many links and so many points of cross reference.

RS: From the similar experiences of exile?

CP: Exile, dislocation, historical homelessness, but also a great distrust of the condition that they find themselves in and a great discomfort with, if you like, pulling on the jacket of the country that they're in. For example, the woman who helped me with the research on *The Nature of Blood,* I wasn't at all surprised when she told me that she has dual citizenship, that she has an Israeli passport too. It's that sense of having been brought up in a society where you always have to be looking for the way out in case it goes wrong again. I think a lot of black people are like that too which is why they cultivated this myth of Africa, or in Britain where they've cultivated this myth of the Caribbean as a place they can return to.

RS: In reflecting on the title of the novel, it seems to suggest that blood ties are important because they are what is needed to sustain people through trauma. As Stephan Stern says, "People are not made to live alone neither when things are good, nor when they are bad" (p. 211). But the privileging of blood ties creates an almost inevitable and natural tendency to discriminate against those who inhabit the same region but remain outside the circle of blood and that violates the more basic reality of the nature of blood—that all human beings, regardless of time, space, race, or creed, share the same blood or life force. How are we to reconcile these two opposing perceptions of blood ties? What is your understanding of the nature of blood?

CP: One of the nice things about being a novelist is that you can mire yourself in ambiguity. You don't have to make a decision. You can explore the grey area. You leave decisions to politicians and teachers. In all the time that I've been writing fiction, I don't have any agenda. The thing about blood is that it is exactly what you just described. It is deeply ambiguous because on the one hand it does create family and bonds which sustain but on the other hand, a radical fidelity and loyalty to it creates the very divisions, the very hostilities, the very exclusions that in a sense lead one to find kinship with others. So it's a sort of horrible circle. In Germany, I went to talk as a favour to a friend called Bénédicte Ledent. Bénédicte has written a book basically, but she knows I don't read anything—reviews, or interviews, or articles. I haven't read her book and I won't read it. At this conference she gave a paper on the relationship between my work and religion and the only question she asked me—she could have asked me anything she wanted because I was there for twenty-four hours and spent most of that time drinking and hanging out with her and her friends—was if I had read the Bible and I said no. I could have said more. What I could have said is that the same ambiguities that you're talking about with regard to blood are present in religion. I'm not a religious person but I do have a position of ambiguity on religion. I don't think that a tight belief in faith is necessarily liberating because, of course, the beginning of the slave trade and the incursion into Africa was perpetrated with a gun in one hand and the Bible in the other. It was basically used as a pretext to civilize the native and that is how people justified the horror of the Middle Passage and of slavery. Yet, I can't find it within myself to adopt a religion-bashing position because what I also know is that in times of great doubt, in the middle of the night, in the middle of terrible circumstances, for people of all backgrounds, including black people, religion is the only thing that has got them through. So you have this terrible paradox that on the one hand it enslaves but on the other it liberates. It maybe enslaves the group and liberates the individual. Maybe it's not that simple. I don't know, but I find myself in the same position with religion as I am with blood.

RS: When Stephen Clingman was introducing you at our departmental colloquium a few years ago, he said that the meaning of your work comes from the gaps between the stories. What effect are you intending in juxtaposing multiple stories that may not have any explicit connections between them? What meaning are you intending for the readers to find in the distances you leap between narratives?

CP: I'm not a great believer in what more rigidly theoretical academics would call the master narrative. It's an increasingly unfashionable position in which doubt has been replaced by certainty. 1 am more interested in hearing from five people "on the ground" than I am in hearing from even the most eloquent politician on the planet. It's up to the individual to subjectively piece together their own version of the world. The gaps are there, if you like, to allow you the latitude to insert your own understanding, and your own meanings, and your own linkages, and your own bridges. I don't want to lead people by the hand or worse by the nose across from this bit to that bit. I want them to find their own meaning and discover their own pain and their own pleasure in putting the puzzle together for themselves. I would like my readers to feel that they are being led to something but they are not being made to drink it. That they can explore, they can walk around, I hope that they can also be emotionally affected by it, but it's what they do after they finish the book that is important. So the gaps are there for them to manoeuvre.

RS: I wonder if you are creating a universalism of oppression in some manner in the sense that you are taking five different stories from very different locations and different times and they do have connections that become apparent when you look back at them all.

CP: I don't really think of it like that. It is up to other people to decide if that is what is happening. It's always a dangerous thing for the author to be too conscious of what he is doing. I'm deeply aware that the way in which we behave as individuals in our own social, personal, historical space has been determined by things that happen in countries and spaces in time that we haven't even thought about. For somebody to view their own experiences as being a) purely within their control and b) shaped only by forces that they can see and understand seems to me to be somewhat naive. History is very complicated and we are a part of bigger things than what we see around us and that's why I find it frustrating and depressing when people compartmentalize off their history. This is why I have a problem with black studies departments which don't necessarily make a lot of sense to me unless there's a white studies department and then I would campaign for the abolition of both of them. There's no such thing. The experience of the sailor on deck is as important as the experience of the slave below deck. That experience of the young boy press-ganged at eleven onto a ship, suddenly finding himself sailing the Atlantic backwards and forwards and dead at seventeen from malaria on the coast somewhere three thousand miles from home and his family is as valid an experience of what happened to the slave below deck. It's very complicated. So I don't really have a universal position, but the individuals I'm interested in eventually seem to meet each other. They find each other. There is some way in which they seem to realize their connection. And if they don't realize as in *The Nature of Blood,* we realize. We should realize in that last scene the huge irony of Stephan's position as a old man now and his attitude towards this woman. After everything we've seen, we should realize how ironic it is that he is beginning to participate in a slightly morally questionable attitude towards these people. And he doesn't know the irony, but we know because we've seen his story.

RS: Your books provide historical understanding and shed light on things that we know but don't allow ourselves to think about very much. They help to provide a larger context.

CP: Well, I think that is the hope, basically.

RS: Your writings address issues at the heart of the postcolonial agenda. You articulate the stories from the past that remain untold, you subvert received history by reworking first person texts, and you expose the assumptions of imperialism that justified oppression. But you also employ a narrative technique that appears to be very postmodern in that it so explicitly disrupts the narrative line. Do you see yourself writing as the nexus of postmodernism and postcolonialism?

CP: No, I don't have any hostility to theory, well, not much. The people that I read and that I gain something from are increasingly people who are doing the same as I am. I read Michael. I'll read whatever he does because I like where it is headed and I like that he distrusts certain narrative certainties in the same way that I distrust them. I'll read Coetzee too for the same reason. But the structural technique is more motivated and produced by an engagement with character and where that character leads me. If the character leads me into a cul-de-sac where I have to employ some narrative strategy to get them to the next stage, which they tend to do because they have their own personal histories, then I'll do it. But I'm not thinking to myself oh, I'm writing after Joyce. I'm not thinking that clearly. As much as I would like to write a novel with a beginning, a middle, and an end, I'm not convinced that I ever can. It would never be that simple because I don't have an investment in the linearity of a master narrative. As much as I love Hardy and Dickens and Tolstoy, they write out of a certainty about the world in which day begets night and night leads to day, and I don't believe that. My experience tells me that that is not necessarily going to happen, and I think the experience of most of my characters is that they can wake up in the middle of the night and find themselves on a train or a boat or a plane from Ethiopia to Israel or from Africa to the Caribbean or from Amsterdam to Belsen and they don't have any control over this. And so I can't really impose the certainty of the master narrative on their lives, and as long as they resist it, then I have to resist it. And that means that I have to find another way of telling the story which means that I just employ every possible technique and method. I read a lot and I fumble a lot in the dark to try and push and feel, to put the bricks into place, and I hope that I am moving towards something which makes coherent sense. That's the hope. But how I imagine it will be at the start is never, in my experience, the way it is when I finish. James Baldwin put it perfectly when he once said, "a funny thing happened on the way to the typewriter," and that is how I feel about writing. I have this notion it is going to be like "this" and then something happens and it ends up like "that."

Interview with Caryl Phillips

Leonard Lopate/2000

From WNYC broadcast on November 1, 2000. Reprinted with the permission of WNYC. Interview conducted in New York City.

Leonard Lopate: Journeys have always been a major theme in Caryl Phillips's fiction but this time around he's written a nonfiction account of his own travels to the three major stops on the transatlantic slave trade and into the history of the African diaspora. His new book called *The Atlantic Sound* is part travelogue, part history, part wide ranging meditation on the legacy of slavery. It's published by Knopf, and I'm very pleased that it brings Caryl Phillips back to New York and Company today. Hi.
CP: Hi. It's good to be back.

LL: You kicked off your travels by retracing the journey you and your parents took when you were just a baby. Is that all part of the diaspora, going from place to place?
CP: Well, I guess so. I mean that journey from the Caribbean to Britain that my parents undertook with me in the late fifties is a journey that they've never really talked about, and I've asked them both together and individually over the years to explain why they left, what the actual physical journey was like, the sense of anticipation. But I think in common with a lot of first generation migrants, they somehow wanted to protect me in some way from the problems perhaps that were associated with migration, the sense of betrayal that they maybe felt when they arrived in England, so they've been quite silent about it. So I thought the only way that I could at least emotionally retrace it was by actually getting on a banana boat myself and going there.

LL: And did that help you understand better?
CP: Well, it's a completely stupid thing to do actually.

LL: It was much later, a different time, a different Britain.
CP: But it was still a banana boat.

LL: At least the banana boat's the same.

CP: It was the loneliest, most kind of traumatic, isolated thing that I think I've ever done. I mean, when you're ten, twelve days without seeing land, you're on a German ship with Burmese crew and there's only three other passengers, one speaks English, the other speaks German. It was bizarre and ludicrous.

LL: But your parents had not come over in such a boat, had they?

CP: They had. Although, actually, by the time I got to Dover and I called my mother and I said, I made it, she said, actually, we came over in a much nicer ship.

LL: And that was to a different Britain, a Britain that was very confused about these people from the Caribbean. It wanted them, because it needed educated people to take jobs that were not being filled after the war but also, there was a strong sense of xenophobia throughout Britain.

CP: Well, it was a particularly difficult arrival, I think, for people from the Caribbean in the fifties because they were, after all, British citizens. My parents arrived with British passports. The nature of the connection that they had with Britain made them feel that they were somehow rejoining an extended family, that they would be welcome as all the slightly dusky members of the family but, nonetheless, part of this British empire.

LL: Because they had grown up in the British system, they probably were more British in their heads than many of' the people who were living in Britain.

CP: Well, my mother told me that every night before dinner, and she was not by any means from an affluent family—I was born in a rum shop, her family were rum shopkeepers in a small village—but every night before dinner her father made them stand while he wound up the Victrola and played "Land of Hope and Glory," so you can imagine the sense of expectation which she carried in her heart.

LL: And then they moved to Leeds. That had to have been a real slap in the face.

CP: Well, hang on a minute, Leeds is okay.

LL: In *The Atlantic Sound,* you visit three major cities involved in the transatlantic slave trade, the first one was Liverpool in England. Now what was its role in the trade?

CP: Well Liverpool is a city which today, of course, presents itself to the world as the home of the Beatles, home of a particularly vibrant type of music and very ironic sense of humor.

LL: Of multiracial harmony?

CP: Not really. That's the thing about Liverpool. It's one of the longest multiracial cities in Britain but it's always had incredible disharmony and I traced that or I followed that back in my own travels and certainly in *The Atlantic Sound* to the fact that Liverpool has a hidden history in the eighteenth century. The city of Liverpool alone controlled three-fifths of the European slave trade.

LL: And it wasn't just the slave trade, it was trade in general with Africa and the products made by slaves.
CP: Sure. It was, I mean, the whole of the industry, the whole of the industrial infrastructure, the architecture, the wealth, the civic wealth, the individual wealth in Liverpool was based upon trading with Africa, but particularly, obviously trading in human beings.

LL: The Town Hall, built in 1754, the height of the slave trade.
CP: Fabulous building but if you look very closely at Liverpool Town Hall, look up at the top of it, you see carved into the façade are elephants, alligators. If you look very closely you'll see a palm tree and then if you look even closer, you'll see human heads. Black, Negro as they would say, Negro human heads. Because of course, Negroes, blacks at that time were regarded as material wealth, produce to be traded, to be sold, to be bartered.

LL: You tell the story of John Emmanual Ocansey in Liverpool, who was he?
CP: He was a man who, in 1881, made a journey from the West Coast of Africa to Liverpool. It turned out his father was a trader and he had decided rather grandly and, I guess in a spread of capitalistic zeal, that he would be able to trade better in Africa if he had a boat, if he had a small steamer. And so he sent money to a man in Liverpool who agreed to build him a steamer; the steamer never arrived so he sent his son, John, who had never left Africa, to Liverpool to find out what on earth had happened to this money. And John Ocansey wrote a book actually, which has been long, long, long out of print but I found a copy of it in the British library and read it and it was full of strange details about this lonely young black man in his twenties wandering around Liverpool, people touching his hair, wanting to touch his skin, being curious about him. And I sort of empathised with him in many ways because it reminded me of how I felt growing up in Leeds, which is only fifty miles away from Liverpool, as a young boy. The curiosity on the streets. The lack of understanding where you come from, and this idea that sometimes people staring at you is not hostility, it's simply curiosity, and having to figure out when curiosity stops and hostility begins.

LL: Did the writer of fiction in you fall in love with this story? This is the kind of thing you could have invented.
CP: I wish I had have.

LL: I mean, it makes a wonderful short story, doesn't it?

CP: I'm sure it's made a wonderful short story for other people and you know, the idea of the stranger arriving. In fact, Joseph Conrad has a terrific short story called "Amy Forster," which really reminds me of Ocansey's plight, which is about a foreigner who gets washed up in a shipwreck in a small English town and he's wandering around and nobody knows where he's come from. It's a very common narrative device and, you know, I think people have made fiction out of it and that's why it was attractive to me.

LL: What's interesting about the Ocansey story is that he is not mistreated. On the other hand, he doesn't really get what he's come for.

CP: No, he doesn't get what he's come for, which is obviously, first and foremost, cash, you know, he wants his father's money back, but he does get something else which is justice. He finds the man who swindled his father and in one of those strange, ironic twists of fate that often litter hidden corners of history, he triumphed in that he took this man to court and the English justice system upheld his case and the man was sent to prison.

LL: After Liverpool you went to Ghana, which is where Ocansey comes from, although it wasn't called Ghana then, it was called the Gold Coast, and one of the most fascinating people you met there is a young man named Mansour. He's really as key to what this book is about as any person, don't you think?

CP: Yeah. Mansour is a young Ghanian man in his late thirties. He was actually a friend of my brother's in London. He had been deported from England for being an illegal immigrant. He worked at a variety of jobs teaching Arabic, driving Domino's pizzas, you know, delivery driver; he'd done a variety of jobs but his ambition in England was to get an education and he failed to get this education and he was deported. When I went to Ghana, I employed him as a driver. He drove me around and much of what I saw in Ghana and much of what I learned about the nature of the relationship of Africans to what we might term Africans in the diaspora, their long lost cousins, was seen and filtered through the eyes of Mansour.

LL: Mansour wants to get out?

CP: Mansour desperately wants to leave, which, of course, makes it rather curious for me to be there, as I was partly there to interview and get to know African-Americans who are desperate to get in.

LL: What happens when a Mansour meets an American who says I've come back to my roots?

CP: Well, Mansour thinks that such an African-American is in desperate need of psychiatric help. As far as Mansour is concerned, Mansour can't wait to get to New York City or Chicago or Atlanta and drive a cab and make some money. He has no idea why an American would willingly give up citizenship, give up a passport, and come and live in a village.

LL: But that's because he doesn't understand the concept of people trying to reclaim a lost identity.
CP: Yeah, that's because Mansour cannot afford romance.

LL: He says, in fact, the only way up in Ghana is out.
CP: Yeah, well, it's not just true obviously of Ghana, it's true of many parts of the so-called third world or underdeveloped world, this idea that you leave and you go to somewhere that can provide you with more economic and educational opportunities. But in Mansour's case, and in the case of many people in West Africa, it seemed to me that there was a particular vigor about their desire to migrate.

LL: But if you look at the history of Africa, most of the most respected leaders, many of the artists, many of the best of the artists spent a fair amount of time in Europe.
CP: A fair amount of time in Europe or a fair amount of time laterally in the United States.

LL: And many went back, some didn't.
CP: And I think that the case of a Mansour, though, is symptomatic of a generation who actually aren't really thinking of going back. The old idea that, as you say, quite rightly suggest, people came, got educated, had experience, were exposed to certain things that they may not have been exposed to at home, then they go back and bring that knowledge with them, that's not, as far as I can see, the modern trend.

LL: There was a Panafest, it was called, near Accra, in Ghana, in which the foreigners were more African than the Africans?
CP: Yeah. Panafest is one of those crushed up, scrunched up words which actually means Pan-African Festival of the Arts and became known as the Panafest. I think it's a biannual event where poets, writers, dancers, musicians come together from all around. But the idea of a family reunion around historical rupture and historical fracture is a great idea, but in theory. It was Olympian in its disorganization and it was frustrating on a level that had to be seen and experienced to be believed.

LL: You say that the desire to return to Africa on the part of black people from the first world, their tendency to exaggerate both the past and the present, has caused you to suffer from diasporan fatigue.

CP: I think when I was enduring Panafest I was suffering from diasporan fatigue.

LL: What was expected of you at Panafest?

CP: I was a sort of roving person with a notepad who had access to talk to whoever I wanted from any of the groups from anywhere in the world. So nothing was actually expected of me. They'd asked me if I wanted to read or do a performance of some sort, but I politely declined.

LL: But what were people doing that was leading to all of this joyous reconnection?

CP: Well, that beat me too. The idea was that somehow there was going to be a discovery that there was a communal past which had somehow been shattered by the act of the middle passage, by slavery, and that people were going to reunite and discover cultural practices in common, were going to discover perhaps, words, ideas. You know, there was nothing specific and that was part of the problem; it was a very vague idea that somehow by virtue of the fact that everybody had in common a shared history that that meant that there would be necessarily a coming together. Now anybody who has ever been at a family gathering or Thanksgiving knows how dysfunctional families are.

LL: Isn't the shared history for many Africans actually American culture? I remember speaking to a number of writers from Africa in London and all they talked about was American pop music, American writers, and I asked them, well, what about Nigerian popular music? There are some pretty famous musicians who have come out of Nigeria, and they didn't want to hear about it.

CP: Well I think that certainly these days American culture has superseded British culture. I think if you asked the same question you'd probably get the same point thirty or forty years ago, although the response may have been to do with British music or British literature or British cultural values. Now, yes, obviously American values, but to be fair that's not something which is purely specific to the African continent. We could say the same about many countries in Southeast Asia as well. No, there are obviously culturally specific things because there are many different languages, and residing within those languages are literatures and religious practices. So there are very specific cultural things, but it seemed to me, in general, a rather romantic notion to assume that this family coming together would be smooth, unfettered by anxiety, and would just move along swimmingly.

LL: One of the historical figures you discovered in Ghana is Philip Quaque. Who was he?

CP: He was a guy who, back at the time when Africans were being taken, not only on ships to the Americas, Africans were also being taken to England to be educated and to come back and, if you like, to rule their people. Many of these people were taken to England and plucked at a very young age out of the bosom of their families.

LL: Christianized first?

CP: Basically, yes. They were often given a very deeply religious education and then sent back to Africa to essentially rule over their own people or to be in some way facilitators to work alongside the English. This man was stationed, again somewhat ironically, actually in a slave fort. He held a ministry; he was a minister, he was educated, he came back as a man in his early twenties, but right underneath his feet, right where he was preaching, right where he was supposed to be giving counsel not only to Africans but to English soldiers, were Africans waiting in the dungeons ready to be shipped off, and it's quite likely that some people that were in the dungeons beneath his feet were members of his own family.

LL: Was the irony lost on him?

CP: He wrote letters. The thing about this individual is that his letters are actually very painful. His initial letters that he was writing back to England to people who had educated him, friends, people he was in contact with, were very pro-the system. But as he got older and as he began to realize how isolated he was, in quite a heartbreaking way his letters became increasingly revealing about his own understanding of the deeply contradictory nature that history had placed him into.

LL: And he suffered a loss of home and loss of self as a result?

CP: Well, I think that's what attracted me to him to be quite honest. Because that idea of a loss of home, that idea of having lost a secure mooring in the world is something which kind of permeates the whole book, obviously beginning with my own journey on this banana boat, retracing my parents' journey. I've always been interested, partly because of growing up in a society such as Britain, which is a very exclusive society, which has a very narrow definition of who belongs. I've always been interested in this idea of home and belonging.

LL: But it's interesting that a lot of people who came to Britain from other places, not just from the Indies, have moved around a lot. Many of them live here now. You spend a lot of time here, Salman Rushdie lives here, people from other parts of the British empire have chosen to live here. Do you think that because of the diasporan aspects of their lives they never really had a sense of a home?

CP: I think that's a very interesting point because Britain up until quite recently has been very resistant to what I call the hyphen. In this country, it's a lot easier to hyphenate American, you're Irish-American, you're Swedish-American, you're German or African-American. You don't hear people in Britain using that term. An African-Britain, an Irish-Britain. Britain doesn't hyphenate. The actual nationality is very concrete and very exclusive. I think for people who have more than one cultural feed or more than one identity in their make-up, it's often difficult to orient yourself properly in British society and I think a lot of people have found it, in some ways, easier over here. It's easier for a writer, if you like, who is an individual, who isn't wedded to a particular routine. A lot of people, I'm afraid, are still trying to struggle to wrestle Britain's face towards a more complex sense of itself.

LL: You also went to Charleston, which was the place where most African slaves were unloaded, but I want to jump a moment to Israel. You found two thousand African-Americans trying to create a utopian community of black Hebrews in the Negev Desert. They didn't return to Africa, they went to Israel instead. Why?

CP: Well, there's a group of people that I found, actually when I was at this Panafest in Ghana, who told me that if I really wanted to see Africans from America, African-Americans who'd gone home, that I should go to Israel. Now of course I didn't believe them when they told me that there was over two thousand people living in a small town an hour and a half south from Jerusalem, but I began to make a few phone calls and found out that actually this was true. So I went there and they told me, they explained to me, that the idea was that somehow the people who had arrived in the United States were the descendants of the Lost Tribes of Israel, so they had actually left originally what is now modern-day Israel, there was no Suez Canal in those days, so they walked into Africa, were dispersed and in a sense, part of their continuing historical punishment was the Middle Passage, being shipped to America. Therefore, a return to Africa was only a halfway return. A true return is to go back to the holy land.

LL: And they wind up in this place that nobody else wants to live in because Israel doesn't really feel comfortable . . .

CP: Well, it's desert. There's nothing there. It's dusty. It's freezing cold at night. It's boiling hot in the day. There is no real organized community. The Israeli government in the late sixties gave them some abandoned barracks, which had been used during one of the earlier wars, but they had to put their own plumbing in. Basically, they had to make a community.

LL: Are they still Americans living in another place? Have they worked out some kind of accommodation?

CP: Well, technically they're not Americans anymore because in order to retain residency there, they had to actually make themselves stateless, so they're not Israeli citizens either. So they live in this curious limbo-land, and for me, the most painful thing was not the older generation who had consciously made this decision to leave, in many cases it was Chicago and Washington, but it was the kids growing up that I found heartbreaking. This idea that the kids were shooting hoops, they watched tapes of NBA games . . .

LL: Spoke English?

CP: They spoke English as opposed to Hebrew, but they were betwixt and between any kind of cultural orientation.

LL: And how did these people survive in Israel?

CP: There's a lot of home produce. Making ice cream, making organic food, raising organic food. They have shops scattered all around Israel and also they have a choir. Quite a well-known choir within Israel and they go around touring.

LL: And some of the kids have joined the Israeli rock bands, I gather?

CP: Yeah, well it's very difficult to leave the community. I'll put it no stronger than that. It's a very tight knit community, but a lot of the younger people who are growing up, not feeling fully American and wanting a sense of home, are trying to integrate into Israeli society and many of them are playing music.

LL: Let's go back to Charleston. In Charleston you write about a white couple. Why a white couple?

CP: Because, as far as I'm concerned, the history of African-American migration and cultural input into this country has affected white people as well as black people. The very act of the Middle Passage, there's many people under the deck but there's somebody on deck steering or sailing that ship and it affected their lives too.

LL: But in this case, we are talking about Judge Waring and his wife Elizabeth. They were whites who went against the tide in Charleston. They entertained black people in their homes, they supported the rights of blacks to vote, etc. And they were forced to leave finally after they had become targets of the KKK. Do you use them as illustrations of how things used to be in a place like Charleston and how they are no longer?

CP: I use them as an illustration as a couple of things. There's a very poignant quote from Robert Frost where he says, "Home is the place, that when you have to go there, they have to take you in." Judge Waring lost his home. He was a man in his late sixties, almost seventy, when he began to make these very courageous civil rights decisions in his courtroom. And as a result, of course, he and his wife were forced to leave the place where he had grown up, where he was a pillar of the establishment. He moved to New York City and he only ever came back to be buried. It was that loss of home that accompanied the moral courage of the man that attracted me to him.

LL: But that was then and you compare the Charleston Festival of African and Caribbean Art today with what you saw in Africa with Panafest.

CP: But what I saw in Charleston was a very cautious display of pride in all things African which somehow seemed to me to be more rooted in a sense of reality, both historical reality and current-day common-sense than what I'd been seeing in Africa.

LL: In a book like this it's easy to try to wrap everything up and draw some conclusions. You say you've resisted having any kind of tight thesis here.

CP: I think that's my novelist's training. One of the things about writing a novel is that, of course, one has the rare privilege of collapsing into ambiguity at the end. There's no necessity to provide answers. It's a similar thing with nonfiction. I found writing a nonfiction book again after so many years slightly discomforting because I have to present myself to the fore, whereas I'm used to hiding behind the characters and feel much more comfortable there. But essentially the actual act of writing nonfiction, the empathy, the amount of energy which is poured into it is exactly the same as a novel and, therefore, the conclusion is the same. It's a certain degree of ambiguity.

LL: Well is there really any way to achieve neat and tidy closure with a subject like this?

CP: I don't think so, because the question of home, the question of belonging, the question of exile has been with us as long as we've been discussing the human condition, and it's not going to go anywhere.

LL: Caryl Phillips's book, *The Atlantic Sound*, is published by Knopf. Thank you so much for being with us.

Rites of Passage

Maya Jaggi/2001

From *Guardian*, November 3, 2001, 6–7. Reprinted with the permission of Maya Jaggi. Interview conducted in Charleston, South Carolina.

In the late 1990s, Caryl Phillips crossed the Atlantic on a banana freighter, recreating the journey to England his parents had made from the Caribbean island of St. Kitts almost forty years earlier. "I couldn't sleep," he recalls. "I spent nights on deck, feeling the vastness and loneliness of the ocean, trying to relive not just my parents' voyage but Columbus's, the slave ships', and the Irish and Russian flotsam migrating to the New World. I realised the mid-Atlantic was where I belonged spiritually, where you'd locate most of my life and work." At only forty-three, Phillips has charted the Atlantic triangle of Europe, Africa, and the Americas in a fast-growing oeuvre that crosses continents and centuries: six novels—including the Booker-shortlisted *Crossing the River* (1993)—travel books, plays, screenplays, anthologies, radio and television drama and documentaries, and essays. One of *Granta*'s 20 Best of Young British Novelists in 1993, he is rare in having been able to make his living as a writer since the age of twenty-one.

His new book of essays, *A New World Order*, combines memoir and travel with topics from James Baldwin and Marvin Gaye to Zadie Smith and the author's lifelong passion for Leeds United football club. His adaptation of V. S. Naipaul's 1957 novel *The Mystic Masseur* is now a Merchant Ivory film. The first of the new Nobel laureate's books to be filmed, it premiers at the London Film Festival this Friday with an international cast, including James Fox and Om Puri. Though Phillips has sharp differences with Naipaul (detailed in his essay, "The Enigma of Denial"), he admires the gentle comedy of his early fiction, and a film that "dignifies the history of the Caribbean, rather than using it as a backdrop."

The spectral triangle of Phillips's work, which embraces the Africa of his ancestry, the Caribbean of his birth, the Britain of his upbringing, and the United States where he lives, covers what the sociologist Paul Gilroy has termed the "black Atlantic." In the U.S., Phillips has been dubbed the "bard of the African diaspora." Yet meeting Phillips in Charleston, South Carolina, the "black Ellis

Island" which was the gateway into America for a third of captive Africans, he reveals more complex affiliations.

In his travel book, *The Atlantic Sound* (2000), issued in paperback this month, Phillips went to Charleston, Liverpool, and Elmina in Ghana, three points that form a triangle of slavery, to explore the notion of "home" central to all his work. Revisiting Charleston for a reading, he makes a pilgrimage to Magnolia cemetery to lay flowers at the grave of Judge Waring, a white judge whose efforts to integrate the state in the 1940s left him ostracised as a "traitor" by the Charlestonian aristocracy. It is characteristic of Phillips's vision that, in excavating the hidden history of this antebellum tourist centre, he draws imaginative links between diasporic wanderers and a white man whose moral stand made him an outcast in his own hometown.

Phillips's interest is in how individuals survive, or succumb to, historical storms and social pathologies. Bénédicte Ledent, lecturer in Caribbean literature at the University of Liège and author of a forthcoming book on Phillips, says his "focus on individual lives rather than systems of thought" breaks down barriers of race and gender. His stylist's prose is married to moral purpose. While its starting point may be the black diaspora, his work illuminates relations between black and white, master and servant, newcomer and "host," men and women.

A chronicler of displacement and precarious belonging, Caryl "Caz" Phillips is himself a "compulsive itinerant" who has clocked up two million air miles during the past decade. Since 1990 he has had a base in both the U.S. and west London, and in 1995 he became the youngest tenured English professor in the U.S. at Amherst College in Massachusetts. He is now professor of English at Columbia University in New York, with a chair at Barnard College as professor of migration and social order.

Phillips lives in Manhattan's Greenwich Village, where his neighbours include the Nobel prizewinning poet Derek Walcott and this year's Booker winner, Peter Carey. "Charismatic" and "magnetic" are terms often used of Phillips, who dresses in black and drives a matching Mercedes. He has a personal trainer and regularly jogged in Battery Park until September 11, when he witnessed the first plane crashing into the World Trade Centre—"the most profoundly wrenching experience of my life after Baldwin's death."

Carey sees Phillips's ceaseless wandering as "acting out a form of homelessness as well as also wanting homes; he has many homes and no home." Yet for Phillips's U.S. publisher, Sonny Mehta, president of Knopf, "Caz knows where he comes from; for someone who always appears to be on the lam, he isn't rootless—that's part of his strength."

Caryl Phillips was born in 1958 in a rum shop owned by his mother's family in the British colony of St. Kitts. He was brought to Britain at the "portable age" of four months. His parents arrived in Leeds a month before the riots in Notting Hill when "black people were being pulled off trains and buses and beaten; far from the streets being paved with gold, they stepped into organised racial baiting." Their experience as part of the Windrush generation of West Indians, lured to fill vacant jobs in the "mother country," fed Phillips's first novel, *The Final Passage* (1985).

His parents, Lillian and Malcolm, had three more sons before divorcing when Phillips was eight. "They were both headstrong, hugely independent—and incompatible. The pressures of migration merely speeded things up." He adds: "Objectively, my childhood was massively dysfunctional and traumatic. I have no happy memories of it. But I never felt deprived; I played with the cards I was dealt."

His mother got custody of the children but when she fell ill, Phillips and his brothers were fostered out together. "We were cargoed around between white families in the north of England; there was always a new set of people who wanted you to call them Mum and Dad." After two years, his mother, a "very smart and courageous woman," decided: "I don't know how I'll do it, but I'm going to bring them up."

A civil servant in St. Kitts, Lillian worked as a bus conductor and clerk in England before she underwent teacher training and became a maths lecturer at Bradford College of Further Education. As the eldest, Phillips took on "enormous responsibility." He woke at 5 am, helped his mother out with a paper round, and ironed his brothers' school uniforms. "I saw my mother operating for years on two hours' sleep. She instilled in me the notion that I had to achieve, that the only way forward England had to offer was education—hard work and discipline. Kids around us were chronic working-class underachievers." The sole black family on the vast Whinmoor estate in Leeds ("full of skinheads"), the Phillips brothers were the only pupils to pass the 11-plus.

But there were social pressures. "I was a rough, problem kid, always in fights, having to slug my way out of situations, and I could run fast—you had to. When someone at school called me or my brothers a nigger, it wasn't my style to complain, but to kick the crap out of them." The "biggest troublemaker but also the brightest kid" at school, he was often stopped by the police, sometimes for running. It was "part of being black in Britain—the price of the ticket." He well remembers Enoch Powell's "rivers of blood" speech in 1968. "The intensity of verbal and physical abuse shot off the scale."

Phillips's mother fell ill again and from the age of fourteen to eighteen, he lived with his father, a railwayman who was training to be a social worker, in Bradford, Leeds, and Birmingham. "We didn't get on: an authority figure moved back into my life. The idea of someone telling me what to do wasn't going to work." There was also a "cultural chasm" between the father and his "be-afroed sons: I was reading Tolstoy and Thomas Hardy and Pasternak, and was passionate about football. He didn't read novels, and was into cricket."

Phillips wrote his first story aged fifteen after seeing a TV programme about Anne Frank. "The horror of the Dutch people who were made to be visible by wearing a yellow star—they were me. They thought they fitted into the society, then they were told they didn't. That ambivalence summed up my life." In his story about a Dutch Jewish boy, "I was trying to work out everything about being black in Britain, parental abandonment, responsibility."

His teachers suggested he leave school at sixteen. "I was deputy head boy and top in English and history. The headmaster sneered that if I worked hard, I might get into a poly. If you look different, people are going to tell you what you can't do. You ignore them." With what his English teacher, Dave Hill, later called "sheer will," he won a place in 1976 at Queen's College, Oxford, where he read English, with ambitions to be a stage and screen director.

Phillips, who had never met anyone from public school ("You learn quickly that they're not any smarter than you, which is liberating"), directed six plays within fifteen months, including Shakespeare, Pinter, and Tennessee Williams. But 1976 saw rioting in Notting Hill, "the first major backlash from my generation." He made weekend trips to "plug into black life" in London's Ladbroke Grove and Shepherd's Bush. After collapsing from "nervous exhaustion," he took a greyhound bus trip across the U.S., deciding to become a writer after reading Richard Wright's *Native Son* by the Pacific. Back in Oxford, he made a pact with himself that "one day I'd order my own books up from the Bodleian stacks."

If African-American literature filled one gap for him, music filled another. The titles of his books often echo songs—*A New World Order, Higher Ground, A State of Independence*. Marvin Gaye, Curtis Mayfield (the subject of his 1995 BBC television documentary, *Darker Than Blue*) and Stevie Wonder were "as important to me as any writers. Not only did they look like me, but their social commitment was wedded to emotions. Eldridge Cleaver and Leroi Jones were angry and righteous. But I learned that you'll always listen to the poet before the politician."

Margaret Thatcher came to power in 1979, the month Phillips graduated. "I left university when Britain was trying to understand why these truculent Caribbean youths were fighting the police; it was clamouring for an articulate second generation who were not throwing bricks. I was perceived as somebody who could explain." But Phillips has always scorned the role of "exotic missionary; my job isn't to explain anybody to anybody. People have always tried to make me into something I'm not."

One inspiration was the poet Linton Kwesi Johnson, who "resisted being packaged in a way I was under pressure to be." Johnson recalls opening the door, at the Brixton offices of the journal *Race Today*, to a "tall, affable, rather good-looking guy who spoke with a Yorkshire accent." Phillips had come to call on the Trinidadian intellectual C. L. R. James. The 1970s riots, says Johnson, "spurred Caz's quest to find out who he was. For our generation, the question of identity was paramount.'"

Phillips spent his summers at university as a stagehand at the Edinburgh festival ("handing Dorothy Tutin her sword"). After graduating, he spent a year there on the dole, living with an artist girlfriend and writing his first stage play, *Strange Fruit*, about a lone West Indian mother and her teenage sons in contemporary England. It was produced at the Sheffield Crucible in 1980, where the *Yorkshire Post* commended the playwright for having "pillaged the white man's theatre knowledgedly [sic]." Undeterred, Phillips moved to London, where two more plays, *Where There Is Darkness*, and *The Shelter*, were staged at the Lyric Hammersmith in the early 1980s.

John Biggins, an actor and friend of Phillips since boyhood in Leeds, recalls how he "walked out of sweeping floors at Edinburgh with contracts to write plays. He had swanky agents after him straightaway; everybody wanted a piece of him. But even at twenty-two, he decided which to do, rejecting people he didn't want to work with."

The dangers of compromise and co-option recur in Phillips's work. He is fascinated by Uncle Tom figures, such as Othello or Louis Armstrong, who are seen, perhaps wrongly, as tame but deluded, the "good black." "There are so many jumping off points in our lives when we're encouraged to choose compromise alley," says Phillips. "I'm interested in what makes people 'make a premature peace with mediocrity,' as Baldwin said. I have compassion for them. I don't despise or think I'm better than them; it may mean your family can eat. But I've never been able to do that myself. It means you're no longer a voice of moral authority." Writers should be "unclubbable," he adds, "not trying to beat the doors down to be accepted or embalmed with a knighthood." In Johnson's view, Phillips has "been his own man spectacularly, not letting other people determine the agenda."

With the royalties from his first play, Phillips visited St. Kitts when he was twenty-two for the first time. "The trip liberated me. It kicked my brain out of a British perspective; I realised the narrative didn't begin in Leeds or Brixton." His

first novel germinated on the inter-island ferry from St. Kitts to Nevis, though it
was five years before *The Final Passage* was published.

He reviewed plays for *Time Out*, and wrote for radio and television. After his
second novel, *A State of Independence* (1986), about a man's tentative return to a
decolonised Caribbean island following a twenty-year absence, Phillips made his
third self-defining journey—across Europe. The resulting travel book, *The European Tribe*, was a coolly indignant dissection of the "sickness in Europe's soul": its
amnesiac rejection of the "outsiders" who are an integral part of it.

James Baldwin told his young friend in the 1980s: "At your age I was angry as
hell. You're cool, you're calm. You're almost frighteningly analytical." For Phillips,
"anger is the worst response because it can only hurt you. I've never been angry
or outraged. That's a label white people put on you because they don't understand
you could respond in a more strategic way." For Johnson, "One of Caz's qualities
is that he's able to temper his anger and express it in a more intellectual way, often
with wit and humour." Phillips's screenplay for the feature film *Playing Away*
(1986), directed by Horace Ové, in which a Brixton cricket team, led by the late
Norman Beaton, takes on the home counties in a village-green away match, was
a comic triumph.

"I'm saved because my first love was always history," says Phillips. "I think
of the ramifications beyond the pain being caused to an individual." His novel
Higher Ground (1989) broke with the more linear realism of his first two novels.
It trawled revisionist history across epochs, from an African slave trader and a
U.S. black power prisoner, to a female Jewish survivor of the Holocaust. In *Cambridge* (1991), Phillips returned to slavery as "an area that has stained British society but which has hardly been scratched at." Through ironic twin accounts of a
nineteenth-century Englishwoman visiting her father's plantation in the West Indies, and a literate slave, the novel anatomised an age, revealing not only how racist myths grew from economic greed, but how white women subject to the marriage market were also in bondage.

The South African writer J. M. Coetzee sees Phillips's work as marked by a
"finely judged balance between . . . immersion in the period, and a retrospec-
tive modern awareness of what was at stake." His fiction, in Coetzee's view, has
a single aim: "remembering what the west would like to forget."

Crossing the River (1993) tracked siblings of the African diaspora across centuries, their experience one of broken families and abandonment. The novel wrote
black characters back into histories from which they are erased, from mission-
aries in Liberia and wild west cowboys, to second world war GIs. Phillips ap-
proaches history "through the prism of people nominally written out of it," hence

his often praised insight into women characters. A novel set in a historical period can be "deeply contemporary," Phillips says. He sees himself as "working against an undertow of historical ignorance."

In 1990, Phillips spent a year at Amherst College in Massachusetts as a visiting writer. Though he craves the "energy and dynamic of a big city," he was induced to become a tenured professor of English. "I loved the teaching," says Phillips, whose students call him Caz. Cordelia Lawton, a former student, recalls work-shops being held in cafes, bars, and truck stops. "He was supportive but didn't pull his punches," she says. "It wasn't a contest of egos, more a roomful of peers." Phillips exposed students to the business end of writing, with trips to publishers where he would "point out the slush pile." He also ran a dazzling reading series in the small town, with writers including Michael Ondaatje, Seamus Heaney, and Salman Rushdie.

Phillips still had a second house in St. Kitts from the 1980s. "For a Donald Trump period, I had three homes—in Massachusetts, St. Kitts, and London. It was financially crazy." Biggins recalls his having "three sets of clothes and furni-ture; he's a truly global operator." But Phillips sold his St. Kitts house in 1993, buy-ing his Manhattan apartment three years later. In 1998, he was head-hunted by Barnard College.

In 1996, Phillips adapted and co-produced *The Final Passage* as a two-part television serial, directed by Sir Peter Hall. At 2.7 million pounds for two episodes, it was one of the highest budgets ever for a drama commissioned by Channel 4. Unlike West Indian writers of the 1950s, such as Sam Selvon and George Lam-ming, Phillips viewed both sides of a mutual bewilderment, it being "the privilege of my generation to be privy to the paranoia of white people: they never had it explained to them what those West Indians brought in their hearts and cardboard suitcases."

His most recent novel, The *Nature of Blood* (1997), exposes Europe's tribal ob-session with "purity" of blood, marrying "in" or "out," through characters resem-bling Anne Frank, Othello, and Shylock. Drawn in through the anguish of the persecuted, the reader's gaze is turned towards the society that persecutes: the Eu-rope that cements its identity by excluding, even annihilating, those it defines as different.

In his anthology *Extravagant Strangers: A Literature of Belonging* (1997), Phil-lips assembled meditations on belonging by writers born outside Britain, from Thackeray and Orwell to Doris Lessing and Kazuo Ishiguro. He was series editor of Faber Caribbean Writers, launched in 1998 to place West Indian writing along-side translations from the French, Spanish, and Dutch Caribbean. The Caribbean, he says, is a "multicultural society going back five centuries, created out of impurity, where Africa and Europe and the Indian subcontinent meet. My roots are in Madeira and Africa, and one of my grandmothers was Indian. But the idea that miscegenation means you go mad is deeply rooted in the British consciousness."

With writing, teaching (limited to a day a week in one semester), editing, and film work, Phillips has a "life that looks like a small industry." He has travelled widely for the British Council, chairing seminars in Paris, Singapore, and New Delhi. He claims never to go on holiday, but checks into hotels to write. "People don't understand it because I live by myself, but a hotel room is neutral space, like a blank sheet of paper." Although his last four books were written in a five-star hotel in Bangkok, "for a long time I couldn't afford that. The criteria are familiarity and control more than luxury. I also love motels."

His itinerancy, he says, militates against relationships with women. In St. Kitts he lived with a lawyer ("the big relationship in my life"), whom he met on the eve of the island's independence in 1983. But "I had my work." Though solitude can be "emotionally draining—like cranking up a cold engine," he says he has never been lonely, other than on the transatlantic freighter in 1997. "It was a new emotion, for which I didn't have words. I realised it might be loneliness."

"I've inherited a genetic independence," says Phillips, whose mother has retired to St. Kitts, and whose father lives alone in Lincolnshire. "I'm not good at compromise. I grew up in a way I wouldn't want to visit on anybody, and I have a passion I wouldn't want to distil." For now, "my head's somewhere else." He takes his avuncular duties seriously, however, particularly the daughters of his youngest brother, Tony, a BBC radio producer. So, too, friendships across the globe. The novelist Graham Swift admires him as a "very serious person who has a tremendous sense of fun."

That relaxed humour coexists with what Biggins sees as the "aura of an older brother, of responsibility and tremendous authority, which comes from a sense of impregnability. What can be fearsome is that he's not prone to a lot of self-doubt or guilt. He has a very strong sense of right and wrong: if you get on the wrong side of him, you're crossed out of his address book." When a guest at a British Council dinner in Germany, which was held in Phillips's honour, dropped a casually racist remark (a "joke" about his eating peanuts), he and other writers threatened to boycott the council. The result was a complete overhaul of its practices by the Commission for Racial Equality. While Swift recalls Phillips being "extremely hurt and upset," Peter Carey says: "Caz won't take shit from anybody. He has no difficulty in not bending on a principle, digging in his heels and not being afraid of the consequences."

In 1989, Phillips went to court to try to stop a Tricycle Theatre production of his script about Billie Holiday, *All or Nothing at All*, which he said was still in draft form. He was also dissatisfied with the director, Nicholas Kent. Though he failed to stop the play, the court injunction ensured that no word of the text could be touched. Phillips, who insisted his name be taken off the credits, says: "I had to put my house up; it cost me £15,000. But it was absolutely worth it on a point of principle." Kent, director of the Tricycle, says he continues to admire Phillips's work, and that "it's always been a regret that we no longer seem to be friends."

Phillips confesses to being a "bit puritanical" about effort. He runs two marathons a year ("never in the same city twice"), and is off to climb Mount Kilimanjaro in December. The draw, he explains, is the "solitude and discipline. It's the same process as writing a book." Once passionate about tennis (he edited a tennis anthology, *The Right Set*, 1999), he no longer plays group sports. A golfer since his teens, he flies off for a week "to play golf on my own, trying to find a neutral place for my characters to start to talk."

In Biggins's view, "Caz is very driven: he sees himself as having a quest to fulfill in his life that outweighs everything." Phillips says: "I never think of a book as an occasion to celebrate. To me, it's always just another piece in the jigsaw. I've never had any doubt that I'm here for no other purpose than to do my work. It's not ambition but obligation."

One interviewer, John Walsh, thought Phillips "vastly solipsistic," putting "large historical concerns at the service of his personal obsessions." Yet while Phillips began writing to solve the "conundrum of my own existence," he has insistently directed his gaze from individual pain to the nature of the society that produces it. He sees Fortress Europe as only the latest episode. "It would be ridiculous to say things haven't changed since 1958. But has the general ethos been uprooted? Of course not. It's a long game, where you're trying to contribute to a strategy, not an instant fix." In New York, he counsels detained asylum seekers. "Can you imagine the silence these people live in? It terrifies me, when they've come into a world of twenty-four-hour talk shows . . .

"I don't have an investment in nationality any more than in the Groucho club," says Phillips, who is now more at ease with his "plural home." As *A New World Order* suggests, the world may be catching up with him. "I used to think I was a freak growing up in England. I always felt unmoored and unrooted. But over the past forty years that's become the condition of so many people." Living in the "global crossroads" of New York, he feels his terrain expanding beyond the Atlantic. He regards both the "back to Africa" lobby and the U.S. "clamour of racial entitlement" with sophisticated scepticism. Swift envies his "ability to be part of Europe and also step outside; he can do that anywhere in the world."

Phillips hangs on to his British passport along with his Green Card. Among his pipeline projects is a stage adaptation for the National Theatre, commissioned by Trevor Nunn, of Sam Selvon's *The Lonely Londoners* (1956)—"the quintessential novel of migration." "I'm not going to give up my right to be a commentator on Britain," says Phillips. "Britain made me as a writer. My anxieties aren't American or New York anxieties, they're British. That sense of attachment will always be there."

Yet there has been a shift. "I grew up where there was a stigma attached to being the newcomer; you were marked as an outsider. The society tried to impose choice on you: are you one of us or not? It's a very British conceit—membership. I resist being labelled, but it took me a while to realise I didn't have to make my life a narrative of resistance. Within myself I contain many worlds; I want to embrace all of them."

Home, Blood, and Belonging:
A Conversation with Caryl Phillips
Paula Goldman/2002

From *Moving Worlds: A Journal of Transcultural Writings* 2.2 (2002), 115–22. Reprinted with the permission of *Moving Worlds*. Interview conducted in San Franciso.

PG: In your book *A New World Order*, you discuss the problem of how to answer the question of what home means, or "Where are you from?" . . . How do you answer that question?

CP: Well, I try to avoid it. I try to avoid giving an answer because it's too big a question. I usually tell people it's where my books are. I say that because for a long time I've lived in more than one place—I've had a place in New York and a place in London, or for some time in the eighties and nineties I had a place in St. Kitts and a place in London—but I've always had to choose where to put my books. So that was always *literally* home.

In a more spiritual—or emotionally fundamental—sense, I try to avoid it because that's what I write about . . . and I don't have an easy answer. The real answer to that question is, just read what I write. Everything is an attempt to answer that question.

PG: To, in effect, *create* a home for yourself.

CP: (pause) It's an attempt to try to convince myself that it's not *necessary* to have a very concrete sense of home. That, actually, those of us who don't have a very concrete sense of home are okay.

We've grown up feeling strange, feeling like the strangers in the classroom, feeling like the odd one out. And I want to write, and say, that it's okay to have a multiple sense of home. It's okay that home can't just be summed up in one sentence. It's okay that you can't put your finger on a map and say that's where you're from.

The desire to have one place and be rooted is a very powerful human desire, but it's something that I don't think is realistic for so many of us. The twentieth century has produced more and more people for whom it's actually *impractical* to have one sense of home. But as yet we haven't caught on to this truth as a *people*. We have yet to accept the fact that the old descriptions which usually have to do with religion or with nationality are actually inadequate for our new condition. We've got old labels but we've got new people. I write for the new people, for whom the old labels don't fit.

PG: How is your work received in the African-American community?
CP: I have no idea. I have no idea because I'm a novelist. The only way I would ever find out if I'm read is by looking at my sales figures, which would tell me I should probably give up. But, hopefully, you can't really judge a specific audience by sales. Realistically, the only way I can find out is by looking around at readings—when I give a public reading, I look in the audience and see who's there. I was in Seattle last night giving a reading—I look around. And, you know, if there were absolutely no African-American faces showing up to my readings, I'd be worried.

PG: How do you divorce those two? You're writing about important political and social issues to the African-American community—a whole section of your book, *A New World Order,* analyses prominent African-American thinkers. So do you divorce the writing and the analysis from the impact of the ideas on the community?
CP: That's one of the things about being a writer, Paula. You don't have any notion about the impact you're having. You have no idea. That's why so many writers want to get into politics, where you do see the effect, as the feedback is much more direct. Writing is very powerful, and you have to believe that you *are* having an effect on the people that read you, even if you don't see it.

PG: How prominent is racism in your daily experience here in this country?
CP: Ah, every day.

PG: Every day? Can you give me some examples?
CP: You're just aware . . . you know, you walk into a place, and you're just aware. I mean, look around here (indicates all white café).

PG: Right.
CP: You walk into certain places where you're the only one. You know, you walk through security at Seattle airport, and you can tell that they want to send you for extra scans. You just know, it's just there—you'd drive yourself mad if you allowed yourself to think too much about it.

PG: Does it change when someone hears your accent?

CP: I wouldn't know. I would be the last person to know. It's just a fact of life. I mean, you're living in a society which is racist. It would be the same for you as a woman if you were trying to function, for want of a better example, in Algeria. You're not going to wake up in the morning and think of gender discrimination, but you know it's there. You have to put it in its place, or it can become corrosive. But you can't put it too far out of your mind; or you'll be vulnerable and get blind-sided.

Unfortunately—you know this as well as I do—a lot of people can't afford the sort of bourgeois middle class equilibrium that somebody like you might be able to muster in Algeria, or that I might be able to muster in the Pacific Northwest. They continually blow up with frustration and anxiety. But we're lucky; I'm lucky because I have ways of dealing with it. I have ways of seeing it come down the aisle, I have ways of protecting myself. A lot of people don't, you know. Money's tight, and they're angry about continual discrimination, and they don't have a way of dealing with it. It keeps happening, and they're not able to be as level headed about it.

PG: That answer provides an interesting segue into another question, which is— The idea of being okay with not having a home does seem to be a luxury. Many communities that feel victimized or oppressed for one reason or another have to latch on to this sense of identity or home around which to organize.

I know for example, that in the Jewish community, there's a strong sense of victimization which provides a lens to view ourselves, and colours our views about Israel. Being able to operate in a multi-national society where you can define your own identity—Is that an economic luxury? Is that something only achieved when one is politically and economically secure?

CP: (Pause) Of course it's a luxury, and of course it's something of a cop-out for me as a writer, who has the economic ability to travel. I don't have a nine-to-five job, I don't have to report forty-eight weeks of the year, so of course I'm able to explore the notion of having more than one place.

But when I travel and investigate others who are also trying to answer these questions, I'd like to think that I'm doing so sympathetically. I may be critical of the romantic desire to achieve a sense of home, but I'm usually moved by the impulse that produced it. The end results of embracing the notion of "home" in a romantic fashion may be kind of nonsensical or difficult to take on board as realistic, but I'm always sympathetic to what made people want to have a sense of home. And my "answers" are always informed by a strong belief in the individual, and by some understanding of the historical problems that produced the individual's desire to belong.

PG: In your book, you analyse a lot of historical figures and even recent historical figures in the African-American community—Who are some current thinkers, leaders, writers, that you admire in that community?

CP: In the African-American community? Can't think of any. Can you think of any? I mean I like Toni Morrison, I think she's incredibly smart. I suppose she could be considered to be a leader. I can't really think of anybody that I would consider to be a politically courageous, intellectual figure. Actually, it's not just in the African-American community. In the *American* community, I can't think of anybody that I look at and I think, "My God, that person is really smart. I wish they were President." I'm sure there are people who I do like, so please ask me, what about so-and-so . . .

PG: Alice Walker.

CP: No.

PG: No?

CP: I mean, she's a bit new age for me, to be honest. I like certain aspects of her work and writing, particularly her essays, but she described E.T. as a "being of color," you know? (Laughs). As some kind of justification for letting Spielberg do *The Color Purple.*

It's all about entertainment, Paula. Politics is about entertainment. So is literature. The only three avenues in America now are to be a movie star, a sports star, or a politician. And they're all interchangeable.

And how do you get—in the space of one and a half generations—from Martin Luther King's speech in 1963 to "We're going to smoke them out of their holes"? Look at the crassness of the English that is employed. It's a steep decline in American leadership, from MLK to George Bush, "We're going to get him dead or alive!" MLK dignified the language. Bush . . . well, you decide. And its not just in the U.S., it's in Britain and Europe as well.

PG: Let's talk about what's going on in the Middle East today. Does the conflict fit into your framework? . . . Am I ascribing to you that philosophy, that there are dangers of searching very fervently for a homeland?

CP: No, you're correct in what you're saying. The Middle East conflict is something which I see in a different light from most people. I see it as an attempt to resolve British colonial ineptitude. You go right back to the Balfour declaration.

British irresponsibility over Palestine, and their lack of responsibility as they withdrew . . . it is very similar to what happened when the British withdrew from Ireland, when they withdrew from India, and the India and Pakistan partition. I mean, today these two countries are *still* standing and looking at each other, ready to start a nuclear war.

The impulse on both sides of the fence—with Israelis and Palestinians—to have a homeland is understandable, given the history of displacement, given the history of dispossession. I don't think I can approach it, as many people can't, without sympathy for both peoples. And it's a perfectly natural human condition, particularly when you feel you've been disenfranchised and when you've been a victim to history, to want to have a place where you feel safe. I don't have a solution for it any more than I suspect you do, but I do have some understanding of why it is there, which leads me back to British incompetence. However, you don't really hear too much on CNN about this historical point-of-view.

It's true with Ireland, and it's true with India and Pakistan, and it's true with great swathes of Africa too: these "British" lines on the maps, nobody took any responsibility for them. Nobody took any responsibility for the emotions which go alongside possession and dispossession of land. The British colonial rulers had contempt for the "native" peoples, including Palestinians.

These days, British anti-Semitism remains powerful. British people have little time for Jewish people. British people also dislike Catholics, hence the problems in Ireland, and they definitely don't like Blacks—and it shows. Just take a look at the globe—there are problems like this all over the so-called "Third World" whose historical roots lead back to Europe, and Britain in particular.

PG: Do you think that might he a bit of a cop out, though, to say that it's the fault of the British? In the sense of—Obviously, there's a historical legacy of very badly drawn borders and a horrible—horrible lack of strong political systems . . .
CP: No, it's not entirely the fault of the British. What's happening today isn't the fault of the British, but the source of the conflict is rooted in the British Empire.

PG: So had it not been for the British Empire, we wouldn't be having these splintering ethnic hatreds happening all over the world? These conflicts, these bloody ethnic conflicts—have been going on for a long time, predating the colonial empire . . .
CP: One should never underestimate people's desire to be rooted. One should never underestimate people's desire for a home, for a place to be safe. But some people are cynical, and the British Empire exploited the desire for rootedness. It's a very powerful impulse. People want a home in which they feel safe. And

sometimes they feel safe only when they're looking at people who look like them. They don't want to be the "other." It's a very deep human emotion, and it's being exploited today in Europe, with the rise of the right in Europe.

One can't get away from the fact that we all have these desires to be rooted, but I've tried, with what I've written, to uproot people's minds to a certain extent, and tried to persuade people to understand that it's time to *let go* of the necessity to be rooted, because with it come all sorts of unpleasantness that can spiral out into what's happening now. For example, the Middle East.

It's all really tragic, but it comes out of what we've inherited as part of our human condition, the feeling that, unless we're able to say, "This is where I'm from" then we're lacking in something. And that's why I said to you that what I'm trying to say in my writing is, actually, "It's okay," because there's lots of us who can't say that we're from just the one, singular place, and take "pride" in this "fact."

That's why I called (my book) *A New World Order,* because the world is changing. The idea of purity is something that we've just got to give up because it's no longer possible. It's not possible within our families—it's certainly not going to be possible nationally. We've got to give it up because the old model is one of great concrete certainties . . . You *will* marry a Black person, you *will* marry a Hindu, of the right caste, you *will* marry another Jew, you *will* marry a Catholic.

You *have* to give that up, because (emphatic) *the world is too complicated.* It is *too* heterogeneous. And if we seek these certainties, it will lead us down the path of trying to create something which actually, realistically, is impossible. And thank God it's impossible.

PG: Is there anything distasteful to you about the catchphrase "multiculturalism"?
CP: I seldom use the term "multicultural" because it always strikes me as something which has been dreamed up in City Hall. It just has this feeling of being a local government initiative: "*What we're doing is a year of multiculturalism.*"

Sometimes all that multiculturalism means is just that we're going to tolerate the fact that we're here in Wisconsin and we've got a few Jews down the road. And we're going to have them tell us about Hanukkah. That would be cool. Or you know, you're living in some little hamlet in Virginia or Kansas, and they want you to come talk about Kwanzaa. That's multiculturalism. So I am suspicious.

PG: Because in a way, it just re-essentializes people.
CP: Of course it does. I mean, multiculturalism doesn't really mean anything. Real multiculturalism is, "Mum, this is Abdul. I'm marrying him." That's multiculturalism. Because it has to be in the family, on a personal level. Otherwise, it's just something that's a social initiative.

PG: So, two hundred, three hundred years from now, we can envision some ideal world where people feel secure enough in their own material possessions, and their own place in society, and the lack of discrimination where they don't have to cling so much to their individual identities, or identities that are carved out for them on the basis of race, ethnicity, gender, whatever. And in the meanwhile, we have a ton of prejudice still going on, a lot of hate crimes . . . very subtle forms of economic prejudice, and not so subtle ones, various wars going on on the basis of ethnicity. What happens? Where is the in-between? What happens to get us there? Works like yours?

CP: No, works like yours as well. That's what happens. What happens is people start talking to each other. People start understanding that essentialism may have been a "neat" idea one hundred years ago, but it's over.

We have absolutely no choice, if we are going to orient ourselves toward the future, but to see ourselves outside of these social constructs of race, religion, and nationality. We have to build a human identity which is much more fluid. So that, when someone asks you where you're from, you can say, "Well, I'm from here, and I'm from here. So now, I'm actually from both these places." And not feel that you've diluted the import of either place.

The Jewish African-American thing that you're doing is really interesting because the history of Jews and African-Americans is the history—you said it yourself—of victimization, a history of being at the bottom of the pile. And the essentialism which has dominated African-American identity, and Jewish identity, has been profound. And therefore, there's been a lot of banging of heads in both communities . . .

PG: But it's a very troubling thing to say—even within the local community that I work in. For me to take this message or this theme of discussion to them, and say, "You know, I think it's time that we moved into a more fluid sense of identity that doesn't focus on victimhood, and that we're able to say we have more than one home."

In the Jewish community, it would be controversial, but it would be okay. Because the Jewish community is very affluent, and is very integrated, and is not—whether or not they recognize it—is no longer in the position of being a victim. That's not as true in the African-American community.

And so, I guess I'm kind of calling the question again—Is it necessary to achieve that status, that sense of security, before one can move into a fluid identity?

CP: (Pause) Well. (Pause) I think you're right. You're right, because, you know, a young kid, who is in the metaphorical "hood" is not going to feel that he or she can abandon their racial identity as easily as someone who is at a university or who is working in computer software . . .

So no, you're right. It is a problem. How do people become more fluid, and become more open? It comes with confidence. It comes with social confidence, it comes with economic confidence, it comes with this feeling that you can let go.

But so many people, and this goes back to what you were saying earlier—so many people don't have a proper purchase on society yet. They see their identity in terms of their religion, and they see their identity in terms of their history, and their history of victimhood. To get them to actually say, "Here's Paula Goldman, you know, let's go hang with her" will lead some to invoke an economic or social argument against it, for example, "Why should we all come to this fancy North Beach café, where she can afford to drink this fancy coffee . . ."

PG: Right.

CP: But does that stop you doing what you're doing? No. It's the same with me. Does it stop me doing what I'm doing? Because people could easily take a potshot at me, and say, "Here's a guy who, you know, drives a nice car, flies off to do this and that, what the hell does he know about suffering?" But I can't be too worried about what others think of me. I'm responsible for what I think of myself. As you are. The fact that you're trying—trying to build bridges—is what counts. And you're moving beyond a narrow definition of yourself.

You see, it's when we hang on to these essentially strict, and narrow, definitions of ourselves—then I think we're in for real problems. *Serious* problems, because as we see in the Middle East, as we see in Ireland, as we see in Rwanda, as we see all over the world . . . As soon as we let something as stupid and superficial as complexion, or what God you happen to worship, or what day you happen to worship—as soon as you let that be the defining factor of who you are, to the exclusion of your capacity to love—you're in very big trouble.

Because all of a sudden you're making alliances with people that you don't like. You don't know them, you don't like them, but the only thing that you know is this superficial thing that you look like them. Or that you worship on the same day as them. And when you talk to them, they're assholes. But you don't think of it.

As soon as the world gives up looking for alliances that are deeper than those based on appearance, religion, or nationality, then we're all in big trouble. And we know we are, for we've seen it before and we know where this kind of thinking leads us.

PG: Thank you.

Other Voices: An Interview
with Caryl Phillips

Stephen Clingman/2002

From *Salmagundi* 143 (2004), 112–40. Reprinted with the permission of *Salmagundi*. Interview conducted in Amherst, Massachusetts, in October 2002.

My discussion with Caryl Phillips, whom I had first met when he was based at Amherst College in the 1990s, lasted more than two hours, and ranged widely across his personal and writing life in fiction, nonfiction, theatre and film. As I had recently written an article (to be published in this volume) on his novel *The Nature of Blood*, I avoided that topic where possible, wanting to have my views neither validated nor invalidated. I also did not want to put those views to Phillips, who is resolute about not reading critical work or reviews on his writing. What strikes me now, on rereading the text of the interview, are a number of things: Phillips's candor; his independence of mind; his sense of humor; and the degree to which the personal, the biographical, and his writing are interlinked.

I.

Stephen Clingman: Thanks very much for doing this interview. I thought I'd begin with something you might not want to hear too much about or even speak too much about any more, and that is the question of identity. You've written, in *The European Tribe* as well as elsewhere, about growing up in England and what that meant to you, the complicated and intense process of self- and social discovery it entailed for you. You feel free to talk about that, but the question that comes to me is: How has all of that become resolved for you *now*? Do you have a sense of belonging now?

Caryl Phillips: No resolution. I think it's still in flux, because as each year goes by, it becomes clearer that I have migrated again. If I wind back the clock to pre-1990, when I came to live in the United States (albeit for one year), there was definitely no sense of resolution or a sense of comfort with identity—personal, social, racial, political—in the Britain that I left. And during the nineties, when

I returned many times each year, one never got the sense that Britain was healing around these questions, and that therefore maybe I was going to resolve something with Britain. What was happening, I think, was that Britain was becoming
increasingly complex and experiencing great difficulty resolving these questions.
So, because of my distance from Britain, and because of my increasingly tenuous
link with Britain, I was not able to *force* any closure there. And at the same time as
I was still dealing with these problems, there were new elements which came from
being in the United States. It began to make me realize that I didn't have to see
questions of identity solely as I had been viewing them—in very colonial, if you
like, or very postcolonial terms. The ley-lines that I was looking along had very
much to do with that old map. Being in the United States made me realize that
these same issues were present here, albeit in a different guise, and they were obviously impacting on my life, and so suddenly, I think the old colonial, postcolonial
struggles that came from being in Britain were being fused with some new questions, which came from being in the United States. So that's a very longwinded
way of saying, "No, there's no real resolution."

SC: In your mind, was there a real sense of departure from Britain when you came
here? Was it a place you were leaving, consciously?
CP: I'd consciously left already. In 1987, I made the decision to leave Britain. It was
Mrs. Thatcher's third election victory, and I was twenty-nine, and I realized that
I'd spent all of my twenties living in a country in which I'd voted three times and
been on the losing side three times. I also felt that the problems of British society
were stifling me. I felt almost as if I was being encouraged to think of myself in a
purely domestic way, whereas I realized that there were aspects of my personality,
my interests, my own personal history, which spilled out from Britain and which
had their origins in different parts of the world. So, in 1987 I went to teach in
India for a couple of months, and then I came back to England. In 1988 I put my
house on the market in London, shipped all my furniture, and went to St. Kitts—
and I was there for about seven months. In 1989, I went to teach at the University
of Stockholm, in Sweden, for six months, then returned to England for a short
period, then returned to St. Kitts. I actually flew to Massachusetts from St. Kitts.
I got my one-year visiting teacher's visa in the U.S. consulate in Antigua. So I considered myself—when I arrived here in 1990—as already having gone through a
period of disengagement with Britain.

SC: In Darryl Pinckney's book, *Out There,* he says, regarding your book, *The
Atlantic Sound,* that it's "a long and bitter farewell to England." Does that sound
right to you?

CP: No, because I don't feel that Britain or Europe constitute resolved business;
I don't feel that I've moved on. As I said, what I feel has happened is that the picture has become more complicated. Let's just look at *The Atlantic Sound*. The
book is very much concerned with the old questions—important questions,
nonetheless—of British-colonial intercourse with the rest of the world, and the
multiple ironies that envelop British history around colonial expansion and imperialism. The prologue and the first section deal very directly with this theme;
the p.s. to this first section concerns a British-colonial subject, or object, on the
streets of Liverpool today. Then we move to the middle panel of the book, in
which we go to Africa to look at questions which are slightly more complicated,
because now the people that we're looking at are largely African Americans—but
they are still people who have been formed in relation to European history. And
then we go to the last section and we're squarely in the United States. So, Darryl
may be reading that movement as a drifting away from Britain or Europe, but I
don't really see it as a drifting away. I just see it as a book in which I begin to fuse
those concerns regarding identity in Britain with related themes that operate in
America, albeit in a different way. It's a book in which I'm still engaged with Europe, but I'm not thinking domestically.

SC: Concerning your sense of location, there's a striking moment in your recent
collection of essays, *A New World Order,* that stopped me in my tracks when I
read it. I don't want to be morbid, but you write there of talking with your lawyer, I think in a fairly literal way, about where your remains will be disposed of.
You mention a midpoint in the Atlantic, subtended by that triangle between Africa, Europe, and the Americas, and it struck me that—well, maybe it *was* literal.
Is that how you feel?
CP: I think these questions came up in my mind for two reasons, One, because most of my family is buried in a very small Anglican church in the village I was born in. It's a very small, poor village of about four hundred people at
the furthest-most point away from the capital in St. Kitts. I was baptized in that
church, as were my uncles, my great-grandmother, you know, everybody. My
family is localized in an almost terrifyingly Faulknerian sense, which led me to
question—when my great-grandmother died at the end of the eighties—what my
relationship really was to the continued genealogical history of this place. And I
began to wonder then, in a somewhat egotistical way—if there were to be a memorial service, where would it be held? Then there was the literal question of
speaking to my lawyer about a will. Like most people, I felt I had to make a will,
and sitting across the desk from my lawyer, my mind returned to the moment

when I was on the banana boat—which I relate in the prologue to *The Atlantic Sound,* when I was retracing the journey my parents took when they came with me to Britain. Although that was a hellishly miserable journey, when I was on the ship I did try to calculate that midpoint in the ocean.

SC: That's a very interesting space, that midspace in the Atlantic: an oceanography rather than a land geography.

CP: Well, I'm not that much of a believer in the importance of being able to claim a rootedness—a landscape, or a geography, which you carry around with you. I'm not the sort of person who thinks, "Well, if I'm not seeing this particular type of tree, or if I'm not seeing this particular type of horizon, then no matter where I am in the world, I'm not at home." The one thing that is constant to me is water. Water seems to me to be something which binds us together. I wrote a piece, once, called "Water." It's one of the pieces that didn't find its way into *A New World Order,* but I remember that I used to read this short piece before reading from *Crossing the River.* In the piece I make reference to "ineluctable ribbons of water that bind us together." I'm interested in what brings us together and what allows us to meet each other, and water, to me, is a pathway along which we continue to meet and encounter each other. I'd rather be on the path than at "home" at the beginning or at the end of the journey.

SC: We had a discussion along these lines in my class yesterday, and one of the participants, David Odhiambo—a writer who was born in Kenya, then moved to Canada, and is now studying in the U.S.—said that when he thinks of water, he thinks of the Middle Passage. And there is an interesting duality about water in the kind of landscape that we've inherited. I can relate to the idea of water as connection, but it does also have this dismal history of what's been done across the waters.

CP: It does. The journey involves loss; it always involves loss. You've left a place; you've left people behind you, left memories behind you. But there seems to me to be a process of reinvention that can happen during the journey. And that process of reinvention before the arrival—the preparation for the arrival—to me is a crucial metaphor for what we do in life, because we must maintain the ability to reinvent ourselves, if only to keep our sanity. When I think back to Equiano's *Travels,* the passages on the ship are amazing, because the guy is renamed. He's called Gustavus Vassa, he's learning English, he's reading the Bible. That idea that there's loss involved in a journey is true, but there are also gains, and an incredible preparation happens on a journey which enables one to cope with the arrival, whether one is arriving at Ellis Island or JFK. Who are you going to be in this new country? So I try and think more positively about what happens on that water.

SC: Looking again, say, at *The Atlantic Sound,* I'm struck by your presentation there of the "black Israelites"—the African Americans who go to Israel, or who then get turned away and end up in Africa. I think you end that section, or maybe even end the book, by suggesting that there's no return ticket. As you say there, "It is futile to walk into the face of history." Given your life—you're someone who has moved, and in fact, *continually* moves—what's the difference between your kind of migration and that kind of migration? Is it the difference between going back and going forward?

CP: To my mind, the main difference has to do with baggage. I'm almost forty-five. I don't have a wife; I don't have kids; I don't have those responsibilities. I'm lucky in that I'm able to make a living doing what I want to do. Obviously, I am privileged to be able to do my job. But most migrations are punctuated by questions of turning the generational hinge, and the problems involved in reorientating children to deal with the new place. It's just a very practical thing. When kids get to five, you have to make some decisions about where home is. I think that's what disturbed me most about the situation with the African Americans in Israel, and to a certain extent in Africa too, because I felt that the people who were going to suffer confusion were going to be their children. If they were adults who had made a conscious decision without children, then I would have said that's fine—they can envelop themselves in whatever fantasy they want. You see, I'm a kid who grew up in a society that didn't want me—that really tried to find all sorts of subtle and unsubtle ways to make it uncomfortable for me to function in that society. And it really affects me when I see kids having to go through that. Obviously, one of the reasons to write is to try to make sure that the society changes its attitude so that kids don't have to go through that any more. I know that's a very grandiose idea and a very grandiose aim. But when I see young kids who are not going to be taken into a society, and whose parents don't seem to be able to help them enter that society—or, in this case, are actually quite unwilling to help them enter the society, then I find it quite disturbing.

SC: You're someone who grew up suffering from prejudice in England. At the same time, you're someone who, as you've just said, is interested in connecting rather than dividing. When it comes to questions of racial identity, you've been someone who, by all appearances, has been prepared to let that go, or to let it be. You say in *A New World Order* that "race matters; sure it matters, but it doesn't matter that much." You've also had some things to say about racial identity in the United States which are probably controversial. Could you talk about that?

CP: I think that in Britain the easiest place for a lot of people in my generation, the second generation, to run and hide would be into the safe corner of racial solidarity. This is not something I ever felt comfortable with, for a couple of reasons. One, my education was such that throughout most of my school life I was the only black kid in school. And then at eighteen I went to Oxford, where, apart from the odd black American Rhodes Scholar or African student, there was no black British presence. So, really through until the age of twenty-one, I was not in a situation where making connections around racial solidarity was even physically possible. I did walk the streets of Ladbroke Grove and Notting Hill when I was a student, and I literally would go into pubs and coffee bars and to reggae concerts just to see if I could feel some togetherness, just to know if I belonged. Did I fit in, or would they look at me and think, "*No, no, you're Oxford.*" I wanted to see what this felt like. But the second reason I never really bought the idea of racial solidarity, was because I grew up in the North of England, and I think that class was always incredibly important to me. I always knew instinctively from when I was quite small—nobody ever explained this to me—but I always knew that race was linked to class in some way. I was working class; I knew that. In the North of England, I went to grammar school at the age of eleven, and I met posh kids for the first time, and I began to understand class then. Then I began to understand something further, which was why the guy who was teaching me history—he was called Mr. Stern, from Berlin . . .

SC: An interesting name . . .

CP: I began to check out this guy, and he liked me. I was good at history. But I could see that he really wanted me to do well. So did my Polish teacher, Mr. Mackiewizc; he was always pushing me. Mr. Mackiewicz took me aside at eleven and he told me, "You should be top of the class; always make sure . . ." So I began to understand issues of class and other forms of group solidarity, for these guys with weird names, who weren't English, seemed to be on my side. They were white, but they were on my side, so I didn't really believe that race was the thing. Obviously then as I began to think about writing and began to think about what kind of things I might write, I read Baraka and Bobby Seale and Julius Lester and all those guys in the sixties and seventies—the angry guys. But I also read Baldwin, who seemed slightly different, and then I read Richard Wright's *Black Boy,* which seemed as universal as *Huck Finn.* So literature, if you like, took me even further away from ever thinking that racial politics was going to be a framework within which to operate.

SC: Did Mr. Stern have anything to do with your character Eva Stern in *The Nature of Blood?*
CP: Maybe subconsciously; it could easily be. I mean, I can see the guy now, though it's over thirty years since I've seen him. Sadly, he's probably long gone now. But I remember so clearly, he had a sort of hostile affection for me, because I was a *brat,* you know, a cheeky little sod. He gave me lines once; he gave me a hundred lines for something I'd done wrong in class. My mother was at college at the time, and she had carbon paper; now, nobody else at the school knew about carbon paper, but I knew about it from my mother—so, of course I used it, but I put it in the wrong way round, so the lines came out in reverse at the back. Mr. Stern was really excited that I had tried it, but he hit me for being stupid. He told me, if you're going to cheat, get it *right!* So, there were all sorts of small things that made me realize that feeling comfort in just being black was never really going to work.

II.

SC: Talking of Baldwin, Wright, and others, in terms of your literary reference points, you have quite a range. Your collection of essays, *A New World Order,* is divided into four sections, on the United States, Africa, the Caribbean, and Britain—a kind of literary geography that mirrors your personal geography. Do you feel you're writing in a black literary tradition, whether in the U.S., Caribbean, or Britain?
CP: It's a good question. I don't really believe that in English there is a black literary tradition. There is an African American literary tradition without any question, but I don't feel a part of that, mainly because it's a very deep and extensive literary tradition, and at the moment I think my voice would be that of an outsider. In the Caribbean there's not really a strong tradition in prose, you know. If you look at the writing in prose in the Anglophone Caribbean in, say, the last thirty, forty years, if you take Naipaul out, you've basically gone a long way towards defusing the tradition. Do I feel a part of that tradition? Not particularly strongly. With regard to Britain, there really isn't a black British literary tradition, and I actually don't think there will be one. And I don't think that there should be one, to be quite honest. I think that what's happened in the Caribbean

where, after the Second World War, you got a flowering of strong and good prose writing—I'm thinking of people like Roger Mais, Edgar Mittelholzer, Samuel Selvon, Wilson Harris, George Lamming of course—is that the tradition then seems to have been hijacked by migration, so that the Caribbean literary tradition has been dispersed geographically to Toronto, to New York, to London, and to Miami to a certain extent. What's developed is a diaspora, an outgrowth. This is a pretty good model for what will happen in terms of a black British literary tradition. People like me, and Hanif Kureishi, and Ben Okri were being talked about in the late eighties and early nineties as "the empire writes back" tendency—but this idea never really went anywhere, because we write different types of books, and beyond our common pigmentation there is little else that binds us together. So, what tradition, therefore, do I belong to, is the natural corollary to that . . . mini-speech. What tradition do I belong to? I belong to a tradition, which I think I won't be defining. Damn copping out, here, but it's true. You will be defining it, scholars and critics like you will define that tradition, because I think there is one, and I can point to the writers who I think are a part of it, but I won't be defining it.

SC: Who would you then point to in that tradition, even if you don't want to define it?

CP: Some of the people I've written about. I think our South African friend, Coetzee. Definitely Michael Ondaatje. I would look to a writer like Pico Iyer, who's about to publish a new novel, Edwidge Danticat, Jhumpa Lahiri to some extent, Rohinton Mistry. They're people who don't fit comfortably into a national tradition, who, for whatever reasons in their work or individual selves would resist being grouped around race, which seems to be an increasingly irrelevant term in talking about literary culture or literary practice. The postcolonial label is something I know that you've grappled with, and as a teacher I've grappled with it too. But that seems to me to be redundant for geographical reasons—as I said before, it's complicated by North America and by other parts of the world, too. It's also been complicated by the fact that we're not really living in a postcolonial age—we're living in a *post*-postcolonial age—so what new word do we use, what new groupings do we get? I don't really know.

SC: Well, let me mention a writer who goes back in time, towards whom you've expressed some form of allegiance. Surprisingly, or not surprisingly, it's Joseph Conrad. There are some interesting turnabouts there. We all know about *Heart of Darkness,* which for so many years was regarded as one of the great European novels. Then Chinua Achebe came and pointed out the imperialist vision, the rac-

ism that's inherent in that book. And then you write an introduction to *Heart of Darkness* in which you defend the novel against Achebe, I think on the grounds that it's about the failures and inherent contradictions of the European modern world. So, that feels to me like a re-mapping, in which lines of allegiance are not obvious, in which the literary map can take many different shapes and forms.
CP: Well, I think so. You see, Conrad's a man of the water—coming back to the notion of water. He's a man of travel, and he's a man who reinvented himself. He changed his name; he had three languages at his disposal; he understood, within himself, the fragility of identity. And he was writing at the tail-end of a period in which the world was still not too much different, in most people's minds, from almost an Elizabethan world order. He comes after novels that were called *The Mayor of Casterbridge* or, before that, *Oliver Twist,* or before that, *Persuasion.* I know Edward Said gives *Mansfield Park* a hard time, because of the passing reference to the slave plantations of Antigua. But that wasn't Jane Austen's brief, you know, because she hadn't been out there. Conrad, he's *been* there. He's been to these worlds, he's been to these places. So, personally I consider Conrad to be a kind of literary partner in crime, because he is man who understood the fragility of identity. And if there's one thing which I think binds together those writers who might constitute some kind of literary community, it's their profound understanding of how fragile identity is when it comes up against a new society. Migration, be it voluntary or involuntary, generally reminds me of how fragile one's name is, how fragile an allegiance to religion can prove to be, the importance of language, the importance of *which* language, questions of gender . . . You know, these are things which it seems to me pretty clear that Conrad understood, and in that sense, we're all descended from him.

SC: There is another world traveler you've tangled with in various ways, and we've mentioned him already—V. S. Naipaul. Naipaul is, in many respects, a Conradian whose problematic relationship with what's called the "third-world" you've pointed out, as have many others. And yet, there's something of an admiration there, I think. You wrote an intriguing piece on the collection of letters between Naipaul and his father, in which you suggested that Naipaul's mistake was to turn away from what provided the impetus to his writing in the first place, which was his relationship to home, his relationship to his father, and a sympathy for the world that he came from. How do you feel about Naipaul? Is that an accurate summary of things?
CP: I admire him, and one thing in particular I respect about him is the way in which he's made a literary life in the face of huge obstacles and in the tireless

pursuit of his vision, even if I don't always agree with the vision. In terms of the question of turning away from his home and turning away from what made him, it's dangerous to accuse any writer of anything, particularly anything negative, but as you rightly point out there is something in those letters that I find disturbing—the idea of rejecting one's past quite so vigorously and without any empathy and—it seems to me—without any real desire to grapple with it or to integrate it into who you're becoming. I wouldn't use the term flawed, but I feel it has actually weakened his body of work. Maybe time will prove me wrong, and perhaps I'm putting this awkwardly, but the process of reinvention—which he has undergone in quite a profound way and written about in fiction and extensively in nonfiction—that process might have benefited from a little more synthesis and a little less rejection.

SC: Synthesis between past and present?

CP: Exactly. There seems to have been a process of exchange, of laying *this* down in order to pick something else up, which seems to me to be only justified by his consistently and—I feel no apology for saying this—somewhat tediously going on and on about how difficult it was. That seems to me to be a total smoke screen. The only way he can deflect one's attention from the fact that he's pushed a whole section of his life away is by trying to explain to you how difficult the process has been. But if it was that difficult, *explain* to us why it was that difficult. If it was that difficult I think it would be in the work, but for the most part I don't detect it. In early work, like *The Mystic Masseur,* the sense of reinvention of that character is looked at with irony and with a certain degree of affection and warmth, almost as if Naipaul knows that this is the game that you play. But later on, there's no irony; there's no warmth. There's a sneer at those he's left behind.

SC: So, there has to be an acceptance of the past, without a shortcut to anger or resentment . . .

CP: Well, I agree, and that's why I think Darryl's curious phrase about *The Atlantic Sound* is totally antithetical to how I think. My feeling is that there will always be a continual engagement with the past, because it's part of your bloodstream, it's part of your make-up, and so you can never really turn away from it. You will examine it from different angles, from different points of view; it will become richer, more complex, perhaps even more problematic and more irritating in some ways, but you will synthesize the past with other elements of your life as you move through the journey of your life. But the idea that there will be resolution or rejection is something which I don't believe. I believe it's actually *irrespon-*

sible to turn one's back on one's past if you're a writer. To go out of your way at a moment when you win the Nobel Prize to *not* mention Trinidad, and to erase it from your past seems to me to be—I'll put it no stronger than this—irresponsible as a writer. Because, whether you like it or not, that's actually what made you. That has gone *into* the making of you. But, having said all this, this is not enough to make me feel there's no virtue there, there's no eloquence, that I haven't learned anything from Naipaul. I've learned a lot from him about being a writer, about the writing life, about how to orientate one's self. He's been particularly useful and instrumental to me in showing that it is possible to have a literary life in which one can operate in both fiction and nonfiction. Because in a British literary tradition, beyond Graham Greene and V. S. Naipaul, there are not that many writers who have given equal weight to both.

SC: How then did it feel to you to superimpose yourself on Naipaul's script, when you wrote the screenplay for *The Mystic Masseur*? What was involved for you in that?

CP: What was involved, first of all, was Merchant-Ivory asking me. I've always admired Merchant-Ivory, because they're about the only film producers in the game who actually have a literary sensibility. And I've always liked *The Mystic Masseur* because it's always been, to me, an affectionate book about Trinidad. I also like the back story, which is about a young kid going to Oxford, and the whole bemusement of that journey out of a colonial world, which I obviously see as mirroring the autobiographical ups and downs of Naipaul's own life. So how did it feel? I felt I had a job to do with the book, and I knew that Naipaul wouldn't like it. I didn't know exactly how much he didn't like it until last week, when I saw the autobiography Ismail Merchant's just about to publish, called, with a twinkle in his eye, *My Passage from India*. Ismail never told me this, but towards the end of the book he reveals what happened when Naipaul found out that I was writing the screenplay. Ismail says in the book—I'm sort of paraphrasing now—that he asked me to write the screenplay because Ruth Prawer Jabhvala thought that I would be the best person to do it, and she didn't feel that she could handle the Caribbean dialogue. She told Ismail to see me, and he was very persuasive, and so I said yes. I wrote the screenplay and delivered it to Ismail, and then I wrote my essay about the letters between Naipaul and his father. At which point Naipaul called his agent and said it was disgusting that I had done the screenplay—he hadn't known that *I* was the one who had done the screenplay—and he suggested to his agent the name of a writer whom he really wanted to write it instead. His agent called Merchant and told him that under no circumstances could this film go ahead with me as the screenplay writer. At which point Merchant told him to get lost, basically. He told him that it was a good screenplay, and that Naipaul was entitled to his own opinion, but Merchant had his opinions, too, and he the filmmaker. So Naipaul refused to come to see the film, refused to go to the private screenings that were set up for him. He sent his agent along and his wife, who were very disparaging about the film, publicly. It created a problem for the film company. But I wanted to do the best job that I could on a book that I admired by an author who, although I might have some questions about, I also admired. If I didn't like the guy or like the book, I wouldn't have done it.

SC: The movie, I thought, has some intriguing differences from the book. The book is much more ironic, at times. You say there's a sympathy there; I think that's right. But sometimes I think there's good old Naipaulian condescension as well, and that, in a way, you warmed it up. Was that a deliberate decision?
CP: Yes. You know, I don't have a long history of writing screenplays; I've written a few, but I'm not the sort of person that sits down and immediately sees what the structural problem is of a screenplay. So I wrote a rather clunky, long first version and spoke to Ismail about it, and to James Ivory, both of whom suggested that it was a bit too detached and that I needed to compress two of the main characters into one. They were absolutely adamant that in filmic terms it would make a lot more sense. But they were both also encouraging me to warm it up a bit, in terms of the humor and in terms of the affection for the characters. And so I did push it a bit more, and that's what happened. I don't know—well, he hasn't seen it, so I don't know if Naipaul objects to it. I would like him to see it, because, you know, as a novelist myself, I would find it quite painful that somebody had made a film of a book of mine, and I just turned my back on it.

SC: It's one thing to judge a movie after you've seen it . . .
CP: Yes, but before you've read the screenplay, before you've seen anything . . . I should add that I wanted to do the film for another reason, which was that the Caribbean is not a zone which is thought of as a location for studies of human character, or for films generally. People think of the Caribbean as an exotic background, yet there are so many terrific stories that have a Caribbean context or a Caribbean setting. There are other novels—I gave Ismail and Jim a copy of *Cambridge*; I've given them about *three*, I think—because I want there to be other films that are made and set in the Caribbean. It's a shock to a lot of people when they actually *see* the Caribbean; they're looking as much at the locations as they are following the story. Most viewers have never really seen it.

SC: Or heard it. It also struck me that the movie had very few European reference points.

CP: Although I've got some problems with the film—and any screenplay writer would, because you write your screenplay, and have your own idea of how the finished film should be—the thing that I'm happiest about is the fact that people have been able to see—physically see—and hear the Caribbean, and imagine it to be a viable backdrop for drama. As you say, it has its own entity; it doesn't have validity through European intercourse. It has its own validity right there and then.

III.

SC: I'd like to ask you about your own writing—not to leave out that aspect of things—and I think that the essential thing to talk about in relation to your books is the question of form. You've said, in *A New World Order,* that every writer's ultimate struggle is a struggle with form. You've also suggested that the writers you relate to are those who are what you call disrupters of national form—and you've certainly used unusual forms in your novels, not least in terms of space and time. There is a shifting landscape in your work that you've made your own. When did you first feel the need for an alternative form?

CP: Well, I think the first time it became clear to me that the old formal models weren't going to work was my third stage play. I had written a stage play called *Strange Fruit* which was very straightforward. I then wrote a second play called *Where There Is Darkness,* where I began to incorporate flashbacks, so if you were going to look for a model or an influence, you would think of something like Arthur Miller's *Death of a Salesman.* But even that didn't seem to work for me. And then in my third stage play, called *The Shelter,* the first half of it is set on a deserted island in the eighteenth century, and the second half in a Ladbroke Grove pub in the 1950s. You can imagine: the audience came back from the intermission, from their gin and tonic and their glass of white wine, and they're thinking, "Well, where the hell did that desert island go?" and we're in a pub with a jukebox. So I began, there, to think time and space. Two years later I eventually completed *The Final Passage.* I'd been writing it for a long time in a very linear way, but when you open the book you see that the first section is called *The End.* So, in a sense, the first words I ever wrote in prose were "the end," and I think there was some kind of leakage out of that third play, where I knew I had to disrupt form. Why? Because the stories I was going to tell, the people that I was talking about, seemed to me to be people whose lives had been disrupted and didn't have a clear narrative continuity, because of migration, because of various forms of displacement. The second reason was that I was seeing historical connections, which didn't make any sense genealogically. You couldn't hold them in one plot. So I knew that at some point I was going to have to introduce the reader to the difficulties, or the annoying demand from me that they think in a slightly different way than they might do if they just picked up a regular book.

SC: To me as a reader these are introductions to a different view of space and time, apart from anything else. I'm just wondering whether, as a writer, the fact the you were working this way introduced *you* to a different vision of space and time?

CP: I think that's a good point. It opens you up to make discoveries, because you don't feel quite as handcuffed by issues of space, time, narrative, continuity. You know, something occurs to you—as Baldwin once said, "A funny thing happened to me on the way to the typewriter"— and at least there's a chance that you might be able to fit it into your narrative framework. I'm never sure; I don't plot out what the structural framework is going to be exactly. I start off always thinking I'm writing something which has Aristotelian unities, and as I'm writing it begins to move in different ways. Then I have to decide whether or not I'm moving with it, and if I can break the vessel but still hold all these different things in my mind.

SC: Characteristically in your novels you might have a character speaking *here* in one space and time and another speaking elsewhere, in a different space and time—each in a specific situation, and both juxtaposed with one another. The totality comes to be the exchange and interchange between these different situations or locations, and that to me then looks something like *dramatic* form. Does that make sense to you? Is there some kind of dramatic form there?

CP: It does, because one doesn't want to obfuscate through just being deliberately gymnastic about the sort of narrative that one's building. You don't want to obfuscate the empathy with character, principally because if that goes, then the whole thing is pointless as a novel. So you need to make sure that the gymnastics don't take away from an understanding of character, but *enhance* an understanding of character. But thematic enhancement is also a reason to do this moving around, because there are certain themes and certain ideas which I feel you can only really understand fully by hearing from somebody or something else. My model—if I have a model—is music.

SC: How so?

CP: You know, there are many images, but one always strikes me. I step out of my-

self and I imagine what it must have been like for others to see me when I was fifteen. I remember walking down the street from school, going into a record store
and buying I think maybe my second copy—I think I wore the first one out—
of Beethoven's Sixth Symphony. It cost twelve and six, or fourteen and six, or
sixty-five pence—I think we had changed to decimal. Coming out I saw a teacher
of mine, and I've often wondered what he thought when he saw me emerging
from Woolworth's with a copy of Beethoven's Sixth Symphony. I remember
passing a girl who was standing at a bus stop holding a copy of Diana Ross and
Marvin Gaye's *Greatest Hits*—which I liked, too—but in my own mind, I thought
I should be carrying the Beethoven. And I'm sure *he* thought that I *shouldn't* be
carrying it. But why was I listening to that? What fascinated me about it was
form and structure, because of the way in which Beethoven kept returning to
the same theme. I can probably whistle that whole symphony *now*. If I hear it, I
know it all; I know every single moment, because it's about how you score emotion basically—how you move and keep a theme going. You keep going forward,
but remind us where we've been; there is a viable parabola, and it rises and it falls
away gently to a conclusion. So, I think it's music which helped most.

SC: Why the Sixth more than anything else?
CP: The Sixth, just because, like any kid, you get stuck on one thing. Kids get ob-
sessional about things, and that was my thing, the Sixth. I remember going to see
Rostropovich play, just when he came out of Russia. I'm sure I was a real geek; I
liked to think of myself as this real hip hooligan, but there was an element about
me that was a bit nerdy. With music my interest was always to do with form, even
though I didn't know it. It was to do with structure and form.

SC: Just to step back again to the idea of dramatic form, if one thinks of a
character on the stage, what we don't have is a narrative frame telling us what
to think of that character. I find that useful for thinking about your characters
as well, because your narrative voice almost never intrudes to tell us what to think
about them.
CP: Which is why I find nonfiction hard sometimes.

SC: But you do it in your nonfiction, too.
CP: Yes, but I find it hard. That—well, you just said it. I try to hide to some extent
in nonfiction, as well.

SC: Why?
CP: I think because—I've never really thought about this, so this is a guess—
I think because I obviously feel strongly about avoiding any danger of polemic.
Like any writer writing about something that they care about deeply, I have an

opinion about the subject and the various situations. I always feel that I have the opportunity in nonfiction to write more directly if I choose to. I could write another book like *The European Tribe*; I could, as I've done on a number of occasions in *A New World Order*, step in front of the curtain and address the audience directly. So I do have that possibility, but I still prefer a more oblique approach. In fiction I think I have to let my characters have their voice, because so many of the people that I write about don't have a voice in other narratives. They're not the master narrators, and they're not the people who have been consulted about what to do next, or about "policy." They've generally been the ones who have been overlooked. So I don't want to get in the way; I just want them to speak. However, as you rightly say, even in nonfiction, my instinct is often to get out of the way as much as possible and let people speak. It's not a kind of coyness about expressing myself, because if that were the case, then we wouldn't have *The European Tribe*, and we wouldn't have some sections of *A New World Order.*

SC: It might be worth getting back to Darryl Pinckney here, who thinks of you as a "recessive presence" in *The Atlantic Sound.* I hope I'm not putting you off Darryl Pinckney, but one senses his frustration as a reader because of your unwillingness to give your own views—for instance on Pan-Africanism, which he says doesn't interest you, even as an idea. So what you see as being nonintrusive, others might see as evasiveness. The question might be, "Is he refusing to say what he thinks?"

CP: I find that strange, because I always think that it's pretty *obvious* what I think. But I know exactly what you mean, because I have had the experience of people telling me they had no idea who wrote this book. And part of what they're saying is, they didn't expect it to be a black guy. The thing is, what *I* think is not always important. Again, I have a forum in nonfiction in which I can speak more directly. And I do, in *The European Tribe*. In the middle section of *The Atlantic Sound* I do say what I think about a particular type of Panafest. But as I said, I have had that experience of people telling me that somehow I cheated. It's not that they're saying, "That was quite satisfying and puzzling." It's almost as if they're accusing me of having pulled a fast one on them. Their response has often been, "Is he deliberately hiding for a reason?" The reason is: I want these people to have their own voice. Remember, many of these people simply haven't been heard from.

SC: One facet of some of the characters you allow us to hear—I'm thinking, say, of Rudi in *Higher Ground* and Joyce in *Crossing the River*—is the kind of acerbic wit that they have, a real punchiness. Both Joyce and Rudi are alienated figures in society, and Rudi can also be quite a pompous figure at times. Does their wit and intelligence come from being outsiders? Is that the voice you're hearing in people who haven't yet been heard from?

CP: I've said it, you know. I was a little smartarse, as a kid—which is why Mr. Stern had to hit me round the head. But he knew that it's a defense mechanism. It's your way of surviving; you'd better be able to think quickly on your feet. When you look at the lives of most comics—I've been reading a bit about comedians lately—these are people who became funny in order to protect themselves, whose humor and whose quick-wittedness was self-defense. I think certainly in the case of Rudi in *Higher Ground* and Joyce in *Crossing the River,* you describe it perfectly: that kind of acerbic wit, which especially in Rudi's case can corrode into just mean-spiritedness, is a defense mechanism. I don't want to deconstruct my own work too much, but I think I know enough about it now to know there are various strategies of defense that people in my books use in order to shore up their crumbling identities. Religion is something that I question in various ways in various books, because religion can both constrict and liberate. Love, obviously, is similar. So—the point you're making about wit—it can get you through a situation, but it can also be your undoing, because you can end up, as a lot of comics do, as very sad and lonely—you know, the Lenny Bruce, Tony Hancock syndrome. It can go both ways. So I'm interested in those mechanisms for shoring-up identity, most of which have an almost Shakespearean double-twist to them. One final point about the fragility around the characters' lives is that, in many cases, they have little control over society. And so they have to prepare themselves in some way, or they're trying to prepare themselves, while some characters simply refuse to prepare themselves for what might happen.

SC: I think that adds real poignance as well. I'm thinking of Joyce in [*Crossing the River*], whose aggressive-defensive wit constitutes her place in the world, at least at the beginning of the story, or the part of the book that she inhabits. Then she discovers a way to let go of that in the relationship she has with Travis, the African American soldier, and then Travis gets killed, and she's left without any defense.

CP: Well, I'm glad you're talking about her. When people come up after a book signing, or when I'm reading and they ask questions afterwards, in the main they are generous and polite. After all, these are not forums for saying, you know, "God, your work is crap!" But I do remember one occasion in which a black woman—and I think it is important that she was black—came up to me, publicly, and was, clearly, extremely angry with me for including Joyce in the book.

I didn't become visibly upset, but I just wanted to turn and walk away, because it bothered me that she was imposing a kind of racially narrow reading of—not just my book, that didn't bother me—but her own *life*. Her life had corroded to the point that it *angered* her, and she was almost shaking with anger that this author had included a white person in the text in that way; and she was particularly upset that Joyce was included as part of the family at the end of the book. But I remember looking at her and thinking, "You know, I don't know what damage has been done to you in your life, but this society's done a pretty good job of beating up on you." And, actually, the reason I wrote the book, the reason I write, is so all of us can open our minds a little bit and actually say, "Oh, so it's okay." So I'm happy to hear you talk about Joyce, because she's one of my favorite people, even though I know you're not supposed to have favorites. She's one of my favorites for all sorts of reasons—partly because it was, you know, not a *risk*, but something I felt really strongly about in a book which might otherwise have easily just revolved around, in the narrowest sense, the iniquities of the slave trade and its legacy.

SC: One of the interesting things to me is that you've got three African children in the book, Nash, Travis, and Martha. At any rate, Travis doesn't get the first-person narrative; the first-person narrative is given to the others in varying degrees, and then to Joyce, not Travis. He disappears off the edge of the frame of the book in a way; he dies without having his own space. And I think that a number of your characters do that. They don't have clear edges to their stories; they disappear into silence. That happens, for instance, to both Eva and Othello in *The Nature of Blood*. Perhaps if that woman who came up to you had seen it in that light, it would have answered some of her questions as to who gets the story.

CP: If she'd had said, is there some larger strategy to who eventually gets the story, who's able to tell this tale, we could have had a discussion. Is this saying something about England? Is this saying something about voice in England? Is this saying something about the way in which history is retold? I mean, why *does* a black American soldier fall into silence in Britain? But it wasn't that kind of discussion; it wasn't that kind of a concern. Yes, Joyce gets the story. She gets the story, largely because her situation—I mean, I don't think I've ever really said this before, but it seems obvious to me that she gets the story because her situation in the novel is c loser to my situation than Travis's. And, I would find it easier, as somebody who grew up in the North of England, to write like her, to speak like *her*, than I would find it to speak like Travis, especially at that time. I'm more familiar with the United States now, and perhaps now I would find it easier to carry a first-person narrative in an African American idiom.

IV.

SC: There might be other readers who object to your voicings: female readers, white readers, or Jewish readers who object to the fact that you inhabit female voices, white voices, Jewish voices, and so on. Yet, if you have any anxiety about impersonation, it's one that you seem to suppress and just get beyond. At the same time, it seems to be part of your philosophy of identity—not only that we can inhabit other voices, but that we *need* to relate to other people.

CP: I like the idea that we need to do it, because I believe that it's the reason I write. I believe I write because I don't want another generation, I don't want another individual to have to suffer, unnecessarily, anxieties around identity, to be ashamed of the question, "*Where am I from*," to feel panicked when somebody says, "Well, who are you?" I don't want to live in a world in which the idea of a complex cultural and historical, racial, religious identity is something to be ashamed of. And I want people to be able to accept the fact that moving across these old lines in a personal way *is* the way forward, is the only thing that we have. We don't have any choice in the twenty-first century but to understand that we are not limited by what we see when we look in the mirror and brush our teeth in the morning; that all we're seeing is a very literal and a very reductive image of who we are. I mean, I don't want to sound like Michael Jackson or Lionel Ritchie—"we are the world"—but it just seems to me ludicrous not to accept and understand that that's where we are at the beginning of the twenty-first century. Because of migration, because of our histories, because of a history of movement—that's what's happening. So, to argue, as I have heard people do, that one is culturally appropriating this or that voice, is not only ludicrous now, it has always been ludicrous. Do you tell Thomas Hardy he should write *Tom of the Durbervilles*, or Tolstoy that he should have written *Alan Karenina*? I mean, it doesn't make any sense whatsoever, and it never has. But it seems to me that to employ the argument now is not only to be foolish but it's to be traveling completely against what is obvious. So in a sense that's my answer to the whole question of writing in different voices. It just seems to me it's important that one shouldn't be afraid to do so, and, as with any character you write about, as long as you do so honestly, and as long as you feel that you have an understanding, and that the characters have trusted you with their story—that's how I think about it.

I always think to myself, this character is speaking to me, because she, Joyce, or he, Rudi, has actually trusted their story to me. And if I feel that I've got to that stage, that level of trust, then I'll start to write, and I won't worry about what anybody thinks. So that's really my feeling; it's at the basis of why I write. It's because those lines which have been set to trip us up—those lines of nationality, those lines of race, those lines of religion, those lines of language, those lines of cultural point of departure—they've been set up there to trip us up by making us think reductively. And it seems to me that if the job of a writer is anything, it is to help to change society. It's to encourage people to change not only the way they think, but thereafter, change the way in which they act. That seems to me to be absolutely fundamental to a writer's job. Otherwise, you know, you really may as well be writing *Days of Our Lives,* the afternoon soap opera.

SC: Just one more word on voicing and narrative, because it is notable how many different versions of these you have. The voices rotate among themselves, and so does everything else: you have epistolary forms, chronicles, journals, sea-logs, first-person narratives, third-person narratives, and so on. I seldom speak about choice when it comes to writers, especially ones I respect, because it seems to me very few things are as deliberate or as schematic as that, but this clearly seems to be part of the way you work.

CP: Well, I think that most of the forms that I would employ, whether it's letters, whether it's intense first-person narrative, are all what I would broadly term "confessional modes." And the confessional mode seems to me to suggest, first of all, a deep necessity to speak, a deep necessity to communicate, which is born of a hurt, a displacement, a sense of exclusion. That kind of confessional mode also— bearing in mind what I said before—further obfuscates my presence, because it's so intensely personal that it makes it doubly difficult to get at who is the controlling narrative presence. But it is, I think, to do with a degree of feeling—like a kid. You don't have anyone to talk to, so you talk to your journal. But it's not just a journal, as you say; there's a journal, there are letters, there are logs—so there are different forms, but they all add up to the same thing, I think.

SC: So, mainly this is listening to someone speak.

CP: Yes. Again, you see I went to university to study psychology. I didn't go to university to do English at Oxford; I went to do psychology, because when I was fifteen, sixteen, seventeen, the books that I used to read were Freud and Jung. I was really interested in what made people work. I was deeply, for whatever perverse reason, concerned with dreams, concerned with the deepest workings of the unconscious. So I used to read Freud and Jung and Adler and all of these people, and I went to university to do psychology, and then realized that my concern with what happens with the unconscious mind was not being satisfied by the course. The psychology course at Oxford was more to do with cutting up monkeys; you know, it was very scientific. So I went to my tutor, having received a mark in the end-of-term exams that was so absurdly low that I won't even mention it, because you'll think I'm making it up. But I was terrible, really, at this, because I had no scientific mindset. I told my tutor that I needed to change; I wanted to do English. He asked why, and I said, "Because I'm lousy at this, you've got the evidence in front of you." He thought for a while and said, "Well, you know, if you're interested, as you say you are, in what makes people work, then you really should do English." He spoke to me about William James, who was the first professor of psychology at Harvard. But, he said, compared to his brother, he knew nothing about people; Henry James was the one who knew about people. And he said, "If you really want to know about people, read novels, because that will take you close." Now when I then started to read novels and switch to English, I realized that the novels I was interested in were those which had a very close narrative, a very interior narrative, and a narrative which had deeply to do with the unconscious, and took you very close to the person. So when I started to write, not only was I a bit more familiar with that form, but I think the people I was writing about were the type who would only be able to express themselves properly in that form.

SC: One thing that involves is the question of language, but in a rather complicated way. I'm thinking of Rudi, say, in *Higher Ground,* or Othello in *The Nature of Blood:* these are Africans, or people of African descent, who enter not only into some negotiation with the American world or the European world, but they also enter into a kind of linguistic space in which they have to take on somebody else's language, or find their own space, their own voice in that language. Their language becomes variable, almost unstable, because they are mediating figures, trying to find their own reality. I'm wondering, could we look at this more personally? For you growing up, being someone who is identified as an outsider, I would guess you almost had to speak a double language. You have to be able to speak the language of the dominant culture and yet retain your own sense of who you are. Are there those links, or do you think I'm making too much of it?

CP: Totally. You've just answered the question, in a sense, because that's exactly what it is. Again, as sometimes happens when somebody else starts to talk about what you're doing, it becomes clear to you what you are doing and why you are doing it. You know, for me, when I went to Oxford at eighteen, it was a really important moment in my life, because I remember getting off the train with my suitcase and saying to myself right there and then, before I'd even left Oxford train station, I will leave here in three years' time, and I'm going to be standing in this same place, but I will have a degree. And I also knew, looking at the spires in the distance, that I had to decide what else I wanted out of this place, otherwise this place would use me. I figured: journalism, theatre, or politics—those are the areas where this place can offer you something. And I already knew I wanted to work in the theatre, so I said, okay, I'm not going to get involved in politics, I'm not going to get involved in anything to do with journalism, and I'm also not going to get involved in sport too much. I'm just going to do the theatre. But I'm going to get a degree, and I'm going to work the theatre side of things, and I'm going to be true to myself. I just was absolutely clear that I am going to be who I am even if it means difficult, problematic times, some of which I've written about in *The European Tribe*. And so I had that mindset before I left the train station. Once I encountered Oxford, for the first time in my life I was offered the chance by the society to become something other than I was. I was offered that opportunity; I wasn't pressured, but it was there. But I didn't want to be a member, because it would have turned me into something that I just had a sense I didn't want to be. So I'm interested in those characters that you've mentioned, not because I have any contempt for them, but because it's basically what's offered to all of us in life. It happened to me, and it still happens to me to this day. It's what's offered to us in life at various points, the opportunity to make one's life a little easier by doing what James Baldwin once called making a premature peace with mediocrity. You kind of *know* it's not right, and you know you shouldn't be doing it. I just had a feeling that I shouldn't do it, that I should just hold off. There are many, many, many people—good people—who don't have any choice. And what happens to them and how that affects their personal history has always been interesting to me.

SC: Can I ask you one last question—about sport?
CP: Yes.

SC: To the extent that you've left so many places, it seems to me that's one place you haven't left, for whatever rational or irrational reasons, conscious or subconscious. I'm thinking of soccer—football—Leeds United, and so on. You talk in *A New World Order* of finding yourself in a crowd of people, suddenly belting out "God Save the Queen" at the top of your voice, surprising yourself. What is it about that camaraderie? On the terraces watching Leeds United is where you must have experienced, in pretty extreme forms, some of the same exclusions you experienced in other areas of your life. And, yet, there's that strange sense of belonging.

CP: What is it about sport that does that? I guess, you know, it's tribal. Tribes are not always made up of people who look the same, they're not always made up of people who necessarily speak the same language. There's a sense of belonging around sport, not only those who play it, but those who watch it, which cuts across a lot of ostensible barriers. You know, when I go to watch a soccer match, or if I go to watch any sporting occasion, and somebody scores a goal, or somebody hits the ball for six, you don't really care who you're hugging next to you. There's something which rises up above those rather stupid and superficial barriers which, in other aspects of our daily life, we believe in, or we're encouraged to believe in. And I think that's what makes sport potent as a kind of metaphor, and that's why your former president, Mandela, is very shrewd about how he views sport as a metaphor for healing. I've been in a situation, many times, where one minute you've been with somebody on the terraces and they're high-five'ing you and you're hugging them, and the next minute they're doing the jungle sounds and the banana noises and monkey noises and what have you, because they don't get it. You know, for a moment they were transcendent; for a moment there was communication, and then it's as if they've retreated into a kind of atavistic behavior, which is normal to them. But for me, I remember the moment when we were high-five'ing each other and hugging each other, and if *he* doesn't remember it, then I guess part of my job as a writer is to find a way to remind him that he rose up above that barrier for a minute. As for the people on the pitch, or the people participating, sport is political. It's Sandy Koufax, Jackie Robinson, Albert Johansson, Lucas Radebe. What happens on that pitch has a profound influence, especially on young kids' attitudes to life. So whether one is a participant on the pitch, or an observer, those lines of demarcation that we've been talking about all afternoon, that are etched in stone in society, that we're encouraged to believe are etched in granite—actually, when we get close up in things like sport, we realize the lines are etched in soapstone and can be rubbed away.

SC: Thank you.

Interview with Caryl Phillips

Charles Wilkin/2002

From WINN FM, December 23, 2002. Reprinted with the permission of WINN. Interview conducted in Basseterre, St. Kitts.

Caryl Phillips is an award-winning and highly respected English professor, novelist, playwright, film producer, and screenplay writer. He has written six novels, three books of nonfiction, several screenplays, and produced many plays and documentaries for the theatre, radio, and television, including the screenplay for *The Mystic Masseur,* an adaptation of a novel by V. S. Naipaul, and a documentary on legendary American musician, Curtis Mayfield. Phillips has lived and worked in Africa, Asia, Europe, and the U.S.A. His awards include the BBC Giles Cooper Award for his radio play *The Wasted Years,* the Malcolm X Prize for Literature for his first novel, the Martin Luther King Memorial Prize for Literature, the *London Sunday Times* Young Writer of the Year Award, and he was listed among Granta's Best British Novelists in 1993. The magazine *Caricom Perspective,* in its Millenium edition entitled "Voices of the Century," honors Mr. Caryl Phillips as a talented author on race and heritage. Born in St. Pauls in 1958, Mr. Phillips migrated with his parents to England before he was a year old. He attended Oxford University. Mr. Phillips is currently in St. Kitts for the filming of a documentary on his life and work which is being produced by Granada TV and Bravo TV for a broadcast next year in Britain and the U.S.A. Mr. Phillips's new novel, *A Distant Shore,* is to be published in April next year. Mr. Charles Wilkin, QC partner in the law firm Kelsick, Wilkin, and Ferdinand, spoke with Mr. Phillips about his life and his tremendous contribution to the arts.

CW: My pleasure to introduce to the studios of WINN FM radio, a famous Kittitian, writer Caryl Phillips, of whom everybody has heard of. Caz, welcome to WINN FM.

CP: Thank you. There's a British film crew who are making a documentary film about my work. It's an hour long documentary which is scheduled to be shown next April on British, and then American, television. The way of making a documentary is to generally focus on an author's life and work, but in this instance, I've tried to push them more towards focusing on the work. If I'm still around twenty or thirty years down the road, the life might be vaguely interesting, but right now let's keep it on the work.

CW: I imagine that the filming of this documentary and the portrayal of St. Kitts in it will have an enormous benefit to St. Kitts in terms of free publicity.
CP: The filmmakers should actually be receiving a free dinner, a free lunch, and a pat on the back from the St. Kitts Tourist Board because they've been here in St. Kitts filming not only historical sites—obviously Brimstone Hill, Old Road Bay, Sir Thomas Warner's Tombstone, the architecture of Basseterre, the Circus, the bayfront—they've also been out on the southeast peninsula looking at various vistas and views. I think they've really done a terrific job of showing the island as the sort of place that you'd want to come and visit—and not to just look into the history, and the very special relationship that the island has with Britain. They also show the island as a great place to relax, unwind, and to take some sun.

CW: What impact is this documentary likely to have on your career?
CP: That's a very good question. It's hard to know exactly what will happen, but one of the reasons I'm doing it is because I have a new novel being published in April and my publishers were very keen that I say yes to this. The same film company actually tried to do a similar documentary about five or six years ago, but I didn't really want to do it because I thought it would be too intrusive. People are always very interested in the lives of artists, of painters, musicians, writers, poets; they want to know about the man or the woman behind the work. I'm quite reluctant to let things drift in that direction, so five, six years ago, I said no. This time I said yes because, with a new novel coming out, such a film does raise your profile and improve your sales, and it makes it possible for you to reach out to the kind of audience that you might never otherwise reach. Television is, after all, the most powerful medium in the modern world. So a television documentary can be significant and bring people to your work.

CW: Let's look at your work a little bit, Caz. You were born in St. Kitts. You grew up in the United Kingdom. And, interestingly, you have described yourself by reference to the metaphor of a tree whose branches have developed and, to some extent, continue to develop and grow in Britain, but whose roots are in Caribbean soil. You want to expand on that for us.
CP: Well, I think that for many people—not just those who write—who are from the Caribbean, there's a sense of some kind of connection to the region no matter

where you travel. There's a sense of belonging to this part of the world. The Caribbean boasts a long tradition of migration, of exporting its talent, exporting its human resources to other people's countries. Sometimes these people return, sometimes they don't return; but whether they return or not, I think many of these people do continue to think of themselves—whether they're sitting in London or Toronto or New York—as people with their roots in Caribbean soil. For me it's always been particularly important to remember my roots because, thematically speaking, a large part of what I've always written about has been connected to the islands of the English-speaking Caribbean. It's been very important to me that I remind people in Britain and in the United States that they can't co-opt me as some sort of exotic addition to their literary tradition . . . I always try and remind them that there's a place from which they can't uproot me and that is the Caribbean. They're never to be able to uncouple me from the Caribbean because I am a part of that long tradition of Caribbean people who've moved beyond, but who continue to feel rooted here.

CW: Tell us what it was like growing up in England in the 1960s and '70s?
CP: Terrible . . . (laughs all around) . . . It was a strange period because my parents, who came over from St. Kitts in the late fifties and went to Leeds, they were what we now term the first generation of West Indian people in Britain after the war. They were the pioneer generation. One of the things about this pioneer generation is that they were very, very keen to root themselves in Britain. They didn't like to talk a lot about the Caribbean, for the Caribbean was the place they had left. Furthermore, they didn't want to confuse their kids who were, after all, growing up in an often hostile British society. They didn't bother with too much talk of "back home" because there was no guarantee that they were going to make it back home or that their kids were going to want to go "back home." Growing up in Britain in the sixties and seventies I felt kind of lost between two places, if you like. I knew that I'd come from St. Kitts. Every time I had to write down "place of birth," I wrote down St. Paul's Village, St. Kitts. But at the same time, I also knew that part of me was British. But then British society was trying to tell me in some subtle, and some not so subtle ways, that I didn't belong there. So I think, in common with most kids of West Indian parents growing up in the sixties and seventies in England, I felt sort of lost between two places.

CW: How different towards Afro-Caribbean peoples is present day UK?
CP: I think very different to be honest. I'm loathe to reach for a metaphor which you would recognize and embrace, but it's a very apt one, and it's that of football. You know, when I think of the Leeds United that I saw during the sixties and sev-

enties, I only really remember one team ever showing up at Elland Road with a black player and that was West Ham. The player was a Bermudan called Clyde Best who took an awful lot of stick from the crowd, including his own West Ham fans. That kind of isolation, that kind of loneliness, which clouded the lives of a lot of people of West Indian origin in Britain at the time, has now completely changed in as much as when you go and watch a soccer match these days, or watch it on Fox Sports World here, all of the British teams have, to some extent, you know, a multi-cultural, multi-ethnic make-up, which includes West Indian players. In other words, Britain has changed. There's more of a sense of it being a multi-cultural or multi-racial society which embraces all sorts of different outsiders, including West Indians. So I think there's been an opening up of the society, and it's become a much more sophisticated, and I think life for a second or third generation West Indian in Britain is significantly more comfortable than it would have been for that pioneer generation.

CW: Caz, you were educated at Oxford University, one of the premiere universities and most famous universities in the entire world. What impact did that have on you and on your decision to write?
CP: It had a profound impact in as much as it completely demythologized for me the notion of class in British society. My parents left this island and settled in the north of England, as did many Kittitians, and the industrial north is almost a country within a country. Yorkshire has a very peculiar, insular, mindset. And so, when I went to university at Oxford I met people who were upper-middle class, who had traveled, who'd been to public schools, who were, to all intents and purposes, the sophisticated inheritors to the traditions of England. They were a new breed of Englishman for me. However, I very quickly realized that these people were no more sophisticated and no more intelligent than I was. That demythologizing of the whole class structure of Britain was very important. In terms of helping me to write, Oxford was also important because, as I always remind students or young people who ask me about their own potential career as writers, one of the things about writing is that you have to read. If you don't read, you're never going to write. And one thing I did at Oxford was I read. I read, read, read. And that reading eventually paid dividend because it gave me some kind of a basis from to which imagine myself as writer.

CW: What other factors influenced your decision to become a professional writer?
CP: Well, I think I was always going to do something in the arts. I went to University knowing that maybe I'd work in the theatre, possibly film, possibly television. I knew that I wanted to do something creative in the arts and probably to do with

the performing arts. But when I was leaving University and beginning to think about what type of plays I might wish to produce—I'd directed a number of plays as a student—I realized that there were no plays, no films, and no books on the subject that I was interested in, and that subject was the emergence of a second generation of West Indians in England. The people who were me, the people who looked like me, who were, at the time of my graduation, basically burning down Notting Hill and Brixton. It was that period of time when I graduated, when the carnival in Notting Hill generally descended into a riot, when all you heard was "Brixton is a problem area," and there was continual confrontation with the police. The fictional narratives about why the second generation felt this way, what their parents (who were the people who came over on the boats) thought about their kids, these plays and stories weren't around for me to direct. And that's when I realized that if I was going to have any career as an interpreter of my own generation, then I would have to write the material myself.

CW: You came back to St. Kitts for the first time as an adult in 1980. Tell me what were your first impressions?

CP: Well, the first impression, I remember, was the body language. I remember walking down Fort Street and my cousin looking at me quizzically. He eventually stopped me on the street corner and said to me, "You know, you're going to have to learn to walk slower." And I looked around at how people moved and how they held themselves, and I realized that there's a big difference between a West Indian in London, or a West Indian in Brooklyn, or a West Indian in Toronto, and a West Indian in this society. There's a body language, there's a way of moving, there's a way of holding yourself, which I didn't understand. Beyond that, I realized I also didn't understand the environment, because if you can't name the trees, if you can't point to a tree and say, "That's a mango tree," if you can't point and say, "That's a breadfruit," you know, "That's a guava," then you're lost. I mean, without the knowledge of being able to name your environment, you're lost. I can stand up in England, I can tell you "That's an oak tree," "That's a beech tree," "That's a birch," that doesn't make me an Englishman, but it makes me feel more acclimatized. I knew within hours of arriving in St. Kitts in 1980 that there was a huge educative process that had to happen before there was a proper sense of connection.

CW: And you returned again in 1983 to cover Independence celebrations for the BBC. How far had your educative process advanced by then?

CP: It's advanced a wee bit because I'd been back, well, I'd been back '80, '81, '82, '83 . . . I mean, I knew, once I came here first in '80, I realized I would have to keep

coming back because so much of who I was and so much of who my generation were in Britain—so many of the questions which were gnawing away and in-
forming the anxiety—the answers were here. They were not going to be found on
the streets of Britain, so I kept coming back for professional as well as personal
reasons. By the time I arrived back in '83, I think I had a more profound understanding of the society. And, it was also important for me that I did come back
at that important turning point in Kittitian history. However, it was also a very
important moment in British history. But if you asked most people in Britain,
they wouldn't recognize it as such. They wouldn't generally know that in January
1624, Thomas Warner set foot here and founded the first British colony. St. Kitts
was the model for all that followed in terms of the colonizing process, and in this
sense it's the mother colony of the British Empire. St. Kitts becoming independent did mark not only a new beginning for St. Kitts, but it marked a point of
closure for Britain too.

CW: How would you compare the St. Kitts of 1983 to the St. Kitts of today, almost
twenty years later?
CP: I think it's a very different place. In some ways I lament the degree to which
we, in St. Kitts, have fallen quite so powerfully under the shadow of the United
States—in terms of television and the other cultural influences which we in
St. Kitts are subjected to. But, it's not just St. Kitts, it's obviously the whole Caribbean region. However, there is no way in which I think a country that is this geographically close to the United States of America can do anything other than take
and absorb American influence. Sadly, it's a very powerful and sometimes per-
nicious influence. A few weeks ago, I was in Japan, and I was talking to Japanese writers and professors out there—they were basically saying the same thing.
They regret the degree to which the United States is beginning to cloud their horizon, but if a nation as strong as Japan is feeling this kind of pressure then we
don't have any choice here in the Caribbean. That's the main change, I think, the
Americanization, which seems to me to be potentially dangerous.

CW: Let's run for a short while now, Caz, to your novels. It's interesting that the
theme of your first novel, *The Final Passage,* is emigration from the Caribbean
to the UK in the 1950s. Its subject is where you began because, as a four-month-
old, you were an emigrant with your parents. So you were in effect depicting your
parent's journey to the UK. And I believe that you relived that journey yourself,
sometime later.
CP: I think most writers' first works draw upon, certainly not autobiographical
fact, but they certainly trace the autobiographical contours of an individual's life.

I mean, there's nothing autobiographical in the novel, but the actual journey itself seems to me to sum up what may have happened to my parents' generation. These days I've crossed the Atlantic many, many times to Britain, at 35,000 feet, with no real understanding of that sense of loss that one feels on leaving an island. And I've also traveled across the Atlantic without that sense of anxiety about what's going to happen on my arrival. When I fly from Britain to St. Kitts, I take the plane to Antigua, and eight hours later I'm in London. But, of course, no matter how many times I make this journey this isn't going to help me to understand what my parents' generation went through. This being the case, a couple of years ago I took a banana boat across the Atlantic. It took three weeks, and the rhythm of that journey seemed to me to be a lot closer to the rhythm of what that pioneer generation undertook. For me, it was a terrible journey, to be honest with you. And lonely. Migrants at least have the pleasure of each other's company, they're able to talk to each other, they're able to swap stories, they're able to stay up late at night and drink rum on deck and speculate. But on this particular journey there was just myself. It wasn't a pleasant journey, but it did, as I said, bring me closer to what it was probably like to be a migrant back in the fifties.

CW: And you depicted that journey in one of your books.
CP: Yes, I wrote a nonfiction book called *The Atlantic Sound,* and the opening section of the book is called "Atlantic Crossing." I basically just write about what happened from the moment I got on the banana boat to the moment I stepped ashore in Dover. The anxiety of being alone, set adrift in the middle of the Atlantic is something that makes you appreciate the courage that it takes to migrate. For somebody from any part of the world to migrate requires some courage, but for somebody from Newton Ground, or from Dieppe Bay, or from Ottleys, a young person in their twenties to pack up their life, leave their friends, leave their family, leave everything they've known, to get on a ship and travel, often not in very comfortable circumstances across the Atlantic Ocean, and to not really know what they're going to encounter—because they'll have just listened to the BBC World Service in the rum shop on a stool at the end of the day—this requires a special courage. Such travelers are expecting to be welcomed, they're expecting to be made to feel at home. They have a British passport in their jacket pocket, the one jacket that they have. And then they arrive in London. And then they face the reality, and they have to soak up the betrayal that comes with colonial migration. It's a very profound thing, and it's something which should be part of the narrative of the life of this island because this island is full of brave people who made that journey.

CW: As you said earlier, your emphasis on work has been on migration and displacement, and also on diversity of people. Your second novel *A State of Independence* in 1986 was the story of a man who had gone to England as a child and returned as a thirty-nine-year-old to St. Kitts thinking, the reverse process now, thinking that he was going to conquer all because of his experiences in Britain, which he thought had prepared him for the return journey, and he had a rude awakening.

CP: Well, I'm sure the island's full of these people too. People go away, and they spend ten, twenty years in another country and then they come back to the country they've left and they think to themselves that they're going to be given preference because of their experience, or the professional credits that they've accrued abroad. What they're forgetting, of course, is that in a period of ten or twenty years not only do they change profoundly, but the country changes too. There are two factors at work here and the idea that the two factors are going to stay stable so that there can be some kind of reunification without rupture and disjuncture is impossible. So, yes, he comes back to his island after twenty-or-so years in England, and is shocked to find that the island has changed and he's not needed. Political change is such that there is corruption, there's preference . . . he's an outsider. And to be an outsider in your own country is a very difficult thing, but so many people here have witnessed it. People are returning, having been away, and some have assumed that there's an easy well-paved path for them to the center of power, and it doesn't work like that.

CW: In *State of Independence,* as you just said, you touch, to large measure, on the realities of Independence. Your book is written three years after St. Kitts's independence and it was felt that a lot of your comments related to St. Kitts and the process of independence and the Americanization of which you just spoke. Some of the reaction to that book, and particularly to the politics you spoke of, was not very favorable.

CP: The idea of a writer in any part of the world sitting comfortably around a table with a politician is generally a fantasy. Writers and politicians tend to have a very uneasy truce with each other. The second thing is the facts of what happened during the independence here, and what happened around the whole process of St. Kitts standing up on her own two feet and beginning to walk in the world, they were problematic. I mean, we're still living with the legacy of some of the decisions that were made back then. However, writers do provide an alternative narrative for the country and that's why writers are often regarded as problematic. In 1956, when the Russians invaded Hungary, ten thousand people were killed. It was Khruschev who said: "We could have saved those ten thousand lives by shooting six writers." Maybe, maybe not, but the truth is writers often do provide an alternative story for a people to lock into.

CW: Do you feel that issue affects the recognition that you have got locally in St. Kitts? Because, let's face it, your are perhaps the best known Kittitian in the world, and yet you don't have the same kind of recognition here in St. Kitts as you do, say in London, or in New York, or in Ghana, even.

CP: I don't take it personally because I try to see it in the context of the relationship between Caribbean writers and this region . . . for the past hundred years the Caribbean has always produced writers who have felt underappreciated in their own countries, and many of them have been outstanding writers. The list is endless: Claude McKay in Jamaica, C. L. R. James in Trinidad, Walcott in St. Lucia, Kamau Braithwaite in Barbados . . . all of whom have ended up living and working abroad, and feeling, to some degree, slighted or forced out of their own native islands. I don't take it personally in any way. I still feel that St. Kitts is a very important part of who I am, and St. Kitts is a very important part of what I write about. My only real concern is that I just wish there was an easier way of contributing. One can contribute by making the books available, and people can obviously buy them. I do teach as well, and I spend a good deal of my year as a teacher in universities. I've tried to come back to the Caribbean to do that at Cave Hill in Barbados. It would be nice to have some more formal way of contributing particularly to the younger people here. It would please me a great deal if there was some way of reaching the emerging generation, and maybe working in some kind of educational initiative.

CW: I saw a former student of the University of the West Indies approach you the other evening with great glee at seeing you, and obviously you had had an enormous impact on her life and she was very proud to say that she had written on your books and that you had taught her at UWI. Unfortunately, St. Kitts doesn't have a campus of UWI but St. Kitts has an external facility for UWI. Has there been any attempt to have you make an impact in that way?

CP: A couple of years ago, I had a visiting professorship at Cave Hill, so I used to go there in the spring for a month or two, depending on what my other obligations were. Back then there was some talk of me coming here to do a talk or do something, but it didn't work out. However, that's the sort of thing that would be terrific. It's a worry to me because if you don't have writers visible, if you don't have writers interacting in the community, then there's no possibility for young people to imagine themselves taking that path, or imagine themselves taking a creative path. I don't want St. Kitts or the Caribbean to end up like a country such as Singapore, because when I was teaching at the university there one of the things that was frightening was that young people had no notion of themselves as anything other than bureaucrats, or working in technological industry. They had no way of thinking themselves as dancers, as musicians, as painters, as sculptors, as poets, because the society didn't encourage that. I know it's different here in St. Kitts because there is good work being done in theatre and in dance, but literature is my own particular beat and I just wish that the young people who want to write, who want to write poetry, write for the theatre, write prose . . . I just wish that there was some way that they, in common with youngsters on other islands, could feel that they had a path, a way forward, if that's the career they wish to pursue.

CW: You've never had a formal request from the government over the years since 1983 to participate in any way through the government's education service?
CP: I've never had any communication with the government, full stop. Again, I don't take this personally because I remember talking to Derek Walcott just after he won the Nobel Prize and he was telling me that the relationship between himself and the St. Lucian government wasn't that great because he had spoken out on different subjects. For instance, he did speak out particularly vociferously on a project involving the pitons, and if he's now recognized and celebrated in St. Lucia (which he is—they've named the square downtown after him and so on), it's a 180-degree turn-around from what it used to be. I think there's a pattern here. I don't think governments in the Caribbean feel necessarily all that comfortable with their writers and I guess that's just the way it goes.

CW: Well, one political personage said to me once, in relation to you, that "one has to be very careful with those people," [laughs all around] "you never know what they're going to write." Which means, in effect, that politicians don't control you and that you have very serious power of the pen.
CP: Well, I think that that's part of the responsibility of being a writer. A great responsibility of the writer is to put a little distance between yourself and politicians and politics. I remember, traveled in Eastern Europe when it was under the Soviet influence. I've been in Moscow, I've been in Berlin, and nearer to home, I've been in Havana. I've seen what happens when the state hijacks a people's history, and in that situation I've also seen how important the writers become because they are often the only people who can present an alternative history. I'm not even going to say an alternative "truth"; they're writing an alternative history and an alternative narrative which provides the people with another way of

viewing themselves to that which the government is offering them. And that is part of my job; part of my job is to provide people with a different way of looking at themselves, and to provide a nation with a different way off viewing itself. And I hope that's something which a book like *A State of Independence* provided. So, yes, a politician who subscribes to a particularly narrow narrative is going to find it difficult to deal with writers who don't doff their caps to anybody's well-peddled line.

CW: You spoke about your contribution through the University of the West Indies. You've also, in the last couple of years, been editor of the Faber Caribbean Series. Could you describe that work to us and its meaning to West Indians?

CP: Well, as you know, in the last ten years, the English-speaking Caribbean has produced two writers, Naipaul and Walcott, who have both been widely recognized. I don't just mean the Nobel Prize that they both won, I mean the many, many prizes, and the great attention that they've received. If one adds to them the writers of the French Caribbean who are very significant world writers, and the writers of the Dutch and the Spanish Caribbean, what you have is a region of the world which has an incredible flowering of literary talent. Most of it isn't made available because the publishing industry is a business, and like most businesses it's a business in recession and having to top-and-tail its budgets all the time. So what we try to do with this series is publish books each year at a reasonable price and make them available to universities and to schools. These are not only the English-language Caribbean books, but the French, the Dutch, and the Spanish, translated into English. In this way the reader can begin to get a sense of the breadth of the region's literature without being hemmed-in just to the English-speaking, so we translate French Caribbean literature, and Dutch and Spanish as well. It's an expensive initiative, but it's worthwhile because, as I say, one of the many great things about this region is the strength of its literature. However, my worry about the English-speaking Caribbean is that, unlike the French, or the Dutch, or the Spanish, the English-speaking Caribbean writers don't tend to live in the region. They have a tendency to become disaffected and move abroad, and this creates a problem because where is the next generation going to come from if they don't actually see their writers?

CW: These books are available in the bookstores here?

CP: Yes, they're available in the bookstores here in St. Kitts, and if there's a difficulty in obtaining them you can get them online. Or, of course, you can also get them if you travel abroad.

CW: Let's turn for a moment to a favorite subject of both of ours . . . sport. You spoke about Leeds United and I know that you're still a fanatic Leeds United supporter. But let's talk about cricket. You wrote a film in England in the eighties called *Playing Away*, which had a cricket theme and, apparently, which was highly acclaimed. Could you describe that to us a little bit?

CP: Well, I wrote this film in the mid-eighties, 1986, I think. I wanted to write something about the type of England that West Indians were living in, which was largely an urban England, which meant that you only knew a small part of England. Which, of course, also means that there's a huge section of England which has no understanding whatsoever of West Indians. If you play cricket in England, you can travel to places in Somerset, in Kent, in Surrey, where the notion of a West Indian, or an Indian, or a Pakistani turning up is profoundly exotic. If you are a West Indian raised on the streets of Birmingham or Manchester or London, you've probably never seen that world. In other words, there's a very strong country/city divide in Britain. So I wanted to bring these two elements of geography and race together. Furthermore, it was right around the time of Band Aid when people were raising money for African famine, so I had this idea that if you had a small village in Suffolk which decided to have an African Famine Week, they might imagine that the climax of their week raising money for Africa might be to invite a cricket team from Brixton to come and play. So, it's a comedy with a dark undertone and we follow what happens when a team called the Brixton Conquistadors travels and, almost like Arthurian Knights of the round table, quests into the heart of middle England to play a cricket match in a small village where the people have never, ever, seen such a rag-tag bunch of no-goods. And so it's basically England meeting the West Indies in a small English village.

CW: The importance of cricket to West Indians in England is enormous. The lack of success of the West Indies team of late reflects itself in Afro-Caribbean . . .

CP: Disaffection. [laughs]

CW: [laughs] . . . Disaffection . . . And I remember in the eighties when we were all conquering. And they actually invented rules at the grounds to keep West Indians "in their place," so to speak. Is the influence of cricket on the Afro-Caribbean people in England dying?

CP: It's changing, that's for sure. Actually, those were my earliest memories in England, in the early sixties, listening to the radio. The names are legendary. Kanhai, Seymour Nurse, Sobers, of course, Wes Hall, Charlie Griffiths. These are legendary names to that first generation of people who went over in the fifties and early sixties. The pride in that team who came to England in the sixties was then repeated in my generation. The pride that we felt in Clive Lloyd's team, the Greenwich, Malcolm Marshall, the Richards team was for the second generation, my generation, profoundly important too because we were still grappling with an England that was marginalizing us and these guys strode to the wicket like Greek gods . . . and won. We're in a new era now where a third generation of West Indian, or black Briton, has emerged whose affection for cricket is somewhat muted, in common, I would say, with the way in which white English affection for cricket has become somewhat muted. So, I think that cricket as a whole within England has declined, but within the Caribbean community there's less of a necessity for cricket as a sort of signifier of achievement. There are now other avenues open and not so much a sort of quietly desperate glance towards the West Indies cricket team as a form of self-affirmation these days. One can get that in soccer, you can get that in music, you can get that in other areas now, so I think this new generation are not leaning too heavily on cricket.

CW: Is there a new generation in England of Caryl Phillipses?
CP: There are! Which is good! There's a new generation of people writing. They're writing about a much more multi-cultural, a much more cosmopolitan England than the England that I grew up in. It's an England in which there's much more synthesis between the Indian, the Pakistani, the West Indian, the Greek, the Cypriot. It's an England which is becoming fully fused in a sense with not just the influence of Caribbean identity, but all sorts of identities. England has become much more open. Perhaps the best known of these new writers is a young woman called Zadie Smith. There are other people coming through and they're all losing a sense of affection for, and dependency upon, the Caribbean. The Caribbean has receded two generations back into their memory and they're able to root themselves in England without having to make self-defining trips to the Caribbean. These days I meet young people all the time in Britain who come out to St. Kitts, or out to Jamaica, or Trinidad, or Barbados, but don't feel any sense of stirring in their souls. They can't wait to get back to Hackney, or to Tottenham, or to Hounslow, or Shepherds Bush—they don't feel the same passion that I felt twenty years ago.

CW: Let's turn for a little while to music. Music has had an enormous influence on you. Particularly soul music and jazz. And, two of your works, of different kinds, have been a documentary on Curtis Mayfield for television and an essay on the death of Marvin Gaye. Would you like to tell us a bit more about those?
CP: Well, I think it goes back to growing up in Britain during the seventies. At

that time I looked for people who could help me to understand what was happening amongst my generation, you know, what was happening on the streets. I
wasn't going to find any clues to that in the work of V. S. Naipaul, for instance. I
mean, he's a Caribbean author, sure, but he's a Caribbean author whose sensibility
was such that he was never going to help me understand what was going on with
the police, what was going on with unemployment, what was happening in terms
of migration, what was happening in terms of social insurrection. So I looked to
the United States and to what was happening in black American society. And it
seemed to me that the people who had the strongest narratives and the most profound insights were people like Stevie Wonder, Marvin Gaye, and Curtis Mayfield, artists who were writing music that was not just passionate, but music that
actually was incredibly socially engaged. So, I guess that, as a young kid, part of
my education was listening to that type of music and trying to understand it all
by some process of transatlantic exchange. Curtis Mayfield may be singing about
what's happening in Chicago or Marvin Gaye could be singing about what's happening in Washington, but I was able to relate that to what was happening in
Brixton, or what was happening in Notting Hill, or what was happening in Leeds.

CW: Caz, as we wind down, you have traveled the world. You have written about
Europe, you have written about Africa, you have written about the Caribbean.
You've taught, or lived, in India, Sweden, Ghana, Poland, Canada, Singapore, the
United States, Barbados. You now spend most of your time between Britain and
the United States. Give us your frank opinion of, what we refer to, as "the quality
of life" of St. Kitts as compared with the rest of the world. Because sometimes
we're very ambivalent. We know the enormous advantages we have living in a
little island like this, but sometimes we feel that our size is a disadvantage, which
it is. Where do we really stand in the world terms of the "quality of life"?
CP: Well, in terms of the quality of life, physically, I think there's obviously something good going on here because I keep seeing people from Europe and from
Canada and from the United States who want to come and retire here. Or, want
to come and work here first, or want to come on vacation here. So, physically, the
quality of life here seems to me to be in excellent shape. I mean, maybe a few too
many cars—it's become almost impossible to park. I'm not used to traffic jams
in St. Kitts, but, you know, I suppose that's progress, and it's come about because
of the importation of particular types of cars. But what really counts in terms
of quality of life is intellectual quality of life, what really counts in a society is
the ability of a society to be critical of itself, the ability of a society to analyze itself honestly. And that sort of takes me back to what I was saying to you about my

fear of Americanization because one of the problems in American society is a lack of analysis. You watch CNN, it's about information. The screen is almost crazily dancing with information. It's almost as if it sets up a visual image that obfuscates any attempt at analysis. And I find, teaching my students in New York, that the most worrying thing about the modern worlds is the lack of a historical sense of self. St. Kitts always had, I think, a profound sense of its own history, because it's a constructed history—whether you're from Europe, whether you're from Africa, you're here on somebody else's soil, and you've had to construct a history, a past, a story which explains how peoples from Europe came together with peoples from Africa, here, on somebody else's soil. American history, or American analysis of self, is not as profound as Kittitian analysis of self has been. I actually think that a Kittitian or a Caribbean analysis of self, and of history, has been far superior to that in North America. But that's changing, and if we, in the Caribbean, and we specifically in St. Kitts, lose the ability to analyze ourselves, lose the ability to criticize ourselves, and become content with just sound bytes, and information, and headlines—which is happening—then I think the society will be in trouble. There's a profound need for stations like this, there's a profound need for independent newspapers, there's a profound need for independent forums where one might exchange thoughts. And maybe now more so than ever before.

CW: You have a new novel to be published in April 2003 called *A Distant Shore*, does it have a Caribbean background?

CP: Not really, actually. It's mainly about . . . well, I guess the clue is contained in the first three words of the novel, which are "England has changed." It's really about what is happening in Britain today, a Britain which is postcolonial, but stubbornly pre-European. And it's about an African migrant who's escaping from a war-torn country in West Africa who—in common with many, many African migrants, and migrants from the former Eastern Europe—is traveling illegally into fortress Europe to try and make his way across Italy, Germany, and France, to the channel, and then get across the channel into England. What is happening in England is seen through the eyes of this African refugee who winds up in England, penniless, homeless, and disorientated, and he has to try and orient himself in this new England. This new England seems to me to be incapable of finding a coherent role in the world at the moment, hence the sight of Tony Blair following George Bush around as though he were his butler.

CW: You wrote the screenplay for *The Mystic Masseur*, which is an adaptation of the novel by V. S. Naipaul, which was released earlier this year and has had excellent reviews. Any other films, any new films in the works?

CP: There's always something going on. I'm going to do another film for the same company, for Merchant Ivory Productions and, I'm trying to write a new film at the moment for the BBC, a feature film. But the thing about writing films is that you never really know whether they will come to fruition. It's a very good process for a novelist to be involved with from time to time, not just because of the audience that you can reach with a film, but because it's sometimes good to collaborate, it's good to get out from the isolated desk. I asked Merchant Ivory Productions, who did *The Mystic Masseur,* which we shot all on location in Trinidad, to put some money into a foundation for Caribbean film. Maybe we can build on whatever small success that film had and generate some funds so that another Caribbean novel can be shot on location here. So, I'm actively trying to do that with them.

CW: And what of the future?

CP: Well, more of the same. More writing, more traveling. The thing about writing is that there's no real career structure as there is with other jobs. You can sense with other jobs that you're ten years from retirement, or twenty years from retirement. You can trace the parabola of how the job has moved from your first day to where you are now and where you might end up. But writing is a strange process. You just keep going forward, and as long as you have something to say then you'll find a way to say it. And I've still got plenty to say, so that's all that matters. Sometimes I look out at the golf course at Frigate Bay and I wish I had nothing to say, so I could go out there with Larry Rawlings, or whoever, and hit golf balls all day, but, sadly, there's only room in life for one obsession.

CW: Well you've certainly done extremely well at your obsession, Caz. It's been great having you on WINN FM. And bringing to our listeners a little bit about your life and your perspective. We thank you very much for taking the time out of your busy schedule. We look forward, hopefully, to seeing the documentary if it is made available here. And, also some of your other works. And we hope that you will get the higher profile that you deserve here in St. Kitts, and that people become more conscious of what a great Kittitian you are. So thank you very much for joining us today.

CP: Well, thanks for giving me the opportunity to talk, Charles.

You were listening to Mr. Charles Wilkin, QC of the law firm Kelsick, Wilkin, and Ferdinand speaking to Mr. Caryl Phillips, a Kittitian who's an award-winning novelist and highly respected English professor, playwright, film producer, and screenplay writer. Mr. Phillips is in St. Kitts filming a documentary on his life.

That documentary is being produced by Granada TV and Bravo TV for broadcast next year in Britain and the U.S.A. Mr. Phillips's new novel *A Distant Shore* is to be published in April 2003.

Transcription done August 22, 2003.

A Conversation with Caryl Phillips

Jill Morrison/2004

From *ChickenBones: A Journal* (November 2003) and reprinted in the *Dublin Quarterly* 1 (September 2004). Reprinted with permission of *ChickenBones*. Interview conducted in New York City.

Caryl Phillips won the 2004 Commonwealth Writers prize for *A Distant Shore*. The 2004 PEN/Faulkner Award for Fiction finalist also for *A Distant Shore*. The 1993 Booker Prize shortlist for *Crossing the River*. He won the Martin Luther King Memorial Prize and the Malcom X Prize for Literature for *The European Tribe*, and 1992 Sunday Times Writer of the Year. Caryl Phillips was born in St. Kitts, grew up in Leeds, and now lives in New York.

Q: *A Distant Shore* is your seventh novel, the latest addition to a body of work that *Time* magazine recently called "one of literature's great meditations on race and identity." How does this novel further these themes in your work?

Phillips: I think the more you write and publish, the clearer it becomes just what your territory is. I'm more concerned with "identity" than with "race." The latter is just one component in the former, along with religion, gender, nationality, class, etc. This is obviously a novel about the challenged identity of two individuals, but it's also a novel about English—or national—identity.

Q: Unlike your previous novels, *A Distant Shore* is set in the present day. Did specific news events compel you to write a contemporary novel?

Phillips: There was no specific news story, but one couldn't help but be aware of the debate about asylum seekers in Europe during the past few years. I noticed that a lot of the pejorative language used to describe them was similar to that applied to immigrants of my parents' generation. I've always felt that I would write a contemporary novel when the right subject-matter presented itself. And, of course, the right characters. I am still deeply committed to the notion of "history" being the fundamental window through which we have to peer in order to see ourselves clearly.

Q: One of the book's main characters, an aging white Englishwoman named Dorothy, seems lost in her own country, like she doesn't know the rules anymore now that immigrants are so much a part of her daily life. Why did you choose to give her one of the major voices in the book?

Phillips: Well, she demanded attention. The complexity of her life, and the corrosion that she was suffering, drew me in. A supposedly quiet, almost anonymous, life, yet one filled with drama and internal anguish. Like so many people out there.

Q: The other major perspective in the book is that of Gabriel, a black African man who journeys to England to escape horrors in his homeland. You've travelled to Sierra Leone, officially the poorest nation in the world and also one of the most violent in Africa. Is this character based on people you met on that trip?

Phillips: No, I went to Sierra Leone after the book was published in England. I didn't base Gabriel's character, background, or journey on any particular African country. However, I did have in mind, Rwanda, Liberia, the Congo, and Sierra Leone. I have travelled pretty extensively in sub-Saharan Africa, but I've (wisely, I think) tried to avoid war-torn zones. But one reads, listens, observes.

Q: Dorothy and Gabriel form an unlikely friendship. What does their relationship signify about cultural shifts in England?

Phillips: Well their friendship is tentative, full of anxiety, riddled with doubt, self-doubt, and conducted under the full and judgmental scrutiny of people who are quick to condemn. This being the case, I don't think there has been much cultural shift in England. People continue to be upright about miscegenation of all kinds—sexual, religious, class "transgressions" are still frowned upon. It's still hard to be friendly to the "other" in many parts of England.

Q: The book is structured chronologically backwards so that readers learn immediately of Dorothy and Gabriel's friendship, and are then taken back in time to learn how their very different lives came to intersect. Why did you decide to use this format?

Phillips: It just seemed to be the best way to tell the story. I wanted to give out the idea that this cautious friendship was actually forged by degrees; painful degrees, as two people from very different backgrounds tip-toed towards each other.

Q: Early on the story, Gabriel is murdered by a group of white teenagers after he settles in their town. Why did you choose to end his life this way?

Phillips: There is still a lot of racial violence in English life—both officially and unofficially. The statistics for racially motivated murder—or hate crimes—in

England are shameful. It seems to me quite likely that a man such as Gabriel, in a village such as the one described in the book, might conceivably meet such a tragic end.

Q: You grew up in northern England, where you were one of the few black people in a white working class town. Have you been back to your hometown to see whether it has changed?

Phillips: I've been back to Leeds many times. The city has changed enormously. It's now economically buoyant, confident, and even trendy. There's a lot of night-life, the club scene is good, and there is great shopping. The place is buzzing. However, the part of Leeds where I grew up is still struggling with social problems, including racism. There are still few non-white faces, and those that walk the streets are subjected to much abuse. So, like most cities, the place has a public face and a private face. The public face is certainly rosier than it was when I was a boy, but the private face is just as sinister.

Q: Films like *Bend It Like Beckham* and *East Is East* show an England where kids mix among different cultures more easily. Is this the case?

Phillips: Well, both films didn't shy away from an albeit tentative exploration of racial problems. However, London (the setting for *Bend It Like Beckham*) is not a city that you can use as a barometer for the rest of England. (It's similar here in New York—i.e., it's difficult to make any judgments about the U.S.A. based on NYC.) Kids in the inner-city areas do mix more readily than those from rural or suburban backgrounds, but the vast majority of England is not "inner city." And even in the inner city one still sees many problems.

Q: Would these films even have been made when your parents came to England from the West Indies four decades ago?

Phillips: No, they would not have been made. Nobody was interested in the story of people who were "foreign" in that most obvious way—i.e., racially different. These "new" films are about people who are curiosities, i.e., British and "foreign." The fact that these youngsters are both participating in, *and* standing apart from, British life makes them objects of curiosity. Their parents—my parents—were always configured by the politicians and the media as a "problem that might one day go away."

Q: After you graduated from Oxford, you met the writer James Baldwin, who greatly influenced your life. Tell us about your friendship with him. What writer would have the same impact on a young black man today?

Phillips: I was very lucky to get to know a writer as generous as James Baldwin.

He was the first writer I knew, and I watched him "handle" the pressure of being a public figure. It's not something I would wish upon any writer! I very quickly understood how important it is to guard one's privacy and keep focused on the work. I understood that the literary world is subject to the vagaries of fashion, the poison of money and celebrity, and all of it means nothing when set against the legacy of the work. I'm not sure who would serve such a role in Britain today. There are young women like Zadie Smith who I'm sure are encouraging a new generation to think of literature as an option.

Q: You've written about the recent fortieth anniversary of Martin Luther King, Jr.'s "I Have a Dream" speech. What is the significance of this anniversary to you?
Phillips: The anniversary reminds one of how far we've fallen in such a short space of time. From the eloquence of that speech to a president who debases his office with utterances such as "Bring them on." Language is vital and precious. It dignifies us.

Q: In addition to books, you've written plays, movies (Merchant-Ivory's *The Mystic Masseur*), TV dramas, and radio scripts. Are you working on a film project now?
Phillips: I'm not very good at talking about what I'm working on. I am doing a film for the BBC, but who knows if it will come to fruition.

Q: You constantly travel around the globe, have ties in England, St. Kitts, and New York. Getting to your own issues of identity, who do you root for during the Olympics?
Phillips: I root for individual athletes. I'm very suspicious of nationalism of all kinds, including sporting nationalism. However, when it comes to team sports, I suppose I still have a soft spot for England. It's where I grew up and went to school. But I've lived in the United States for nearly fourteen years, and I feel increasingly a part of this society. I can see how I've changed and grown here, and I'm happy to have had this opportunity.

Fighting the Silence Born of Injustice

Gail Bailey/2005

From *Canvas Magazine*, April 16, 2005. Reprinted with permission of the *New Zealand Herald*. Interview conducted in Florida.

Caryl Phillips, winner of last year's Commonwealth Writers Prize for *A Distant Shore*, has been around the world and back. In conversation with Gail Bailey before his visit to New Zealand, he talks about his unlikely journey from a tiny island in the Caribbean to becoming one of Britain's most acclaimed writers.

When I ask Caryl Phillips what it means to be from St. Kitts, he answers my question with several of his own. "I often think about what would have become of me. Would I have been one of the people working in the bank? Would I have left, gone to Canada? What would I have done?" This kind of speculation seems only natural from a writer who has dedicated most of his career addressing the ramifications of migration, whether it be forced—the transatlantic slave trade, the Holocaust, or fleeing from civil war—or strategic—leaving the Caribbean for Britain, the U.S., or Canada.

It is the latter migration that has had a major impact on Phillips. Born in St. Kitts in 1958, his parents left for Britain when he was only a baby. Growing up in Leeds in a mostly white environment meant living with the divide of two cultures: "One felt very much split. Sometimes you felt British and sometimes you felt from the West Indies. It had a profound effect growing up with a sense of two identities. It meant that you never really felt comfortable. You always felt slightly like a bit of an observer."

Being on the periphery of society, though, has served Phillips well. His novels, beginning with *The Final Passage* (1985) to *A Distant Shore* (2003), capture the disturbing complexities of the lives of characters that are often at odds with a social order that resents their very presence. Characters like Solomon in *A Distant Shore* bear the brunt of a tragic history that inevitably consumes them. The past usually gets repeated—in an almost endless cycle of injustice and persecution.

A refugee with mysterious African origins, Solomon, befriends Dorothy, a

139

distraught, middle-aged white woman. Set in a small English village, the novel tells the story of this unlikely friendship only to unravel the secret pasts that have forced Solomon and Dorothy to seek refuge in Weston—a town that wants nothing to do with them. It is only when tragedy strikes that their true selves are revealed—a little too late, though. While together, Solomon and Dorothy remain silent about who they really are. Yet, it is a shared sense of unbelonging that is the basis of their relationship.

At a time when most of Europe is attempting to restrict its borders, *A Distant Shore* has received high praise and insightful criticism of its portrayal of a Britain that is downright bleak.

"England has changed. These days it's difficult to tell who's from around here and who's not. Who belongs and who's a stranger. It's disturbing. It doesn't feel right." These are Dorothy's words at the opening of the novel. Her anxiety, says Phillips, is a reflection of a wider state of "panic" that is presently being experienced in England.

"I deliberately wanted to choose somebody who you might not think that she would never feel not at home in Britain because she looks so much like she belongs. It happens very quickly and it needn't happen in just British society. I think in many societies, the movement from inside to outside doesn't necessarily have to do with race. It can have to do with class, money, religion, with anything. One minute you thought you were standing right at the centre of society and that everybody respected you and the next minute you realise that actually you're marginal."

When one talks to Phillips about the state of British society or Europe in general, it is evident that it is a subject that heightens his own problematic relationship with a country that is home and, yet, not home.

"One of the things if you grow up in a society feeling voiceless—which I grew up in Britain definitely feeling—you then begin to question why that is and then, of course, you hit against the injustice of the Atlantic slave trade. And then you begin to realise that the silence, that profound silence about who you are and what you are does come from an injustice. Therefore, for me, writing a character, writing a novel, telling a story is very much about combating that silence. It's very much about giving people a voice to tell their own stories, so that they can write themselves into history."

I talk to Phillips via telephone from his new home, the U.S. When we spoke, he was in Florida, "escaping winter." New York, though, is where Phillips spends one semester teaching at Barnard College.

"A great mongrel city, New York is an easy place to feel at home," says Phillips.

"In New York hardly anybody asks you where you are from. Everybody feels like that is such a redundant question. I think that's a sort of relief for somebody with multiple identities."

When he is not teaching, Phillips spends the rest of the year writing and attending writers' festivals and conferences. He has homes in St. Kitts, Britain, and the U.S.

It was fifteen years ago that Phillips was first in New Zealand for Wellington's Writers Festival. It was also the 150th anniversary of the Treaty of Waitangi. Phillips says that it was an interesting time to be in New Zealand. "I did get a sense that there was a literary and political culture here that maybe I hadn't quite anticipated how vigorous it would be."

As part of Auckland's Writers and Readers Festival, Phillips will discuss *A Distant Shore,* as well as the overarching themes of his novels: the troubling complexities involved in the postcolonial condition, which inevitably encompasses the search for place and belonging.

Phillips's narratives are just as complex, known for their highly fragmented and elliptical nature. Novels like *The Nature of Blood* (1997) alternate between several narratives and characters, from Eva who is recently released from a concentration camp to the plight of an Othello-like character in sixteenth-century Venice.

Time magazine's Donald Morrison calls Phillips "a writer of wrongs" and J. M. Coetzee says that Phillips's novels bring to light "what we like to forget." However, Phillips is hesitant over the phone to agree with such "grandiose" descriptions, but he does acknowledge that throughout the past twenty years of his career he has been trying to articulate the issues of certain sectors of society that have been completely ignored.

"My reason for writing a book is obviously, yes, I want people to read the book and to feel differently about the world around them at the end of the book . . . In other words I'm saying that I want to change the way society is, because I'm not comfortable with the world around me. Yeah, I could be a politician, a social worker, a doctor, but I think writing a book is a very practical way of doing that. It's just that the effect takes a long time to be seen, to be seen in a writer's lifetime. I do believe that books change people's mind about things, and that's why so many writers all over the world are jailed by oppressive regimes."

Addressing the nature of seeking refuge and all the horrors that lead people to seek asylum is not just topical but important to write about, says Phillips. He has spent a considerable amount of time in West Africa and throughout the years has been to a number of camps and detention centres.

News reports about increasing right-wing sentiments regarding asylum seekers incenses Phillips, especially since he has known people who have tried to seek asylum in Britain. He says that essentially "we have a responsibility and we've always had a responsibility to take in people who are suffering, to take in people who have been persecuted, to take in people who are not able to contribute to their own society and would like to contribute to our society. That's just a basic, human, familial responsibility. What you're doing by not taking people in is in many instances leading people to be persecuted. And you're actually doing something damaging to your own society, for it is often the immigrant who is the engine, the person who regenerates, stimulates society."

In one of his recent projects, Phillips has written the foreword to *Book of Voices*, a short story anthology that seeks to raise awareness of the plight of writers in Sierra Leone. He was there in January to be a part of fundraising for the reestablishment of Sierra Leone's PEN office that had to close during the country's civil war.

By the end of our conversation Phillips's voice sounds tired and sombre; he is recovering from the flu.

It is not lost on him that the crossings that took him from St. Kitts to Britain and now to the U.S. is one that he could not have ever predicted. "The nature of my journey often seems to me increasingly improbable. When I was born in 1958, there was no expectation that any of these things would happen to me. It seems very fortunate, but it also seems like a very unlikely journey."

Dancing in the Dark: Caryl Phillips in Conversation with John McLeod

John McLeod/2005

From *Moving Worlds: A Journal of Transcultural Writings* 7.1 (2007), 103–10. Reprinted with the permission of *Moving Worlds*. Interview conducted in Leeds, England.

In 2005 Caryl Phillips published his eighth novel, *Dancing in the Dark*. Set chiefly in New York City in the early years of the twentieth century, it engages movingly with the life of the Bahamas-born Broadway entertainer Bert Williams who in his heyday was one of the best-known of such figures appearing on stage in a number of music-hall revues and performances. Much of Williams's fame rested upon his difficult decision to wear blackface on the stage; Phillips's novel explores the emotional and psychological consequences of the nightly action of "blacking up," and engages with the larger problems of race and identity which both defined and degraded Williams's increasingly troubled, and troubling, life. Brilliantly imagined and superbly crafted, it is a poignant portrayal of Williams's life and loves—his partner George Walker, his wife, his father—often told through their voices.

On 11 November 2005, Caryl Phillips returned to the city where he grew up and visited the School of English, University of Leeds, where he read from his novel and showed a short film made by Williams which depicts him in blackface performing one of his famous comedy routines. After his reading Caryl Phillips discussed with me his new novel, and the issues it raises, before taking questions from the audience.

John McLeod: Caryl Phillips, thank you for such a generous rendering of the book for us, as well as for some wonderful readings. If I can begin by picking up on a phrase that you used a few minutes ago where you talked about Bert in terms of "self-erasure." That seems to me a particular challenge for a writer: to explore or to imagine the life of someone who spent a lot of his life trying to rub himself out or being erased by others. It is a challenge which perhaps only the novel or the novelist can meet. I was wondering if you felt that, as a consequence of writing this novel, Bert had swung more into view or if he remained an elusive figure?

Caryl Phillips: Well, he swung more into my view and, hopefully, he will also swing into the reader's view, but I think that the historical character is still a source of contention. For instance, there are two biographies of him. Actually, there was a kind of biography published a couple of years after he died. It wasn't really a biography, but more a collection of anecdotes that was put together in the States in about 1924 (he died in 1922). There was a first real biography published in the 1960s and another in the 1970s. Now the most fundamental fact that a biographer has to pin down is where somebody was born, and these two biographies both arrived at different places: one said Antigua and one said the Bahamas. Now that, to me, is mind-boggling that anybody could write a biography and get the place of birth wrong! But that doesn't speak to any incompetence on the part of the biographer; that speaks to the degree of difficulty in getting behind the façade of this character. So when I say that he swung into view for me, yes, because the actual facts, the nuts and bolts, of his life were not as important to me as the emotional texture of his life—as the heart of the man, the loneliness of the man, the courage of the man. Yes, I am 99.9 percent sure he was born in the Bahamas, and I think that is an established fact now, and I know where he died, and I know certain things about where he performed, and I know the Shaftesbury Theatre where he performed in 1904, and I know that he performed in Buckingham Palace for the King, and I know he taught Edward VIII to dance—the King who abdicated—so there are certain facts that I know. But I am not a biographer, so it is paradoxically a sort of gift to me as novelist when a character remains so elusive because it clears a whole space for me to imagine. Furthermore, he also had no children, so I'm not really afraid of litigation at the moment! I'm not really worrying about some great-grandson who is going to come knocking on my door and say, "You clown, you got it absolutely wrong about great-grandfather Bert!"

The truth is, I can't imagine ever writing a novel again about a real-life character, because I'm not sure that anybody would ever fascinate me so much yet present me with the gift of having no baggage, if you like. The epigraph to the book is from an interview that Bert Williams did—I'm not sure in what year, but I think about 1911—and the epigraph is "Nobody in America knows my real name and if I can prevent it, nobody ever will." This quote is from the period when he was on stage with Ziegfeld Follies, he was the only black guy on the programme, he was the most famous entertainer in America, and yet he didn't want anybody to know anything about him. I think the question that bugged me was—why? Why? I think, to be honest, it was shame. I think a deep sense of shame.

JMc: From my reading of the novel, Bert struck me very much as both a lonely character having to deal with a great deal of pain and shame, but he was also, the word you used there, a very courageous man. He was trying to make his way and manoeuvre in a very small space at times, and often at the mercy of other people's fantasies, other ways of seeing him. Do you think it is fair to call him a courageous man?

CP: I think he was very courageous. You know it is not very pleasant to think of somebody, one hundred years after the event, participating in an act that suggests it is not only degrading to him, but degrading to a whole group of people. So it may seem somewhat peculiar to hear me describe him as courageous. But he was a performer and he began his performance career at a time when that blackface image was acceptable. And it was not only acceptable, it was probably the only way that a black person in America could have any access to utilizing his performance skills because a black person was not going to get access to the big stage unless he bought into that deal. Blackface became problematic as the times and the mood changed. The somewhat rusty hinge of the nineteenth century creaking into the twentieth was traumatic for African-American life; so many things changed, and a lot of transformation was generated by the publication of W. E. B. Du Bois's *The Souls of Black Folk* in 1903. The book changed the perception of what a black person was in America for a whole range of people, and at precisely this time Williams is performing in blackface. He has a choice: take it off and his career is possibly over, or keep performing and risk alienating a whole bunch of people. At what point does an individual artist have to turn his back on his art for the sake of an imagined community? In other words, when does an individual artist have to take on the burden of responsibility? Now that is a question which has plagued many, many performers, black, white, of all creeds and religions.

In the twentieth century this question has become a particularly difficult burden on the shoulders of African-Americans, and it remains so to this day. One of the reasons that I wrote this novel now is because of hip hop. Because this same debate surrounds rap and hip hop. At what point do you tell an individual, "You are letting the side down"? "You should not do that because your responsibility is not to your art, your responsibility is to your imagined community"? Bert Williams had to tread this line a hundred years ago and deal with all these same debates, and I think he dealt with them with courage and dignity. It doesn't mean that I agree with him or that you as a reader will necessarily agree with him; but the struggle that went into grappling with this debate and what it cost him . . . personally, that's what really interests me.

JMc: I think that was one of the striking features of the novel, certainly for me, the personal cost and the difficulty of maintaining or forming key relationships with his wife, with his father. It seems to me that the novel was exploring all kinds of personal and difficult issues around the issue of race, and the ways in which race can complicate and problematize some of the most intimate aspects of a person's life.

CP: I think that is absolutely correct. And it makes it increasingly difficult if that person has a public life too. Again, you see this right through the twentieth century. You see it in the life of a person like Jackie Robinson, the baseball player. You see it in the life of Nat King Cole. You see it in the life of Marvin Gaye. Personal problems played out publicly—and all of these people died very young, by the way, from stress-related causes, as Bert Williams did. It is not an easy thing for anybody to do, to have to balance out the difficulties of personal responsibility with one's loyalties to a group. But to have to play that out in the public glare and to have to grapple with a stereotype which is imposed upon you, which can stifle you as an artist or stifle you as an individual, is a tremendously difficult thing to do. And he dealt with it. I mean he dealt with it and he didn't deal with it. But he did the best he could in the circumstances. As I said about before, I'm a novelist so my job is not to judge him. I don't have any judgement about the guy. My job is to understand him, and that is actually much more difficult than judging him.

JMc: This might be an appropriate juncture to think about what one might call the public life of the novel. You talked earlier about the shameful episode of Caribbean or African-American people wearing blackface in the early twentieth century. I know you've spent a lot of time giving readings and talks about this book in the United States recently. I guess the question I want to ask is how has this book been received by its American audience and its American readers?

CP: Well, I think it opens up, or has opened up, a lot of conversations that I think people find uncomfortable. One of the conversations is about the relationship between West Indians and black Americans, which is a very vexed and difficult relationship. You know, so many black Americans in public life in the United States on close examination are not African-Americans. Colin Powell, the basketball player Patrick Ewing, Harry Belafonte, Sidney Poitier—they are all West Indians. And that is a very difficult relationship because there is a deep-seated animosity, and there has been for many years, between the black American community and the West Indian community. Because Bert Williams was a West Indian immigrant, this is central to his dilemma, and it's also central to a lot of the criticism he received, because people were saying, "This crazy West Indian, he doesn't really understand *us*. Does he not understand that he is making us look bad? He doesn't get it because he is from the Caribbean." This ongoing debate has surfaced at most places in the United States where I have recently done a reading or given a talk.

The other thing which crops up is the idea which we've touched upon already; in other words, the whole question of representation today. People have been very quick to ask me about hip hop and what I think about the responsibility of 50 Cent, or what I think about the responsibility, or the irresponsibility, of some rappers. At what point do they have the right to say "motherfucker this," or be misogynistic, or be homophobic? And at what point does Bill Cosby, or whoever, have the right to say "why don't you shut up, 'cos you're making us look bad"? So that debate has cropped up many times.

And then I think the third thing is a slight anxiety and unease about why Bert Williams has been so profoundly forgotten. Why is it that people don't know about him when, if you were in New York, or if you were anywhere in the United States, one hundred years ago, every single person, black, white, whatever you were, you would know who Bert Williams was. You would absolutely know. I'm trying to think of somebody who is as famous as him today . . . probably Will Smith. Everybody in America knows who Will Smith is. Bert Williams was more famous than Will Smith is today. Why has he been forgotten? People are trying to grapple with that, and then trying to grapple again with the morality of just forgetting the whole disturbing issue of minstrelsy. So those are the three areas that have come up pretty consistently.

JMc: We like to think, particularly in a university context, that we are much more aware of, and we know much more about, the contribution of black peoples to history and culture in America, Britain, and Europe. But I wonder if there is a kind of complacency for some people about that? We like to think we know, but actually there are so many stories that have been forgotten; so many other figures like Bert Williams that we need to know much more about or need to remember.
CP: There are loads of them. I mean my own interest in reclaiming history obviously comes from having grown up in this country where I was surrounded by stories of people who had been forgotten. Luckily, now, there are any number of good writers, historians, and academics who are trying to address this, trying to reexamine the gaps, crevices, fissures in British history. But my own interest in looking at these gaps or omissions comes directly out of having grown up in this country and having been educated in this city with a sense that my own story, my own narrative, was not included in anything. Therefore I have always

been vigilant about such omissions and I continue to be vigilant. The fact that this book is set in America doesn't really matter. It's about the same basic process: being vigilant about one's history and suspicious of the narrative that is presented to me as the narrative of the people, as the narrative of the region, as the narrative of the town, as the narrative of the country, I'm suspicious of it all. And therefore I'm going in and occasionally trying to do a little historical repair work. The impulse comes from having grown up in Leeds—in England.

JMc: I was just thinking there about the comment you made before—about the sense in which one of the things you were doing in writing about the past, was also perhaps addressing some of the issues about the present: hip hop and 50 Cent, etc. One of the major characters in this book, for me, was New York City; and I wondered if there was a similar relationship you're exploring in the novel between the New York of the past and the New York of the present?

CP: It's a good question. New York is close to me because New York is my home. New York City is where I've lived for many years, and one of the reasons that I've chosen to live there is because of an idea that is very central to American life, which is the act of reinvention. The ability to reinvent yourself is theoretically at the heart of the American idea, so that you arrive in the United States, albeit at Ellis Island usually, not an auction block in Charleston—that is an altogether different act of reinvention. But you arrive and they spell your name wrong and you say, "No, you bonehead I'm from Palermo and this is what I'm called," and they still spell it wrong and, by the time you reach Lower Manhattan, you are called Jim and that's what you have to deal with (you know that *really* you are called Giovanni). The ability to participate in this act of reinvention—which is part of the excitement and part of the thrill and the mythology of America, that you can arrive and begin again—continues to draw countless hundreds of thousands of people there all the time. In a sense that is the strength of the place.

Now, a hundred years ago, New York City was full of small theatres, vaudeville theatres, where people performed sometimes twenty-four hours a day. These theatres were all over New York City, and this was just before cinema. Remember cinema was born in New York City, not in California—it went to California for the weather, but it was born in New York. And what were people doing? They were pretending to be somebody else. So, the Jews were pretending to be Irish people, the Irish were pretending to be Germans, the Germans took the piss out of the Chinese, the Chinese people took the piss out of somebody else. And that's what they did, they pretended and played out the act of becoming Americans, which is why vaudeville happened, which is why the theatre happened, which is why films happened, which is why Chaplin, who was an immigrant himself, and came over, and immediately began to play at being somebody else.

The only people who couldn't play were black people. But then the only people who have never been able to play in American life are black people. Because they are the only people who never wanted to come there in the first place. Everybody else wants to be in America. There is not a single African who said, "Yeah, OK, I'll be a slave." Not one. No African got to the auction block in Charleston and said, "Yeah, OK, call me Kunta Kinte, that's fine." Because they didn't want to be re-invented. They were perfectly happy where they were in what became known as Dahomey, or Benin, or Ghana, and they didn't want to go anywhere. So the act of reinvention for African-Americans has always been problematic; it has always been difficult, and it continues to be difficult to this day.

Seizing a sense of identity continues to be an absolutely central conceit of being an African-American. Why do you think 50 Cent is called 50 Cent? That isn't his real name. Why do rappers reinvent themselves? Because it is the form which allows them to play at becoming the types of Americans that they want to be. Now a lot of this takes place in New York City because New York is the crucible of American immigration, and these acts of reinvention, as treacherous and as difficult as they are, are still being played out on the streets of New York. So, for somebody who is interested in identity, somebody who is interested in race, somebody who is interested in migration, it is an interesting place to be. It's not the only place to be, but it is a particularly interesting place to be, I think.

JMc: Do you think that Bert Williams found in New York City in the early twentieth century a space where he could engage in self-invention or reinvention or take some kind of control over his world? It seems to me that there is a relentless sense in the book that he is always being reflected in somebody else's mirror.
CP: That is a very good question. Where could he go to chill?

JMc: He goes to the bar, and that leads to my next question. He likes a drink and a lot of the characters in the book . . .
CP: It's a total coincidence John! No, he took solace in escaping himself and he found a great deal of peace and a great deal of tranquillity by being by himself in a bar that he considered to be safe. It is on the corner of 135th Street and 7th Avenue. It's called Metheney's. He took solace there. The key is that it was a safe bar.

One of the most famous stories about Bert Williams is the one that W. C. Fields told of Bert and himself going into a bar in St Louis, Missouri, in about 1914. Again you have to remember that at the time Bert Williams was the highest paid entertainer in America. The two of them go into a bar after a show and W. C. Fields says, "We'll take two whiskeys." The barman says, "OK," and puts one whiskey in front of W. C. Fields, and Fields says, "I said two whiskeys," and the barman says, "Well, there's your whiskey, but for him a whiskey is $50"—which would be the equivalent of about $1,000 today, more than that probably—and Bert Williams reached into his pocket, pulled out $500 and said, "I'll have ten." So he had ways to deal with it. But that is why I said Metheney's was a safe bar because it wasn't just *any* bar, it wasn't just drink that was providing solace, it was *that* bar that was two blocks, less actually, from his house. He died a very lonely and isolated and difficult death, but then many American performers do. If it is not whiskey, then it's drugs, or, if not that, then hypertension.

So, was there a place? I don't think so. The poignant thing is that he did find some degree of solace, however transitory, right at the end of his life with his wife. I think there was some kind of reconciliation but by then it was too late.

JMc: This is my last question before opening up to the audience. Bert Williams is a figure who has clearly inspired you, as a writer. Do you think he could be an inspirational figure for people at the beginning of the twenty-first century?

CP: Well, I hope so because part of the problem of living in the Western world now, certainly part of the problem of living in the United States and being a teacher in the United States, is that people have no respect for the past. People have no understanding of their own history and, in fact, they think it's cool not to. What do you say when you insult somebody? You say, "You're history!" They have that much disrespect for history, but if you don't understand where you've come from and you don't understand the difficulties that have preceded you, then you have no idea of *how* you got to where you are. And if you don't know where you are, then you don't know where you are going. So you have to be cognisant of history—you have to learn that the anxiety that is currently ensnaring your life, the predicament that you find yourself mired in, has usually been tackled by somebody else, and one might learn something by being aware of what happened before. So, I think that understanding the past is always important. What one learns from it, or what the reader deduces, or what I deduce as a writer, is kind of up for grabs. The engagement is what matters.

Caryl Phillips

Michael Krasny/2005

From KQED's *Forum*, October 17, 2005. Interview courtesy of *Forum*, a production of KQED Public Radio, San Francisco, California, Michael Krasny, Host.

MK: Bert Williams was known as the first popular black stage performer in America's early twentieth century. This Caribbean-born vaudeville performer at one time was just about the highest paid entertainer in the United States and was best known for playing a burnt-cork-faced, dim-witted, so-called "coon." He was in a comedic talent league that included Buster Keaton, Charlie Chaplin, and W. C. Fields; Fields, in fact, called Williams "the funniest man I ever saw and the saddest man I ever knew." Caryl Phillips's eighth novel, *Dancing in the Dark*, focuses on Bert Williams. Born in the West Indies and brought up in England, Caryl Phillips won the 2004 Commonwealth Prize for his last novel, *A Distant Shore*. He was a Guggenheim Fellow and a recipient of the Martin Luther King Award and also the James Tate Black Memorial Prize. A fellow of the Royal Society of Literature and a professor of English at Yale, Caryl Phillips was described by the *New York Times* as one of the great literary giants of our times, and he joins us in the studio for this morning's opening hour *Forum*. Good to see you again. Welcome.

CP: Thanks a lot.

MK: Glad to have you here. Well, let's begin by talking about why you did this book. Williams was certainly an extraordinary figure: first black mega star, earliest black entertainer here in the United States to make it to the top. But you've done nonfiction, and you did a lot of research for this book. Why novelize his life?

CP: Well, I think because the material which was available for me to work with largely represented the public face of him. It was reviews of him, the occasional interview, playbills, scripts of his stage performances, but I couldn't really find any of what I tend to call the "confessional material": the diaries, the letters, the journals. And having scrambled around for a number of years in various libraries in New York and individual collections, I realized that there just wasn't much of this material. So it left a sort of gaping hole in the life where a novelist could imagine those quiet, interior moments that perhaps might cause a problem for a biographer but create a challenge for a novelist.

MK: The challenge being the inner-life, as you suggested, and maybe getting behind the mask?

CP: Well, I think that's exactly the area that a novelist would find the most compelling area to go—those quiet private moments when a person who is so public and so well known spends time sitting in a bar with a drink by themselves, sitting in a dressing room before a performance, late at night by themselves wandering the streets. These moments seem to me to really get to the essence of who this man was. Not the public moments, not the moments where he's been interviewed, not the moments where he's in the spotlight, but those moments where he's questioning himself.

MK: Let's talk about those private moments or that inner-life, but before we do, just to give the listeners a sense of who he was and maybe to localize it a little bit, Williams was probably best known for, well, the "Two Coons Act" that he did with George Walker. They met here in San Francisco in fact.

CP: They did. They met on Market Street in 1893; they were both very young, both teenagers and down on their luck. George Walker was busking with a banjo in a corner; he'd come from Lawrence, Kansas, and he was trying to make a living here in San Francisco. Bert Williams had grown up in Southern California and had gravitated, or migrated, north to San Francisco. And the legend is that George Walker was busking on a street corner, and Bert Williams saw this colored boy who was roughly his own age and they started talking. They realized neither of them were doing very well and they thought that maybe if they teamed up things might improve, and if they didn't improve, at least they'd have each other for company.

MK: Playing "African Savages" was one of the first roles that they moved into?

CP: Well, very soon after they met, they were asked to impersonate Africans. There was a great exposition that was happening here, and, the "African Savages" who were traveling from Africa to come and be exhibited—a somewhat bizarre, anthropological gaze was about to be focused on them—were late because the boat was late. And so what the actual producer of the exposition did was he rounded up as many young, colored performers as he could and paid them to impersonate Africans. So that was Williams and Walker's first real performance role here.

MK: When you think about impersonating Africans, the irony is that the success that Williams had was related to the minstrel shows. The burnt cork and all is what white people were doing, and suddenly a couple of black entertainers are doing the same thing but doing it in a way that was . . . well, let's talk about Walker and Williams and what they did on stage.

CP: Well, what they did on stage, which was so disturbing, was that they pandered to a certain stereotype of what black people in late nineteenth-, early twentieth-century America were supposed to be, which is lazy, slovenly, not too bright, very much in touch with their emotions and not too much in touch with their intelligence. That's one stereotype and Bert Williams played into that. George Walker, on the other hand, played into another African-American stereotype which is a guy who is a dandy, a bit of a showoff with earrings, diamond-tipped walking cane, flashy clothes, gold teeth, a womanizer, and sexual athlete. So they found themselves playing to these very deep stereotypes of what black people were, which were really the main performative strategies which were available to black people at that time. And both of them, if you like, kind of perfected those stereotypes.

MK: And really, in a sense, those stereotypes were precursors, at least in terms of what Williams did, for figures like Stepin Fetchit and Amos 'n' Andy, even though around the same time we had Paul Robeson and Charles Gilpin who were real figures coming to the fore.

CP: Well, actually, it's interesting you should mention that. I think Robeson and Gilpin really came into their own in the second decade of the twentieth century, and in fact, towards the end of the second decade of the twentieth century at the time when Bert Williams's career was winding down. He died in 1922. After this I think there was a huge shift in society's attitude towards African-Americans, both in larger American culture and certainly in the performative, commercial American culture. In 1903, when Du Bois published his book *The Souls of Black Folk,* things shifted. And then another shift happened at the end of the First World War when African-Americans returned to the U.S.A. having had the experience of going to France and having experienced what it was like to step out of American society. The emergence of Robeson and Gilpin was part of a larger awakening of African-Americans to the idea that—you know what? We're no longer going to buy into these stereotypes. The pain, of course, for Bert Williams was that for most of his performative life he felt trapped by this role that society had created for him.

MK: We're talking to Caryl Phillips. His book is *Dancing in the Dark*. Again, I want to get into that sense of pain as you as a novelist have conceived it here because it's so central to your novel; however, you mentioned Du Bois and, of course, this is also around the time the great debate between Du Bois and Booker T. Washington was going on. Booker T. Washington actually credited Bert Williams, as I understand it, with doing more for the race than he had done?

CP: Which, I think was a somewhat tongue-in-cheek comment. I think he meant it, but in the context, I think he was trying to say that the performer, the person who occupies the commercial stage, has a great responsibility when it comes to affecting people's perception of the black community. I was reading the other day about Harry Belafonte and the work that he did in the middle of the twentieth century working with Martin Luther King. I think there's always been a kind of very tight, symbiotic relationship between African American performers and social change. We can look at the comments that the rapper Kanye West made only last month about what's happening in New Orleans. I think there's always been a tremendous amount of pressure on black performers, and, in some cases, the performers have felt an obligation to be more than just performers and to be representatives of the race. A lot of the criticism which fell on Bert Williams's head was that he wasn't prepared to be a representative of the race and he acted very much as though he was above it. "I am just a performer. Stop trying to make me a representative of all African-American people." He took a lot of heat, frankly, for his position.

MK: At the same time you certainly give us a picture of a man who probably was terribly inwardly tortured, at least as you imagine him to be, by the sense of this stereotype that he had to perform in a kind of unwritten contract with the largely white audiences he had to perform for, particularly on Broadway. In fact, he performed in England in front of King Edward. But the theaters had what they called, as I understand it, "Nigger Heaven" (Carl Van Vechten has a novel by the same name) where blacks would sit by themselves—

CP: —in the balcony.

MK: —in the balcony. And so he was performing essentially for white people.

CP: He was, and his career was essentially funded and made possible, certainly towards the end of his life, by the support of white producers such as Florenz Ziegfeld in particular because Williams was the only black member of the Ziegfeld Follies. That dilemma, that idea of having a career which was largely dependent upon white America's patronage, but at the same time not wanting to be alienated from the black community, if you like, I think did cause him a tremendous amount of pain and a tremendous amount of inner-torment. And that's largely what the novel is about. It's about that hidden battle, that hidden sense of almost unimaginable pain that this man suffered from being, on the one hand, the most visible and the most public black person in America and, on the other hand, a growing sense of vilification and criticism which he was enduring from the black community because of the way in which he was comporting himself vis-a-vis white America.

MK: And from his father. You get into that whole relationship. Did you base that on biographical knowledge again, or . . .
CP: Some biographical knowledge. His father was, like him, a West Indian. Bert Williams was born in the Bahamas in 1874 and he came to the United States in 1885 when he was eleven years old. The father was very determined to make a better life for himself and for his family; hence, the migration. But like many West Indians who came into the United States, he was a man of great pride and dignity and he wasn't really prepared to buy into what we could call the racial climate of the time. He felt completely insulted by what he encountered in Florida, so that's why they migrated west to California in the hope of finding a less preju-diced and a less hostile environment here in California. Well, the truth of the matter is, his father remained a man of great pride and what I was able to discover about the father was that there was a huge schism between himself and his son Bert Williams when the father realized that the son was "blacking up" in order to perform.

MK: The sense of how you, again, imagine what he goes through in terms of his pain and torment is also really linked to a great deal of shame, and the irony of it is that this is a very dignified man as you portray him.
CP: Not only a dignified man, he was an extremely intelligent man too who spent great portions of his adolescence reading. He was very well known in Harlem at the height of his fame for being a man who you could find in the local bar on the corner, but he would always have a book. A man who was very proud of his Af-rican heritage, and a man who really had a great pride in who and what he was. He hoped to go to Stanford when he was seventeen, but the family couldn't af-ford to send him to Stanford. That was his great ambition, to be an engineer and to study at Stanford University. But, not being able to afford the fees, he actually became a waiter, a singing waiter, at the local hotel. But he still remained an avid reader despite the traipsing up and down the country playing the lumber camps and so forth. And right to the end of his life he was a great scholar, a dignified man, and a reader.

MK: You also give us a portrayal of what James Weldon Johnson called "Black Manhattan of Harlem"; in fact, in the prologue you go to some length poetically to talk about how Harlem doesn't know Williams anymore. Williams is a presence who is absent or an absent-presence or something like that.

CP: Well, I think that doing the research for a novel is always actually more pleasurable than actually writing a novel. You feel like a sort of literary detective unearthing this, that, and the other, and often you can get stuck on the research because it's fascinating. I think you're absolutely right to identify James Weldon Johnson and his book *Black Manhattan* because that was one of the central texts which I returned to time and time again for research. But I also live in New York City, so I was able to go and walk those streets. I was able to look around at Harlem today and think about what Harlem was like a hundred years ago, and that's really where the opening pages of the novel come from. This idea of the absence of Bert Williams on those streets, not just the physical absence in terms of people having no consciousness of who this man was, but the physical decline of the place, the lack of pride in the place compared to what Harlem was like a hundred years ago. I know there's a great push today to re-gentrify Harlem, if you like, but a hundred years ago the crime, the drugs, and so on that are now problems in many parts of New York, not just Harlem, they weren't there, and, as I say in those opening few pages, this would have disappointed a man as dignified and as proud of his African heritage as Bert Williams.

MK: So your walking around Harlem was a catalyst in addition to the research. I mean was it a necessity for you to pull the narrative out by actually doing that? By going into Harlem?

CP: Yeah. There's so little of Bert Williams's private life that I could get hold of, so actually walking those streets, standing outside of the house which he spent a greater part of his life—the house in which he died—on Seventh Avenue at 135th Street, just standing outside of it and trying to imagine what it was like, and what the house would have looked like a hundred years ago, these quiet acts of literary osmosis which I was engaged in, they became as much a part of the research as sitting in the New York Public Library leafing through old programs and reviews. I mean it was very poignant, to be honest, walking around the streets of Harlem. Today the guy's house is a hairdresser's, and I knew if they went in and asked them who Bert Williams was, they probably would not know that this was home to the most famous black entertainer in America. In a sense, that broke my heart too.

MK: Quiet acts of literary osmosis—that's a memorable phrase. Thank you for that. Do you know, just jumping ahead, Spike Lee was in town last week. You know his movie about the minstrels?
CP: *Bamboozled?*

MK: Yeah.
CP: Yeah.

MK: What did you think of it, just out of curiosity? It's also about masks and playing these stereotypical roles and needing to do that for performance sake.
CP: Well, I enjoyed it because I think he's hitting on something that's very important in contemporary African-American life, and which was important in Bert Williams's life too, which is the degree to which African-American performers are subject to certain stereotypes and how, in a sense, the crisis of race and the problem of the color line has always been played out in American life on stage. The first film ever shown in the White House was *Birth of a Nation.* The first great successful commercial musical in this country was *Showboat.* The first and, to some extent, most important talkie was *The Jazz Singer.* You know, all these issues around race and transformations have been played out at crucial times in American history on stage and on screen. So I enjoyed *Bamboozled* because it seemed to be, in a contemporary sense, putting its finger on that problem again.

MK: It also makes me mindful of a famous line of Richard Wright's which I'm sure you know, "The Negro is America's metaphor." In a sense, the Bert Williams story tells us a lot about America. I know you come to America as an immigrant, so you have that advantage of seeing it through foreign eyes at least before you became settled in New York City and so forth. But there is a sense of history kind of in an archetypal way speaking about America, isn't there?
CP: I think I do know that Richard Pryor quote—

MK: Richard Wright.
CP: Sorry, Richard Wright quote. You know I was thinking as I was listening to you, I was thinking of Richard Pryor's album. I was listening to it this week. He made an album some years ago, *Bicentennial Nigger,* which is very, very biting, but it gets right to the heart of the issue of how central the figure of "the Negro" if you like is to American culture, American entertainment, American politics. Looking at America through the prism of race is one way of really approaching the central dilemma of America, but Richard Wright also understood this. As did

another American writer: James Baldwin, who again seemed to fully understand the importance of America coming to terms with her history only once she'd come to terms with the fact that the only group of migrants, the only group of arrivants, who came to this country but who did not want to be here were Africans. Everybody else came to America to reinvent themselves, to become somebody else. That's the great strength of this country. The great platform upon which this country has assumed a certain moral authority in the eyes of the world has been its capacity to allow an individual to reinvent him or herself, including renaming themselves. But for African-Americans that act of transformation has been particularly difficult because African Americans didn't want to come here in the first place. And I think this problem still haunts America to this day.

MK: It's also the idea of invisibility that Ralph Ellison works with. When you mention Baldwin, I'm thinking about something that Baldwin said that W. E. B. Du Bois said as well and that is the idea of dual consciousness—that somehow it's not who I am, it's what I am. I'm seen always as what I am.
CP: Right.

MK: I'm invisible if I'm seen at all.
CP: Well, it's the fact of being able to participate in a society and sometimes feeling of it, and sometimes feeling not of it, and never knowing when the change is going to descend upon your shoulders. Looking at America, as Du Bois said, through a veil so that sometimes you feel that you're participating and sometimes you feel that people are just observing you and you're somehow held in kind of performative bondage. I still think that this is a problem today in American society. I still think that for many, many people, particularly African-American people, this notion of participation and invisibility remains a difficult area of negotiation in their daily lives.

MK: Again, if you just joined us, we're talking with Caryl Phillips. His new book is called *Dancing in the Dark*. It's all about the great entertainer Bert Williams; it's about race and the paradox of being black in America, and being at the top as he certainly was in the entertainment world. It's an amazing story. Actually, somebody should do this as a movie, don't you think?
CP: I would love to see Bert Williams's life on a larger stage. I think it lends itself very clearly to being filmed.

MK: Jamie Foxx comes to mind. . .
CP: Exactly.

MK: I'm speaking this hour with Caryl Phillips who has written a book called *Dancing in the Dark* about a great so-called Negro entertainer Bert Williams. This is an opportunity to talk to a man whom "Booklist" describes as in a league with V. S. Naipaul and Toni Morrison—that's heady company. Nice to be put in that company, isn't it, Caryl?

CP: Yeah, it's very flattering to be put in that company of those two writers. I've always admired their work and I've also admired the sort of over-arching arc of their careers, particularly Naipaul whose politics I've not always agreed with, but I've loved the way in which he's balanced fiction and nonfiction and made a career out of treating nonfiction as seriously as his fiction.

MK: Do you treat nonfiction as seriously as you treat fiction?

CP: Absolutely. There are very few writers these days who write nonfiction and fiction. I mean in America one thinks immediately of someone like Mailer who is a very serious fiction writer and a very serious nonfiction writer. And you know, in Britain, maybe Graham Greene who approached both with the same degree of seriousness of purpose. But, I've always regarded nonfiction, serious nonfiction, not an interlude or a break from my fiction, but an equally complementary aspect of what I do.

Caryl Phillips: Reflections on the Past Twenty-five Years

Renée Schatteman/2006

Printed with permission of Renée Schatteman. Interview conducted in Florida.

RS: We're here today on March 31, 2006, with Caryl Phillips. Caryl, thank you very much for offering to do this interview. To begin, if you consider 1980 as the starting point of your career with the production of your play *Strange Fruit*, then 2005 would mark your twenty-fifth anniversary as a writer. In those twenty-five years you've produced eight novels, three works of nonfiction, three stage plays, and a number of screenplays. To start with a very large question, what comments would you have about what: you have accomplished in this period? Is it what you hoped to do and what you imagined, or has it taken you quite by surprise?

CP: When I started out writing, I was trying to write a play, but in the back of my mind I wanted to one day write a novel. So, having completed the play, and having seen it produced in 1980, this was a great sense of achievement for me. And then publishing a novel in 1985 was also a great sense of achievement. I remember feeling that I'd done it—what I wanted to do. I wanted to be able to write a novel and have it deposited in the library—the Bodleian Library in Oxford. That was what I'd always felt would constitute the idea of success. As a student I wanted to be a part of the Bodleian library on a more permanent basis. To be honest, since then I haven't really had that same feeling of achievement. Those were the two moments when I really felt that I'd done something. Everything else since then has been part of a larger project, if you like. It's not about one book; it seems to be a larger project which, maybe somewhere down the line, I will feel a sense of resolution or a sense of peace about.

RS: So, if you think in terms of the larger project, do you see connections between your various texts, and do you feel as though you are building upon ideas as you move from one text to another?

CP: I don't feel connections between the texts in the sense that one is necessarily leading to the other. However, I think that I'm increasingly aware of the fact—

how could I not be as a teacher at a university—that other people are beginning to see connections between the texts. But for myself, I see with increasing clarity the territory that I'm trying to work in. I'm never sure if it's going to be a book of nonfiction, or if it's going to be a book of fiction, or if it's going to be an essay or a collection of essays. But I'm increasingly aware of the territory that I'm trying to cross and re-cross. In that sense, inevitably the texts do speak to each other. Or maybe I should put it this way: they will eventually all speak to each other. But right now it's pretty much a matter of just staying on the scent of whatever it is that is pulling me forward.

RS: The year 2005 also saw the publication of your eighth novel, *Dancing in the Dark*. This novel could be seen as a work that's primarily about the United States and about an American story. In your other novels the U.S. is often featured as part of your triangular concerns between Africa, Europe, and North America, but none of your earlier works allowed the U.S. to be the setting for your primary story. Does this reflect a new development in your relationship with the United States? Are you more rooted here? Has your new position at Yale University, for example, given you a new sense of home? So perhaps speaking from the location of *Dancing in the Dark,* you can talk about your feeling about being here within the United States.

CP: Well, I think the announcement that the book was on its way obviously set up question marks even before it was published. My British publishers were wondering why suddenly there was a book about an American. And my American publishers said, "Finally you're writing something about us." In a practical sense, it was the first book of mine that had been initially edited in America. Knopf sent the galleys back to England. I encouraged this, not so much because the novel was set in America, but because it had American spelling and it would have been a nightmare to work with copy editors in Britain and insist on the American spelling and so on. So, the fact that it is an "American" book did open up a few new doors and few new conversations. But the other central dynamic of the book for me—sitting right here, where I wrote it, in this room—revolved around the fact that the man, Bert Williams, was a West Indian. So, the novel is very much about Bert Williams's and his father's difficult communication as people of the African diaspora within the United States of America. I think it would have been perhaps a slightly different book, and perhaps a project that wouldn't have fascinated me so much, if this had been a book about a man who was born in Philadelphia and his parents and grandparents were also born in Philadelphia. I think I would have still been interested in the notion of minstrelsy, and how one negotiates identity in America as a person of African origin, but I think the fact that Williams was a migrant from the Caribbean who then had to negotiate issues of diaspora and identity to live within the United States placed the novel, if you like, in conversation with my other works in a much more powerful way.

RS: Right. And it also suggests, as is the case in many of your books, that place is not necessarily situated in one location, and that one place has implications of other places and other stories that interact with that place.

CP: Yes, these questions of place, location, belonging, and stories that are set in a particular geography, but which have a resonance somewhere else—these questions are true for much of what I've written, and certainly true for *Dancing in the Dark*. However, I'm sure some people will still look at it as an American novel. I'm sure some people will say, "You know he came lo America to teach in 1990, so he's been here fifteen going on sixteen years now, and finally he's comfortable writing about America." But it's not that. Obviously, it would be wrong to say there's not an element of feeling more confident about my own standing and my grasp of this country, because you don't spend so long in a country, and you don't teach so many generations of students, without your knowledge of that country appreciating pretty significantly. But I had written about America before I came here. I'd been interested in America before I came to this country. However, if you stay in a country for a certain amount of time, you eventually unearth local stories. You know that section in *Crossing the River* called "West"? I don't think if I had still been in Britain I would have come across that story. So, you spend time here, you find you understand the place a little better, but this does not necessarily indicate any deeper meditation upon, or claimed ownership of, narratives that reflect the American condition. However, you know more, you hear more, you see more, and it adds to, rather than displaces, that which you already know.

RS: I'm wondering how it is to experience America, at this moment, under an administration with such a conservative ideology where, for example, in this past week the House of Representatives made a suggestion to make illegal immigration a felony. I'm thinking back to the fact that you talked about leaving England partly because of Margaret Thatcher and the climate that she had created there. Is it difficult writing about the ideas that you write about in the climate that you find in the United States right now?

CP: It's a good analogy. I'm glad you brought it up because people in America and people in Britain have said to me, "How do you cope living in George Bush's America?" And I say, listen, I coped with Mrs. Thatcher's Britain until finally I was fed up, and I had had enough of it. A lot of the central political ideology in this country is, to my mind, as nauseating as it was in Britain in the eighties under Mrs. Thatcher. The difference is in Britain in the eighties, I was a very visible person because there were not that many second generation black people in literature, or in arts, journalism, and the media generally, so there was a real pressure upon me to comment, to participate, to be a kind of "rent-a-quote." Here in the United States of America, I feel the same degree of kind of outrage and annoyance about a lot of what happens, but people are less likely to approach me for my ideas on what George Bush is saying, or what Condoleezza Rice is saying, or what happened in the Senate the other day. There are countless numbers of people who have a much higher profile and who are much more deeply invested in this country than I am, so they become the people who you see popping up on the *Charlie Rose Show*, or Bill Maher's show. It's never going to be me because there are others. So, in a sense, it makes it slightly more comfortable for me to get on with my job. I always find it quite difficult to get on with my job in Britain.

RS: So, perhaps the detached mode that helps you as a writer is something that you can participate in more here?

CP: Yes, I feel that very much in this country. It's very rare that anybody will ask me what I think of the United States. Obviously, in a larger interview, they might mention something in the same way you've done about immigration, but there haven't been that many cold calls from the *New York Times*. However, it's different in Britain. Even yesterday, V. S. Naipaul said something about how awful Henry James was as a writer and how Jane Austen was an amateur and how England is going to the dogs—and the *Guardian* immediately emailed me and wanted a quote. So, even now, after all these years of being here and imagining myself to be relatively invisible in Britain, there's still that sense that when somebody does something, I'm expected to comment on it. In this country, I can pretty much just get on with what I'm getting on with.

RS: If you would indulge another question about *Dancing in the Dark*, one thing that sets this story apart from your recent novels is that you seem to be concentrating on one person's story as opposed to looking at multiple people and putting their stories side by side. Did the experience of writing about one character affect your relationship with the character since you sustain that relationship throughout the whole text? And did it affect the way you presented the story?

CP: No, I think my own perception of it is that, to some extent, I was writing about four characters. I was writing about Bert Williams, and George Walker, and the two wives. Clearly, Bert Williams was the central, driving, determining character. The novel opens with him and ends with him, so in that sense, yes. But

I still felt that we were getting glimpses into other people in a way which wasn't too conventional, if you like. So, yes, it was much more of a novel in which you looked through the one prism and could follow one character, but there was still some leaping about and jumping off here and there into other people's interior lives.

RS: A lot of people have asked you about the development of your ideas and your form in your career as a novelist, but I'd like to ask you about your sense of your growth as a nonfiction writer. Do you see any significant differences in the three works of nonfiction that you've published? Do you feel as though you've come to understand the nonfiction form more fully as you've advanced in your career?

CP: Yes, I understand it much better now by virtue of doing it more often, particularly during the last few years. I have no idea how many uncollected essays I now have, but I guess I have another book sitting out there which differs somewhat from the style and the format of *The European Tribe*. *The European Tribe* is much more discursive and much more about traveling with an open mind, if you like, and just recording what happens and reflecting upon it. Through the mid to late nineties, when I first began to write nonfiction for the *New Republic,* I sort of went the other way and started to do nonfiction essays, many of which are collected in *A New World Order,* which involved a terrific amount of library research and a lot of reading. I'm thinking about the essays on people like C. L. R. James, and V. S. Naipaul, and Eduard Glissant. These are nonfiction essays that really have an argument and structure to them, whereas the earlier work in *The European Tribe* is much more attuned to discovery. And then I think, probably from about 2000 onwards, when I started to write for the *Guardian,* I wanted to somehow blend the style of *The European Tribe* which was a travel-oriented narrative with something which involved library research and argument. I first went in that direction in *The Atlantic Sound,* where I was trying to both hit the road, if you like, and take a library with me. That felt a lot more comfortable to me. When I wrote *The European Tribe,* I wasn't in a university atmosphere. I was doing some short book reviews for newspapers and magazines, but I didn't really want to write anything that was an extended critical response. My writing was very much about me trying to find out where I was, and, at that stage in my life, I felt reasonably comfortable placing myself in the narrative. I was, in that sense, fearless about saying, "Here I am." I think once you've published a few novels, and you become more aware of the weight of what you're saying, and critical feedback, where to place the "I" can become very difficult. That's why it was great for me to start writing for the *New Republic,* because I was writing scholarly responses that were sort of subjective but they relied greatly on objectivity and research. But, as I said, after 2000, I wanted to rediscover the personal pronoun again but not lose that analytical ability. So that's very much what *The Atlantic Sound* was about—trying to reclaim, re-find, and rediscover the personal pronoun but not to lose the critical angle. I think the uncollected essays, that will hopefully be someday published in book form, speak to this synthesis.

RS: Your fiction is very research-oriented as well. There you take the personal story line of someone's life, but you interweave so much historical perspective into it that shows the large body of research that you've done. So do you think that your fiction and nonfiction are moving toward each other?

CP: Yes, I think they are moving closer together. Nonfiction, to me, has always been an important part of what I do; I've never considered it to be a secondary thing. The manuscript that is sitting right here on this desk is a nonfiction book, but I have spent exactly the same amount of time going through the details, checking facts, and re-imagining situations as I would with a novel. So, it's the same process. They are coming together for me much more fully, which is why I don't separate them anymore on the inside flap of the jacket. I just say to the publishers, listen, let's not bother dividing them up. Of course, that can be a problem for the marketing department, but that's okay because I'm not in the marketing department.

RS: They talk today about how we're entering into the age of memoir and nonfiction and how works of literary value are not selling nearly as well, so I like the way that you complicate that by saying that the two genres really have a lot of interconnectedness.

CP: First of all, I think that it's true that literary fiction is not selling. I don't think as many people are writing literary fiction, but it's also not being published as it once was. The figures speak for themselves. There's no way that the publishing industry in any country, whether it's the United States, Britain, Australia, or Canada, can look at the number of literary novels that were published five or ten years ago and say that they publish the same amount now—they just don't. Are people reading the same amount? No, they're not. People are reading, but they're reading other material; they're reading airport lounge material. So, people are writing a different type of fiction or they're writing memoir, or popular nonfiction. You're left as a writer with the same choice that faces many people when fashion changes: you either adapt or you die. That's what will happen to literary fiction. If I was the type of writer who only had an interest in high literary fiction, I think my writing career would be in danger, as is the case for lots of writers. But, you know, luckily I'm interested in other narrative forms, genuinely interested and not interested out of a sense of panic. However, I have no desire to find myself in the airport lounge along with thrillers and romance novels. So we'll see what happens. I do know that there has been a radical change even in the twenty-five years that I've been writing and publishing. There has been a change in the way in which people view literary fiction, let alone in the way people consume it. And some of it has to do with declining attention span because of technology. People don't seem to have the time or the interest to "lose" themselves in fiction. However, there's no point in moaning and wringing our hands and saying, "We're writers; we have to write." Well, you know what? The world goes on.

RS: Well, some would argue that it also has to do with the fact that people are so desperate for the truth since they aren't necessarily being given the truth by authoritative powers around them that they're grasping for whatever appears to have the mark of authenticity to it.

CP: Yes, I think that that's true, actually. It seems to me that people are interested in information. They're interested in being given facts, but they want them in a palatable, quickly accessible, easily digestible form. You see this when you turn on the T.V. The T.V. news bears no relation to what T.V. news was like a generation ago, because it's now just fact. Up the side of the screen and along the side of the screen—there's all this stuff coming at you! We turn on the computer now, and it's not a reflective zone. It's not a place to sit down and mull things over; it's asking you to make decisions all the time; it's all about information and about getting the facts; it's all about "Google" this and "Ask Jeeves" that. Literary fiction doesn't work like that. It's not about information; it's not about facts; it's about ambiguity; it's about *not* knowing; it's about exploration; it's about taking your time. It's in trouble because it's the antithesis of what the prevailing mood is in society. You see this in the theatre now. A lot of the plays that are on Broadway—new plays, even off-Broadway plays—don't have intervals anymore. They are now eighty minutes long, so you pay $120 to go see this half-a-play. I don't mind because most of the time I don't like them, so the fact that you're back on the street by 9:15 is okay by me. But, it's not like going to see a Eugene O'Neill play, or a Tennessee Williams play, or an Arthur Miller play where you've got an act and an interval and another act and sometimes another interval. These days it's all to do with speed—let's get to the conclusion! Well, literary fiction, more so than the theatre, is about taking your time, is about not making judgments, is about providing room to allow your readers to dwell in the gray areas. It's not spoon feeding, and it's not tying it all up in a neat bow and a ribbon saying this is where you're supposed to be. I'm afraid that every time I turn on the T.V., whether to watch the news, or whether to watch *Law & Order,* or whether to watch *American Idol*—which I don't watch!—it's all about speed, and judgment . . . judgment. Everything ends in judgment and it's so crass: you press a button and you vote the person off. And it's really good if they cry and you don't give a damn about what they feel. This is the culture and yet at the same time you're trying to write a novel about exploration and feelings and patience. I'm sailing upstream with half a paddle basically.

RS: But there's the hope that we have become so glutted on all the information around us that we need to cleanse our palate, and there's the underlying belief that we know that that information ultimately isn't foolproof either.

CP: Well, that's what I believe. That's what I have to believe; otherwise, I'd fall into despair. Obviously, what I hope is that not everybody out there is interested in an "easy-access-narrative fix." I try to maintain some hope, and I don't want to sound like an old fuddy duddy, bemoaning the good old days already. I don't know what will happen, but a lot of what will happen, I'm afraid, will depend on the publishing industry. People will always write literary fiction if people are prepared to publish it. As long as those doors are open, then good writing will be done. Sometimes I sit around with other writers talking about these issues, but the feeling at the end of the day is that there's nothing that you can do about the situation except go on and write new work. And if it reaches an audience, that's fantastic. If it has difficulty reaching an audience, it is either because the public doesn't want to know or because the publishers are not pushing it enough. Either way you simply carry on and have a think about what to do next.

RS: I know that you've talked about how you get a great deal of comfort in talking with other writers who are of a similar ilk. I just wanted to push you on that a little bit. Do you think there is among intellectual writers like Michael Ondaatje and Salman Rushdie a new movement moving towards almost a transnational, transcultural way of thinking of the world? I think, truthfully, you've done this in your own writing for a good long time and may have been ahead of the group on this. Anthony Appiah has just put out a book about *Cosmopolitanism: Ethics in a World of Strangers,* suggesting that we need to be very careful about the way we've always placed so much emphasis on difference and that, in the long run, differences can be very dangerous as they have given rise to sectarian violence or also imperialism. I'm just wondering if among this cohort of writers that you have befriended, you think there's a similar strain that runs through your work along these lines.

CP: I think one becomes friends with certain people because you recognize something in them, or something in the way in which they live their lives, that strikes a chord with you. Back in the 1980s, there were people that I was aware of who I subsequently became friends with, including writers like Rushdie and Ondaatje. I considered James Baldwin to be a part of that group, not only because he lived in France but he obviously slipped the noose of identity a couple of times, not only with reference to his own sexuality but with his mobility, and his visibility as a black man in the South of France. There were people who it was very difficult to attach a label to and make it stick, and I found a sense of comfort in reading their work. I found a sense of comfort in the fact that I was able to become friends with some of these folks. As I look around the world today, though, I think that there are many, many more such writers who are not only living a kind of transnational life but are writing across transnational borders with a great deal more ease, and without apologizing or explaining why. It just seems to me that this issue has become far less problematic, and today it is easier to be that kind of writer, or to be that kind of an individual. I began as a writer feeling very much like a minority, like a sort of weirdo. But my own background and interests, which necessarily cross borders, now feel almost mainstream in a certain way. I'm happy that the world seems to have turned and embraced some of the issues that have preoccupied me for a long time. However, I don't think the world has fully embraced everything by any means, which is why there is still a lot of writing to be done. I don't think it's quite acceptable to be so vigorously transnational yet, but at least the issues are there to be debated and they are not resisted with quite as much hostility.

RS: Do you think there are women writers who fall into that camp too? The names of male writers come to mind more readily.

CP: Apart from the obvious sort of American hyphenated models such as Bharati Mukherjee and Maxine Hong Kingston, or Cristina Garcia, I think there's an older generation of people like Katherine Mansfield, Christina Stead, Jean Rhys, or Ruth Prawer Jhabvala. Ruth is a German Jewish girl who grew up in England and went to India and began writing in India and now lives in New York. Her work—short stories, novels, and the film adaptations for Merchant Ivory—is very much concerned with migration and culture clashes. Anita Desai is very much concerned with these issues too. These are women whose lives have crossed borders, and then within the United States there are a number of women writers who are easily described as transnational and hyphenated.

RS: I think what might complicate it is that understandings of home perhaps get gendered differently.
CP: Women writers get treated differently anyway, whatever they're writing about. They're often undervalued and underappreciated by the reading public unless they're writing a particular type of genre, whether it's "chick lit" or romance fiction. A serious women writer is always going to live in the shadow of the surrounding male writers. I mean you see that in Canada where as great as Alice Munroe is, and as great as Margaret Atwood is, when people mention their names there's still a sort of slightly apologetic kind of shrug because they're not Michael Ondaatje or one of the older guys like Robertson Davis. In Britain, I was very good friends with Angela Carter who I think was head and shoulders above any writer of her generation male or female, but she was always in the second paragraph after Martin Amis and Ian McEwan and so on. I'm not passing any adverse commentary on Amis or McEwan, but that's just how Angela Carter was perceived.

RS: Let me move toward concluding here. I wanted to ask you now that you have been selected to have a collection of your interviews included in the Literary Conversation Series published by University Press of Mississippi and will be joining a number of esteemed authors in doing so, what can you say about the interview form and your experience with it? You've been very generous over the years with your time in providing many interviews that show your intelligence, and your wit, and your charm, and I think these interviews offer a great supplement to your readers in understanding your fiction and nonfiction. But I'm wondering what do you get out of it? Does the interview format and your experience with it provide you any further understanding of your ideas, or is it something you see as basically a service?
CP: Well, that depends—there are two types of interviews. There's the sort of interview that you do as part of a book promotion that is short and sometimes it's pleasant because you find yourself clarifying things in your mind, but the basic thrust of the interview is to try to sell the book in some way. I don't really get asked to do these interviews that often because I'm not very good at them. My publishers don't ask me to do too many of those. The other kind is the one where you feel it's like being in the classroom and you've been asked an intelligent question and you have to think it through. It gives you the opportunity to think about what you *really* think about the subject, about an author, about a particular book,

about yourself, about your own development—questions that I never ask myself when I'm sitting at my desk. So those type of interviews I don't mind doing so much because I do feel you sometimes get some clarification as to where you are and what you're doing. Again, not always, but then again not every classroom that you go into do you come out of it thinking that you learned something.

RS: You're just hoping the students did.

CP: You're just hoping they stayed awake! But the longer interview is an interesting form because it allows you to ruminate on certain things. The only other thing I would say about such interviews is that once that rumination is done, the only time I would ever revisit the interview and read it would be if I was checking it for accuracy, which I've done for maybe 30 percent of the interviews I've ever done; either because I have time, or I know the person, or I thought the person did a particularly generous job of preparing.

RS: In many ways you seem to be a fairly private person and yet on the other hand in your interviews and elsewhere you're very open about your intellectual life.

CP: Yes, but people don't know anything about my private life.

RS: That's true, that's true.

CP: I'm doing an interview on Tuesday for a French TV station and they emailed me from Paris today to confirm it. I've had to tell them a number of times that they had better find some place to do this interview because they are not coming into my apartment in New York. I don't let anybody interview me there or in this house in Florida. I know you, so that's fine. But I just figure that people make up what they want to make up anyway, so let them make it up. I'm not going to give them too much information.

RS: It's just an interesting tension of a writer's life that a writer by nature has to be a very private person and yet the job also can thrust you out into the limelight and give you that public attention.

CP: Well, you learn a bit about yourself over the years. To start with, it's exciting when somebody wants to talk to you, it's exciting when somebody wants to write about you, it's exciting when somebody wants to take photographs of you, because all of this has never happened before. Like anything, it's a novelty, and because it's never happened before, you don't know how to deal with it. It's usually only after your confidence is betrayed a couple of times by things you say "off the record" to somebody, that are then published and disseminated, that you realize you have to be careful. Some people don't feel the necessity to be vigilant, and they live out a lot of their private life in a public space. Other people close down absolutely. They won't give any interviews; they won't do anything. I think I try to strike a balance where I remain open to talk to some people, even though I do feel that, particularly earlier on in my life as a writer, people did take advantage. But the choice is there: you close down, and you just say I'm going to be a recluse and not do any of this, or you try to organize yourself to remain open while at the same time you keep a part of yourself locked away. That's the way I've tried to do it. The other big danger in the United States, of course, is that one lives in a culture of celebrity. You know some of my cohorts and colleagues actually enjoy this fact, but to my mind celebrity is the most poisoned chalice of all to sup from. I've learned, I hope, to turn down a lot of things that smack to me to be about personal promotion in the crassest sense. But my publishers have told me that my intransigence has cost me book sales; it has cost me the possibility of developing a new audience, but I don't care because there are some things I know I'm not going to do. Even simple things; for instance, I don't like book parties. I just don't feel comfortable at them because I feel as though everybody's on show. I don't network—that's what they say, "You don't network." But you just have to figure out for yourself what your own personality is like and what you're able to deal with.

RS: Well let me ask you one more question. If we consider this being the midpoint of your writing career . . .
CP: . . . with a bit of luck.

RS: Yes, with a bit of luck. But do you have any thoughts on what the second half of your writing career might bring?
CP: I'd just be happy if there is one. The older you get the more you realize it's just a roll of the dice after a while. You just have to do the best job you can with each book. Here's the thing, you begin writing—or you should begin writing—because you have something to say. If you don't have anything to say, then you shouldn't bother. There are already enough books out there, arid it's a very hard job, so do something else. But you should begin because you have something to say. Certainly I did, and then I made a pact with myself at a certain point that if I had nothing further to say then I'd stop. I didn't want to be like a kind of crazy boxer who keeps stumbling into the ring out of habit and trying to go fifteen rounds with another novel. You have to have something coherent to say. If you have a relationship with yourself and the changing world around you, you inevitably accept that you never really know if what you're going to feel in your life is either urgent or vital from one moment to the next. Things are constantly changing, personally and socially. So will I always have something to say? If the interchange

between my inner growing sense of who and what I am, and the world outside, continues to be dynamic and challenging, and if I'm lucky enough not to get ill, then I will continue to write. What I'll write I don't know. However, I never take it for granted that the energy between my inner growth and the changing world is always going to produce an impulse to write. For instance, from 1997 to 2003 I didn't publish a novel. I could obviously have written a novel in that six-year period, but I didn't write a novel because I didn't really feel that spark. Right now, the situation has changed because I feel like there are lots of things that I want to write, and say, but when I'm done I could be back in that six-year trough, and this six-year trough could last for twenty years. So I just don't know, but right now my mind and heart are full of work.

RS: And you published two or three novels after that six-year period?
CP: I published in 2003 and I published in 2005 and I'm going to publish a book next year too, but not a novel. Right now I feel I've got plenty to say, but I don't know how it will play out.

RS: Well, thank you very much for this time, and as always it's a pleasure to talk with you.
CP: Thank you.

Degrees of Damage: An Interview with Caryl Phillips

Kevin Rabalais/2006

From *Glimmer Train* (2007). Reprinted with the permission of *Glimmer Train*. Interview conducted in New York City.

Born in 1958 on the Caribbean island of St. Kitts (population 40,000), Caryl Phillips moved to England as a child, was raised in Leeds and later educated at Oxford University. In 1985, Phillips published his first novel, *The Final Passage*, which received the Malcolm X Prize for Literature. His other novels include *Cambridge; Crossing the River,* winner of the James Tait Black Memorial Prize and short listed for the 1993 Booker Prize; *The Nature of Blood* and *A Distant Shore,* which received the 2004 Commonwealth Writers Prize; and *Dancing in the Dark.* Phillips's nonfiction includes *The European Tribe,* winner of the Martin Luther King Memorial Prize, and *The Atlantic Sound.* He is also the author of plays and screenplays. In 1993, Phillips was named one of *Granta's* Best of Young British Novelists.

Kevin Rabalais interviewed Caryl Phillips in his home in Midtown Manhattan on July 6, 2006.

KR: Unlike your more recent work, your first two novels, *The Final Passage* and *A State of Independence,* were traditional narratives, linear in structure. Did you have a model in mind for those early books?

CP: In retrospect, compared to my later books, they appear to be linear and relatively straightforward in terms of narrative chronology. But in the early eighties when I began *The Final Passage,* I was conscious that the very first words I wrote were "The end." So even then I was conscious of playing with time and narrative chronology. I knew that you couldn't really tell the story of those Caribbean characters using a traditional, nineteenth-century, Dickensian, naturalistic narrative. As soon as you have characters who migrate, who cross water and become culturally plural and lose something, their dreams and their whole sense of themselves is thrown out of kilter.

KR: What were you learning as you wrote those first two novels?

CP: Like most writers, I didn't have any money. I kept having to break off and write a script for television or do some journalism or something else to make money. So it took a long time. But in that process of taking time off from the novel, I was reading a lot—American novels, British novels; and, specifically, Caribbean novels—because I wanted to get the atmosphere, the flora, and fauna correct. Having grown up in England, I wasn't really able to name the Caribbean trees or describe the sunset properly. But none of the novels I read seemed to give me a structural model. I was stumbling to find my own way to something which suggested a coherent narrative, some kind of structural movement which reflected these people's lives.

KR: What role does reading play in your writing now?

CP: Like most writers, if you write enough, you lose the innocent pleasure of reading. It's a very extraordinary book that shakes you into some world that you remember, perhaps, from when before you were a writer, a time when fiction was magic and could transport you. You're too often aware of the scaffolding behind the story. The type of writers that I read then and the type of writers that I return to now are, for want of a better term, the engineers, people like Faulkner and Marquez, Twain and Conrad. In terms of nonfiction, I return to Baldwin for the narrative attack in his essays. These are not always people I want to read for pleasure, but I read them to try to understand how to move a story, how to get four wheels on a narrative and get it moving. It's very rare that I come across a new book that has something inside the narration that interests me or whose structure interests me.

KR: Are there any writers who have surprised or shaken you lately?

CP: I think that W. G. Sebald is the last author who surprised me. He surprised me because he articulated something which I feel increasingly not just in my own writing, but as a reflection of where I think we're drifting as readers and writers in the early twenty-first century. This is the collapse of the difference between fiction and nonfiction. Sebald seemed to articulate that confusion around fiction and nonfiction and find a form that synthesized the two. The writers that I tended to look at who were very influential to me when I was beginning and, to a certain extent, are still now are people like Baldwin, Naipaul, Bellow, Mailer, and Graham Greene, writers whose careers exist in fiction and in nonfiction. These are writers who seem to place an equal weight upon their nonfiction and fiction, In some cases, like Baldwin, they will probably be best remembered for their nonfiction. But Sebald surprised me because here was someone whose career you couldn't really divide between fiction and nonfiction. J. M. Coetzee's work is also like that, to a certain extent. I think his autobiographical trilogy is a pretty carefully calibrated piece of nonfiction by a fiction writer. In some sense, I think that Coetzee is probably the last writer of pure fiction who surprised me with how he positions himself as a writer and how he negotiates that issue of fiction and nonfiction.

As a young man, I was very attracted to the form of the Polish writer Tadeusz Konwicki's books. His work, like the work of many Eastern European writers and artists, employed narrative strategies that made sense to me. These were writers, artists, and filmmakers who lived in a world where they never knew what was happening from day to day. It was like a bizarre, surreal dream. One minute they were German. The next minute there were tanks in the street and they were Russian. Within their lifetime, they had no idea how to combat this bizarre series of transformations. That's like being a migrant, basically. One minute you're hot, sitting in the Caribbean, and then the next minute you're cold and sitting in London.

KR: After *The Final Passage* and *A State of Independence,* your work took a new direction. The structure of your novels changed drastically. Do the experiments in structure of these later novels have to do with this drifting that you mention?

CP: The structures grew out of the subject matter. To be honest, looking back now, I don't think I would have had the confidence to write books such as *The Nature of Blood* or *Crossing the River* as a first or second novel. With *The Final Passage* and *A State of Independence,* I felt like I had done something that was reasonably conventional in terms of chronology. After that, I didn't want to mimic the form. I wanted to push at the edges of how you tell a story. To find a contentment with an ability to tell a story and then repeat that form, just pour new characters and new plot points and situations into it—it just seemed a little too premature to have found a solution to how to tell a story. I wanted to keep pushing at the boundaries. Luckily, the subject matter that I found myself dealing with kept demanding that I address the issues in the stories with something that was formally more challenging than before. I got a couple of books done, and maybe it was time to spread my wings a bit. But I'm not sure that I would have had the wherewithal or the courage to have done that initially.

KR: In that sense, in terms of the technical problems that each novel presents, does one book grow out of the next?

CP: I always feel that the biggest challenge for me is not "What's the story?" or "What should I write next?" hut "How am I going to tackle the next piece of work?" I've been very lucky in that I've always known that there's a rich reservoir of stories and people floating around that I want to write about. Some are purely imaginary. Others are based on fact. Rather than have a sort of template which I can go to and say, "OK. This is how I tell my story" and then pour the new ingredients in, to me it's always been a challenge of "How are you going to tell this one? How are you going to approach this?" Maybe some people are constantly searching for character or plot or subject matter. But I've been lucky. I've always felt that I've had subject matter that I will get to eventually. It's always there.

KR: How does structure develop for you?

CP: It grows organically. I always ask myself, "What is this book going to look like? What is the shape of it going to be?" I have an idea of what that shape will be, but I never really know until I start. A very concrete example of this comes from the book I'm writing now. To all purposes, it's comprised of three essays. The central essay is about eighty pages long. It's based on the life of a boxer who lived and died in Britain in the mid-twentieth-century. I first came across his story twenty years ago and have spent a long time thinking about him. I finished the essay, and then about four weeks ago I realized that the place he said he was always happiest is a holiday resort in north Wales that he owned for a short time. I knew instinctively that I had to go there. I didn't want to have to go there. I was busy with other things. But I knew I had to write something about it. I didn't know if the trip there would produce just be a few lines of color in the piece or if it would spawn ten more pages, but I went there instinctively. While I was there, I realized that the boxer had three daughters who are still alive. I knew that I had to interview them. That's the real story. Now, the book has been held up because next week I'm going to fly to London and interview them in the hope that it will provide a deepening of the story.

This is pretty much how my fiction goes, as well. My plan with the essay was to write eighty or ninety pages about this boxer's life. But in the writing, you begin to uncover new ideas. Even in nonfiction, the same thing happens. The form of the essay changes. I become restless. I begin to just sense the form. Either you submit to this instinct to further develop and further refine the form, or you stick to your original idea and work within certain parameters. In the case of *Crossing the River, The Nature of Blood,* and several other of my novels, I began to trust my instinct and submit to it. In other words, if I discover something in the journey, then I'm prepared to tear up the original template and follow to see where it leads. With the development from my first novels to the later works, the one thing I learned in that journey is not to be afraid to follow your instinct. And you must make the reader follow you. In my earlier books, I had a much more conservative sense that I must serve the reader. After that, I decided that shouldn't be the case. If my instinct tells me that I need to do something, then I follow it.

KR: Each of your books brings its own demands and teaches us how to read them in their own way.
CP: The British writer Margaret Drabble said to me not long ago, "The thing about reading your books is that with each book I learn how to read the next book because you're teaching me how to read them." I knew she meant it as a compliment because she's a generous, spirited person, but it took me a while to figure out exactly what she meant. At this time last year, I was in Dublin, and Roddy Doyle was introducing me at a reading. He said, "The thing about your books is that they're not easy. Can't you make them easier for us? We want to read them before we go to sleep, but we just can't because we're not going to slide into them. Why are they so hard?" Again, it took me a while to discover what he meant. But yes, he's right. Why are they complex? Why are they so challenging?

KR: Why do you think so?
CP: I think it has to do with that transition that I tried to articulate earlier, realizing at a certain point that I wanted the reader to follow me. I always had a reasonably cogent idea that the books in themselves constitute a body of work, I always figured that if the reader sees the bigger picture it will become clearer. If you follow book by book, maybe they are difficult individually, but based on Drabble's point, if you manage to stumble through one then perhaps you're not so surprised when you get to another one. From one book to the next, you begin to realize that certain conventions will be ignored and certain counter-conventions are prevalent.

KR: The way you speak of a body of work is similar to something that David Malouf once said. He compared the arc of his body of work with the shape of a story collection.
CP: I'm not sure that I'd make a statement as confident as David's, maybe because I'm not as far on in "the collection of short stories" as he is. What I would say is that I am reasonably sure of what the collection will look like at the end. Writers are a bit like dogs in a sense. As you go on, you stop at this tree. Then you move on and stop at another tree. You are always marking your territory, but it takes a while, if you are thinking long term, before you're actually aware of what your territory is. Again, I was lucky in that from quite early on I had a sense of the themes I was grappling with. I had a sense of territory that would reoccur and

that I would want to cover again and again. I've always had a sense of one or two books down the line. I know where one book is leading. I'm not finishing a book and then twiddling my thumbs. I'm usually finishing and thinking, "OK. I have a sense of what the next one will be." As far as a collection of short stories, as David Malouf has suggested, well, I'd like to think my body of work has that kind of coherence and planning, but I don't know yet.

KR: When did you first read about Bert Williams, the Caribbean-born entertainer at the center of *Dancing in the Dark?*

CP: A few weeks ago, my assistant from ten years before was in town and I gave her a copy of *Dancing in the Dark*. I said, "You *did* do research on this, didn't you?" She said, "Yes. I dug up all of this stuff for you." I laughed. She said, "I wondered what took you so long to write this novel." I said, "I had other things to do." That, actually, is quite typical of what I mean by planning.

I remember talking to somebody in 1998 about the first essay in the collection I'm writing now. I remember saying, "Listen, I'm going to write something on so and so." I sent him a draft recently, and he said, "I thought you had forgotten about it." I said, "No, no, no." It was bubbling all along.

KR: You really do have a backlog.

CP: Sometimes you have an idea for something, and it doesn't get to the front burner right away. Anything can happen. Somebody else can bring out a book on the same subject, or, as happened to me once, I was talking to another writer who was passionately concerned with a certain area, and I took all of my files of research on that area and handed it to him. I said, "You would be better at this than I would." It felt good that somebody else wanted to write about that character.

KR: Are you working simultaneously on projects?

CP: In the past, I've started something and broken off to do something else, and then come back to it. Maybe it's just a function of an addled brain. These days I try to focus on just one thing, although, for instance, when I finish this book, I know that I'm going to write a play based on somebody's book. I've been working with the writer and the director. In the past, I might have tried to do a draft of it in between these essays, hut now I tend to try and get one thing out of the way before moving on.

KR: Do you think of the books in aural or visual terms?

CP: Music has always been important to me. I hear it, and 1 then know how I want the narrative to move, when it should go from quiet to slightly more turbulent, and then to a moment of suspense. As a kid, I loved the straightforward pop songs of the sixties and seventies. So many of them were narratives with a beginning and middle and end. I'm thinking about people like Stevie Wonder and Marvin Gaye. Their songs all had a story to them. But I was a bit of a weirdo, as far as my teachers were concerned, because I also liked Beethoven's symphonies. One minute I would listen to Marvin Gaye and the next to the 6th Symphony. It made no more sense to me than it did to anyone else, but in retrospect I can now see the larger movement. With the symphonies, I was learning something about pacing and movement, and in the smaller, pop songs, I was learning about how to tell a story.

KR: That's the larger scale of structure, but how do you work on the level of the sentence?

CP: I hear sentences completely, before I write them. That's the thing which annoys me most about reading contemporary fiction. I can't read most of it. I'm always complaining to one of my good friends, the British poet Glyn Maxwell, "Why can't people hear music in words?" He laughs and says, "Because they're not poets. They're novelists." But novelists should be able to hear music in words, too. They should be able to hear the way words flow. When they can't, it's the kind of thing that stops me reading dead in my tracks. If I come across sentences that are just clunky, then I don't really want to pursue the work. The author must have a reasonably well-attuned ear. I wouldn't say that I sit there and the words flow naturally. Sentences must be worked over. I have to go back and rework and rework, but the ultimate, driving impulse for me is, "Does it flow? Does each word move within the sentence, and then from that sentence to the next sentence with a certain elegance?" If it does, fine. If it doesn't, I need to drag the whole thing down and begin again.

KR: Does your inability to read contemporary fiction have anything to do with your decision to write, primarily, historical fiction?

CP: It has been an issue for me in the past because of the subject matter I was dealing with. I felt like I had to do historical repair work. It was not on people's radar. People didn't fully understand the connections my work was making, and they weren't really aware of what I felt was the contemporary resonances of understanding the way the past feeds the present. I felt obligated to write about the past. I was always trying to write about the present, too, but I had no problems refracting it deeply through the past. I feel less of an impulse to do that today because people in the past ten to fifteen years have written about contemporary relations in Britain, raising an understanding of issues that have to do with nationality and belonging. We now have a much better sense of how this is rooted in the British past. I don't feel the same necessity to do that historical repair work, which is perhaps why a novel like *A Distant Shore* has a contemporary setting. The next novel I will write is also contemporary. I wouldn't say it is over, but it's not as pressing on me. Even a novel like *Dancing in the Dark* didn't really feel historical. Obviously it did in terms of certain nuances and period research. But I always felt as though I was writing about a character who could be alive now. I felt I was writing about what it was like to live in a celebrity culture.

KR: In that way, *Dancing in the Dark* is much more of an emotional history of the time and characters than a historical novel.
CP: That's what I was trying to get at, I think. It's certainly not a biography and doesn't prevent anybody from doing the nuts and bolts research and try to produce a more detailed and scrupulous biographical study. My novel is much more of an emotional portrait of celebrity, a man who was an exploration of the words *celebrity, notoriety, race,* and *belonging.* That, to me, seems to be the story of what happens in America time and time again. But in that sense it's all contemporary. Though many of my novels have been historical, I felt they were necessary because there wasn't anything else like them. If I was going to make whatever point I wanted to make about a contemporary world, I had to at least introduce some of the past.

KR: As someone who writes nonfiction and fiction, did you ever consider writing a biography of Bert Williams? Do you think that we can understand his character better through the novel?
CP: I obviously think you can understand the character better through fiction because I'm biased. That's my job. I'm not a biographer. I respect proper biographers and people who know how to immerse themselves. And there are a few people who are good at doing both. Peter Ackroyd is terrific at doing fully fleshed out biographies and writing fiction. I don't think I have either the patience or the skill to immerse myself in a character's life without my imagination kicking in. Ackroyd came under some criticism years ago when he published his Dickens biography because he began to imagine certain passages. I understand why he wanted to do that, but he was offending the purists, who wanted to know why they were having to deal with imaginative interludes in a biography. Well, they were having to deal with them because Ackroyd's a novelist and he can't think about a character for a long period without wanting to speculate. I suspect some of that

would happen were I ever to try to write a biography, so I've just gone straight for the imaginative speculations.

KR: How does the process unfold for you?

CP: The Internet has changed everything sporadically. Ten years ago, my assistant would have had to do a lot of legwork, interlibrary loans, photocopying. These days, it's a bit easier in terms of pulling things off the Internet. The one thing that hasn't changed with research is the basic nuts and bolts of it. What would generally happen is that I would say to the person I was working with, "Bert Williams. African-American theater between 1870–1900." My assistant would get books from the library. I would look through them, though I wouldn't read them all from cover to cover. I would put Post-Its in the pages that seemed most relevant and photocopy them so that all of the books could go back to the library, and I would then have a pile of three- or four-hundred pages of photocopied material. I would read those pages and mark what was relevant. The assistant would type that material onto a disk, which I would label something like "Bert Williams" or the name of a location. In the end, I always have a file that runs between 100–200 pages. I keep that as a research bible before I start to write the novel. When I start to write, if I get stuck, I'm able to look up something—modes of transportation in New York—and I will know when the subway was dug, when the El stopped running, when cars replaced horses, things like that. All of this stimulates your imagination. If you write about Bert Williams walking through New York City, you want to know whether he would get splashed by a horse and carriage. These are minute things, but they keep my fictional mind alive because I'm able to keep fact-checking. Then other things would crop up along the way. I would have three or four questions each time I met with my assistant. I would say, "Can you find out if a gentleman would wear a frock coat in New York in the 1890s? Were there ashtrays in bars or did people flick their ashes on the floor?" Small details usually stimulate larger points. These are all backup things to sort of assist me as I write the fiction.

KR: The language in your novels also stays close to the period about which you are writing. What kind of research does this require?

CP: I spend a lot of time checking words to see whether they were in usage at the time I'm writing. There's one website, etymology.com, which I find very helpful. For instance, in the eighteenth-century essay I'm writing now, I describe one of the characters as having an interracial marriage. I was reading it yesterday, and I thought, I don't know if they'd have used the term "interracial." My assistant is in Israel on holiday at the moment, so I had to go and look it up myself. It took about twenty minutes, trying to find out if that term would have been used in the late eighteenth century. In terms of the actual voice of the characters, though, that comes down to imagination. You can't research that. But in terms of the accuracy of voice, you certainly can check and double-check.

KR: That accuracy is also present in your fiction, as well.

CP: Words betray. It's one of the things that any writing workshop will teach you. Words betray character. It's not only what a character does, it's not only what happens to that character, it's how the character expresses himself. He must have a nuance and a weight different from other characters.

KR: Earlier, you mentioned your admiration for J. M. Coetzee's work. In a *New York Review of Books* essay, Coetzee wrote about the structure and polyphony in your work "as imaginative forays into a single body of work, the history of persecution and victimization in the west." He proposes that your work has a single aim: "remembering what the West would like to forget."

CP: At this stage, if I were to say what the aim of my work has been, I think it's increasingly an exploration of the meaning of "home." That's obviously connected with what Coetzee is saying. Home is connected to persecution and memory and loss. But it can be as simple, or as vague, as loneliness or isolation. If you looked at my work toward the end of the nineties, you may have seen large historical themes played out, small lives coming into contact with large historical themes. But I think these days, either as a progression or development from that, I'm much more concerned with lives, loneliness, isolation, and grappling with the meaning of "home," not necessarily on the grand, global scale, but often on the domestic scale. I spoke earlier of the case of Bert Williams. Here was the pure, profound loss of a man sitting at a bar in Harlem, with drink after drink, being thoroughly unmoored despite being at the center of the culture because of his celebrity. There's no great global persecution in that, but there is, I think, a preoccupation with home and loss and belonging.

KR: You've mentioned that you have a problem with the terms "loss" and "home," noting that "any Diaspora involves a sense of guilt and loss." Is writing a means of trying to combat or understand that loss?

CP: Certainly I've tried to understand what it means. I think of the modern condition at the beginning of the twenty-first century, and I see a certain displacement and cultural plurality which involves having a multiple sense of the meaning of home, I try to write about this and not just in a contemporary sense but historically as well. I don't know if you can combat or compensate for the loneliness, or for the sense of being unmoored, adrift, and bereft, simply depressed in one's life. I don't know if reading a book, let alone writing a book, can ever repair that degree of damage.

Only Connect: An Interview with Caryl Phillips on *Foreigners*

Bénédicte Ledent/2008

Printed with permission of Bénédicte Ledent. Interview conducted in St. Kitts.

Bénédicte Ledent: Much of your writing is about foreigners—the Othello figure in *The Nature of Blood*, Solomon in *A Distant Shore* and Emily in *Cambridge* are just some examples. What is special about the foreigners depicted in your latest book, Francis Barber, Randolph Turpin, and David Oluwale?

Caryl Phillips: I think that the only thing that is special about them is that they are all foreign in approximately the same way; they are black, male, and nominally British. Their race, gender, and nationality play a great part in the way in which their various identities are constructed and offered up to them by British society.

BL: What is the role played by gender in their identity construction?

CP: Men have a certain confidence in some situations; in other situations they are perceived of as a threat in a way that a woman would not be. I think gender considerations, like the other variables of identity construction, vary according to place and time, but gender always exerts a real influence. One doesn't hear of many black women being present in eighteenth-century Britain; boxing is, of course, a largely masculine pursuit; and vagrancy (a key element of the Oluwale story) was, until quite recently, largely considered to be a male problem.

BL: *Foreigners* has been published on both sides of the Atlantic. Surprisingly, the full title of the British edition, *Foreigners: Three English Lives*, which clearly encapsulates the paradox at the heart of the book, was shortened to *Foreigners* in the American edition. What motivated such a change?

CP: Actually, there was some discussion in the U.S. about publishing the book as a novel, but the full title was suggestive of nonfiction. As soon as one puts a colon, or a subtitle on the cover of a book of prose, the natural tendency is to assume that it's nonfiction. I think that the change in the title had more to do with strategies of marketing than anything to do with the fictional or factual qualities of the text. I've long been interested in the interface between fact and fiction, but the industry seems to have a much more practical concern with this question as opposed to my own theoretical musings!

BL: Did American and British audiences react differently when you gave readings?
CP: I didn't do that many readings from the book, and when I did I tended to mainly read from the Oluwale section. I found the audiences on both sides of the Atlantic were moved by his situation.

BL: The setting of your early novels was often unspecified. For example, *The Final Passage* takes place on an unnamed Caribbean island and the locales in *Crossing the River* are rather vague. Your most recent works of fiction have on the other hand been more specific about location. *Foreigners* seems to pursue this need for spatial accuracy, in particular in the section set in Leeds where one can almost follow David Oluwale step by step. What was the purpose of this very precise contextualization?
CP: I felt it important, particularly in the case of David Oluwale, to get the facts right. A great deal of the narrative relates to a court case and testimonies by various people. I was led by this legal quest for accuracy. Similarly in the case of Randolph Turpin, one has documentary footage, newspaper reports, and even books that have been written about him. I also interviewed two of his daughters. This being the case I also felt obliged to be accurate. With Francis Barber I felt a little more latitude to imagine and evoke; recreate, if you will.

BL: Why?
CP: This is largely because—with reference to Barber—there are no newspaper reports, court records, photographs, newsreels, or people alive who I might interview. This being the case, I'm not burdened by evidence on my desk.

BL: *Foreigners* is very original, both formally and thematically. It nevertheless contains some motifs which can be seen as pervading your writing. One omnipresent idea in your work is that good intentions may have disastrous consequences, which is notably illustrated in *The Nature of Blood* through the transportation of Fallashas to Israel in the 1980s. In "Dr. Johnson's Watch," the famous Dr.'s well-meant generosity towards Francis Barber might very well be one of the causes of his downfall. How do you interpret this form of irony?
CP: I certainly recognize that one of the great ironies of existence is that a gesture of affection, or a sacrifice of a deeply practical nature, may well not necessarily lead to salvation. That it might actually contribute towards somebody's downfall is, of course, a depressing thought. However, this kind of irony nearly always provides a writer with dramatic material.

BL: "Made in Wales" reminds one of your interest in sport, particularly in boxing, as a metaphor for life in society, and maybe for the Black British condition itself. I don't know if you agree with this last point. "Made in Wales" might bring to mind the fate of a boxer like Frank Bruno; it also briefly refers to the nineteenth-century prize fighter Tom Molineaux, on whom you wrote a film script in the mid-1980s entitled *The Ebony Imposter*. Was Turpin's fate very different from theirs?

CP: Turpin's fate was pretty much the same as their fate. There's a huge discrepancy between the fame and adulation that a prize fighter can achieve at the peak of his powers, and the depths of obscurity, poverty and loneliness into which he can plummet once his career is over. Fighters are almost always being controlled by somebody—generally for economic or class reasons, or both. I think one of the greatest openings of an American novel is the fight sequence near the beginning of Ralph Ellison's *Invisible Man*. I've always been interested in sport as a metaphor for what is going on in society, but boxing seems to offer us a pretty consistent window (across three centuries) through which we can peer and see some of the problems that are plaguing a society.

BL: You are known to be a football fan. Have you ever thought of writing fiction in relation to this sport?

CP: I've never thought of writing fiction about football; or in fact anything dramatic at all on the subject. Some years ago (1986) I wrote a feature film about cricket called *Playing Away*. A similar idea for a film (or novel) connected with football has not occurred to me, although I'm a much bigger fan of football than I am of cricket.

BL: Another usual metaphor in your writing is that of the family. David Oluwale's ultimate homelessness seems to be conveyed through the absence in the narrative of any family, whether parents, wife, or children. If I'm not mistaken, Oluwale was married in England at some point, wasn't he? Why did you leave out this supposedly happier part of his life?

CP: I'm not sure it was a happier part of his life. And nobody seems to be able to say, without contradiction, that he was married. I put adverts into newspapers in Leeds and Sheffield trying to track down the wife and the children—however, I wasn't able to come up with anything. In a way, the difficulty of tracking down a cohesive family that might have offered him support and provided him with purpose seemed to fit with the details of his life that were clearly on record.

BL: Did this lack of consistent information about Oluwale prove problematic when you were writing the book? Was it also the case for the other two lives?

CP: I don't think the lack of consistent information about Barber bothered me too much for, as I've already stated, I was already on an imaginative course with his story. It was a problem with Turpin, which is why I finally decided to travel to Wales and track down people who had actually known him. Of course, they merely complicated the story, as opposed to providing definitive answers, but the drama of the journey to Wales, and the subsequent encounters, helped me to shape and finish the essay.

BL: One of the major points of contention among scholars working on your work is whether you should be regarded as an optimist or a pessimist. By putting the tragic stories of these three men side by side, do you suggest that things have not really changed between the eighteenth and the second half of the twentieth century? In other words, even if the inclusion of Turpin's family in the middle section leaves some hope for the future, do you suggest in *Foreigners* that there is no way out of racial and social determinism?

CP: I do think that there has to be some way out of racial and social determinism, and I hope that what I'm doing is a contribution of some kind towards a better future. However, I don't underestimate the cyclical nature of these things, and I also don't rush to embrace a kind of reckless optimism of the kind that many politicians and some social policy professionals like to espouse. Such as the idea that, at the start of the twenty-first century, there is no real racial or gender discrimination in Britain because many laws have been passed to tackle these issues. It takes many, many generations to change people's opinions, alleviate their fears, and make them comfortable enough to embrace difference. One cannot simply legislate these things, nor can one measure change by looking at statistical superficialities. The human heart is capable of many things, including stubbornness.

BL: *Foreigners* can be read as a tragedy, like much of your work—with the possible exception of *Playing Away*, which may be described as comedy. Gravitas is no doubt the most appropriate answer to the serious topics you tackle. However, have you ever thought of adopting the comic mode in your fiction? Your friends know that you have a great sense of humour.

CP: I find it easier to attempt humour in dialogue, whether for the screen or stage. I think that gravitas is a tone which seems appropriate to a lot of my subject matter, but not all by any means. For instance, there seems to me to be some lighter moments in *A Distant Shore* and even in *Dancing in the Dark*. They are not comic by any means, but there are moments of warmth, empathy, and irony. And I can imagine, in the future, some tonal shifting in the fiction, although I doubt if it will ever be comic.

BL: The reviewers have repeatedly commented on your book's hybrid, almost unpindownable nature. I know that you do not read reviews, but as an academic yourself, you might understand that some critics need to classify the writing they discuss. Labels like "creative nonfiction," "historical fiction," and "creative biography" have been used to describe *Foreigners*. Is there any one that seems to apply to your book better than others? And why? How would you define your book?

CP: I try not to worry at all about labels. Personally I would describe it as nonfiction, but in an attempt to resolve this problem I've dispensed with the division between fiction and nonfiction on the header pages of my books. Of course, this won't solve anything because people will still feel the urge to label, be they academics, bookstore owners, or publishers. This being the case, "creative biography" might be a suitable label for *Foreigners*.

BL: In a recent interview with Kevin Rabalais you expressed an interest in W. G. Sebald because you said his work articulated "the collapse of the difference between fiction and nonfiction," which you thought was increasingly typical of twenty-first-century writing. Does this development mean the death of the traditional novel?

CP: No, I don't think the traditional novel will die. It will merely reconfigure itself and privilege different methodologies and strategies of narrative construction. I think, almost inevitably, these will be less complex than some of the modes that we absorbed, as readers and writers, with the onset of both modernism and postmodernism. The fact is we're becoming less patient, more easily bored, and probably more judgemental. In other words, we're becoming increasingly stupid.

BL: Isn't the role of literature to go against these deleterious trends rather than yield to them?

CP: Of course, that's the role of literature. It's not necessarily the role of publishing.

BL: Will your next novel also bring fact and fiction together? Or is it too early to tell?

CP: No, I don't think it will.

BL: Like *Foreigners*, *Dancing in the Dark* is a generically challenging book, fictionalizing the life of the Black American entertainer Bert Williams. It deals with the twin concepts of celebrity and race, also at the centre of "Made in Wales," the section of *Foreigners* devoted to Turpin. However, *Dancing in the Dark* views Bert from the inside, while Turpin's story is told from the outside. Did this mean a different involvement with the character when you were writing the book?

CP: Yes, I felt deeply for Bert Williams in a way that I never did, or sought to, with Turpin. For me, fiction is very much determined by the connection that one feels with character, and the ability to place character before plot. In the case of Turpin, I was always aware of the chronology of his life. In the case of Bert Williams, after a while, I didn't care much for the sequential details of his life for I was thoroughly invested in the man.

BL: Which was a more painful process for you, I suppose?

CP: It was certainly emotionally more difficult, although the technical aspects of writing the narrative remained equally challenging.

BL: *Foreigners* is based on a tripartite structure, like *Higher Ground*; it juxtaposes three stories which might be read independently but are densely interconnected. Why did you choose this particular form? Does it confer a special role on the reader? Does it also imply running the risk of being partly misunderstood?

CP: I think every author runs the risk of being misunderstood to some degree, but that shouldn't trouble him or her unduly. To ask the reader to read thematically and build bridges and dig tunnels between sections of a book that don't otherwise look as though they are, on first glance, connected, is to perhaps ask of the reader that they do a little extra work. I chose to have three sections because there were three people who interested me; I think if there had been a fourth person I would not have shied away from including him, or her.

BL: Are there other famous figures that you did not include in this book but might consider writing about in the future?

CP: I don't think there are any other people who come to mind. At the moment I can't imagine myself doing another book which is so biographically-based.

BL: Each of the three sections uses a different narrative strategy. Was your choice intuitive or did it rest on rational criteria? Or both, maybe? Could you briefly explain the formal genesis of the three parts?

CP: The choice was intuitive, and then as I entered further into each section I tried, very deliberately, to develop a formal tone that was different from the other two sections. But the main thing is the intuition. The language of the Barber section fascinated me. The high civility of the English language when used to describe acts of cowardice and betrayal. In the Turpin section I was trying to fashion something akin to sports reportage. Finally, the Oluwale section, which is the most complicated of the three, is a fusion of styles which attempt to reflect the emotional shifting of register that I felt when researching the story, from my interest in dry courtroom reportage, to a deeply personal feeling of connection with Oluwale's story in some way.

BL: Your fiction is known for giving a voice to those who have been left out of history books. *Foreigners* does retrieve the stories of three men who have been silenced but, paradoxically, their voice is never directly heard in the narrative, except for a few words uttered by Francis Barber in the first section. Why?
CP: Perhaps this has something to do with my notion of the difference between fiction and nonfiction in the simplest sense of the terms. In nonfiction I always feel that I have to be more present as an agent of narrative purpose. In some senses, I hope I can be trusted with their stories and the characters can just relax. In fiction, I am not present and very importantly—the characters' voices must be heard.

BL: A voice which is most probably yours emerges in the second and third sections of *Foreigners*. Was it a problem for you to be audible in that way?
CP: It's always a problem for me to be audible; my preferred mode is silence, or invisibility.

BL: Why?
CP: I've no idea why. Other authors seem to be very adept at being visible narrators, but I've always preferred to be behind the scene. Even when I was very preoccupied with the theatre, I wanted to be a director but never an actor. The idea of walking onto a stage filled me with a kind of horror; it still does.

BL: The language in "Dr. Johnson's Watch" is modelled on eighteenth-century English. How did you go about writing that section? Were the problems that you met the same as when you wrote *Cambridge,* for example?
CP: The problems were pretty much the same; accuracy of vocabulary, rhythm of the language, the syntactical music of the period. I remember the labour with these issues when I was writing *Cambridge* and the work on "Dr. Johnson's Watch" was similar.

BL: "Dr. Johnson's Watch" contains a lot of adjectives. Was this a deliberate choice? Why?
CP: I try to be very precise with adjectives, and with imagery in general. I want the reader to be able to "see" clearly. Once I have a reasonable sense of character, it's this detail of visual fine-tuning that takes me a lot of time and many drafts.

BL: How many, on average?
CP: At least five or six, but sometimes more. There are some pieces which are re-

written and reworked a dozen times. It's not a very economical way of working, but it's the only way I know how.

BL: Are there words or categories of words which, in your experience, require more of your attention than others? I know that this sounds very technical, but I imagine it is part of the writing craft too, isn't it?

CP: I think I pay particular attention to verbs. Sometimes, in an effort to keep the narrative flowing, one can revisit the same verbs too often and too clumsily. I try to be cognizant of the difference between, for instance, "run" and "hurry" or "slouch" and "slump."

BL: Thank you very much, Caryl, for agreeing to answer my questions.

Index